Long-Distance Genealogy

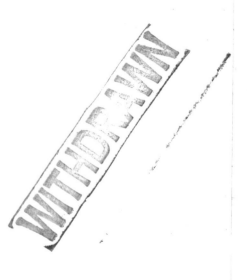

Long-Distance Genealogy

Christine Crawford-Oppenheimer, MLS

BETTERWAY BOOKS
CINCINNATI, OHIO

www.familytreemagazine.com

Long-Distance Genealogy. Copyright © 2000 by Christine Crawford-Oppenheimer. Manufactured in the United States of America. All rights reserved. No part of this book may be reproduced in any form or by any electronic or mechanical means including information storage and retrieval systems without permission in writing from the publisher, except by a reviewer, who may quote brief passages in a review. Published by Betterway Books, an imprint of F&W Publications, Inc., 1507 Dana Ave., Cincinnati, Ohio 45207. (800) 289-0963. First edition.

Other fine Betterway Books are available from your local bookstore or on our Web site at www.familytreemagazine.com.

04   03   02   01   00   5   4   3   2   1

Library of Congress Cataloging-in-Publication Data
   Long-distance genealogy / Christine Crawford-Oppenheimer.
      p.   cm.
   Includes bibliographical references and index.
   ISBN 1-55870-535-X
   1. Genealogy. 2. United States—Genealogy—Handbooks, manuals, etc. I. Title.
CS16.C78   2000
929′.1′072073—dc21   00-040332
                                                  CIP

Editor: Sharon DeBartolo Carmack
Production editor: Brad Crawford
Interior designer: Sandy Conopeotis Kent
Icon designer: Cindy Beckmeyer
Cover designer: Karla Stover
Generational photo by Arthur Tilley/FPG International LLC

About the Author

Christine Crawford-Oppenheimer, MLS, has been doing genealogical research for more than twenty years. Her training as a librarian and archivist is useful to her not only in her day job but also in her second profession, genealogy.

Ms. Crawford-Oppenheimer has spoken frequently at national conferences and seminars; she has addressed topics as varied as basic genealogy, networking, family health history, and the published *Pennsylvania Archives*.

Articles she has written have appeared in the *National Genealogical Society Quarterly, The Pennsylvania Genealogical Magazine,* the *Western Pennsylvania Genealogical Society Quarterly,* and other magazines; she writes a column for the *Armstrong County* [PA] *Genealogy Club Quarterly*.

DEDICATION

To my fourth-grade teacher, Patricia Webb Oertley, from whom I first learned how much fun writing can be; to the memory of my father, who first inspired and nurtured my interest in genealogy; to my mother, who always knew I could write a book; to my husband, who stood by me in all the travails of putting a book together; and to the memory of Nancy (Rollins) (Rollins) (Green) (Smalling) Wilson, whose story first piqued my interest in genealogy.

Acknowledgments

This book probably would not exist if William Brohaugh, new media director at F&W Publications, hadn't, out of the blue, invited me to write it, allowing me to fulfill my childhood dream of becoming a published writer. I turned for advice to Sharon DeBartolo Carmack, who told me that she had good experiences with Betterway Books. Little did I know that eight months later, Betterway would hire her to be my caring and sympathetic editor.

Lady Jane, Lydia, Davy and Jäger gave me support and purrs as I worked, often coming to my office to sleep on my files, desk, or lap. As I tried to balance a full-time job with the demands of writing a book, Jim also encouraged me and put up with a messy house and many meals of Chinese takeout. Come to think of it, he often suggested the Chinese takeout!

Icons Used in This Book

 CD Source
Databases and other information available on CD-ROM

 Citing Sources
Reminders and methods for documenting information

\di'fin\ *vb* **Definitions**
Terminology and jargon explained

 For More Info
Where to turn for more in-depth coverage

 Hidden Treasures
Family papers and home sources

 Idea Generator
Techniques and prods for further thinking

 Important
Information and tips you can't overlook

 Internet Source
Where on the web to find what you need

 Library/Archive Source
Repositories that might have the information you need

 Money Saver
Getting the most out of research dollars

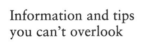 **Notes**
Thoughts, ideas and related insights

 Oral History
Techniques for getting family stories

 Printed Source
Directories, books, pamphlets and other paper archives

 Reminder
"Don't-Forget" items to keep in mind

 Research Tip
Ways to make research more efficient

 See Also
Where in this book to find related information

 Sources
Where to go for information, supplies, etc.

 Step By Step
Walkthroughs of important procedures

 Technique
How to conduct research, solve problems, and get answers

 Timesaver
Shaving minutes and hours off the clock

 Tip
Ways to make research more efficient

 Warning
Stop before you make a mistake

Table of Contents At a Glance

Table of Contents

Preface

C hances are you picked up this book because you're doing or are interested in doing genealogical research on ancestors who lived some distance away from where you live. Sooner or later, almost all genealogists find that they need to do long-distance research, searching for ancestors as close as a few counties away or as far as several states away.

Perhaps you've read books on genealogical research that blithely instructed you to go to the courthouse or newspaper office or library where your ancestors' records are. It discussed the sources genealogists should use, but didn't explain how to get these sources. You have a problem: The place where your ancestors lived is too far away for you to get to easily. The distance may not be great—even a town one hundred miles away can be a problem. Most genealogists who work full-time are at work during times when records repositories are open. Or perhaps your ancestors lived two hundred or even two thousand miles away, making your search even more difficult. What do you do now?

DON'T PANIC!

Researching from a distance can be frustrating, especially for the new genealogist who doesn't know how to locate repositories or the fine points involved in achieving success when contacting them. But you *can* do genealogy from afar, if you're willing to pay a small amount of money for stamps and photocopy fees or for renting or purchasing research materials. You can attack the problem by looking for (1) actual documents and information about your ancestors and (2) people who are researching the same lines and might already have collected information they can share with you. This book will tell you how to research your family history even if your ancestral home is far away from where you live.

HOW CAN *LONG-DISTANCE GENEALOGY* HELP YOU?

In some ways, *Long-Distance Genealogy* is a beginning genealogy text. It describes many useful strategies for the genealogist and discusses basic records that the genealogist should pursue in the search for family history. However, its emphasis is not only on *what* to access but also on *how* to access material from a distance. *Long-Distance Genealogy* will show you techniques for locating information to document ancestors who lived in an area of the United States that you can't conveniently visit to do research. It explains what materials genealogists can access from a distance (most of the materials that genealogists can access in person) and the best ways to go about getting at information through correspondence (both with individuals and repositories), library research, interlibrary loan, microfilm and CD-ROM sources, and the Internet. It discusses how to locate others who are researching the same lines and includes suggestions on how to get maximum results from a research trip. It discusses when you should consider hiring a professional genealogist and how to choose and get the best results from one.

WHAT WILL THIS COST?

One thing you should know from the start: long-distance research involves money. At the very least, you'll have to pay for stamps and envelopes. You'll probably also pay for photocopies of documents, book excerpts, and articles; fees some repositories charge for research; magazine subscriptions; and queries in magazines that charge by the word. **But working from a distance can be much less expensive than going to your ancestral area to research,** and you can make decisions to limit the amount you'll spend. Almost all hobbies cost money, but how many give you the gratification you'll get from building your family tree? The fun you'll have in tracking down your ancestors and the satisfaction you'll feel as you fill in yet another blank space on your pedigree chart should make it worthwhile for you. If not, consider looking for another hobby!

Money Saver

MY STORY

How did I get to be an expert on long-distance research? I first became interested in my family history at age twelve, when my father aroused my curiosity. He asked, "Did you know that one of your great-great-great-grandmothers was married seven times?" I was fascinated and wanted to know more. My father instinctively suggested that I follow the first step of good genealogical research: interviewing relatives. I wrote to relatives on his side of the family, including my grandmother, who wrote more letters to some distant cousins I didn't know. I became interested enough that I wrote to relatives on my mother's side, as well, asking for details on her line. But I had a major problem. I lived in Saudi Arabia. I had no access to any kind of research facility. And at that time, there were very few genealogy how-to books, and none were aimed at children. Having collected the information from my relatives, I moved on to other things. Luckily, I did save all the letters those distant cousins wrote, and I harbored a small flame of interest in my lineage.

Soon after the television dramatization of Alex Haley's *Roots* engendered a national rebirth of interest in genealogy, I began working at a library agency where a co-worker ordered census microfilm on interlibrary loan. I didn't know that census microfilm existed and asked for details. Once I found out that these microfilms were listings, put together every ten years, of all family groups in the United States, I was hooked. (Remember that I grew up in Saudi Arabia. At the time this encounter took place, I had not yet been counted on a U.S. census. The first time I was counted on one, I was twenty-nine years old! Think of this later, as you try to figure out why your ancestors aren't on the census you think they should be on!) I pulled out my collection of letters, started ordering censuses, and discovered family group sheets and pedigree charts.

But I still had a problem. Now I lived in eastern New York. Geographically, my closest ancestors were in eastern Pennsylvania, two hundred miles away, and the area I consider my ancestral homeland, western Pennsylvania, was four hundred miles away. Tennessee, Ohio, Kansas, and Illinois were even more remote. I made occasional visits to western Pennsylvania, but for most of my research there and for the other areas, I had to develop long-distance research tactics. That's how I learned the techniques that I describe in this book. Some of the repositories and people who received my early research letters will probably be delighted to see how much I've learned!

SCOPE OF THIS BOOK

This book has some limits. It only deals with research in the United States, although some of the techniques also apply to foreign research. While it is a full guide to many aspects of genealogical research, its main focus is on how you can get or see copies of records and other materials from distant locations. There's less emphasis on using these records, so you may want to buy other books to supplement this one. The book doesn't cover organizing your research, so you may want to buy a book on that subject, such as Sharon DeBartolo Carmack's *Organizing Your Family History Search*. This book doesn't discuss computer programs for genealogy. If you're interested in computer software for organizing your family information, you can find details on programs in a book such as Marthe Arends's *Genealogy Software Guide*.

ARE YOU DOING *REALLY* LONG-DISTANCE RESEARCH?

Are you an expatriate American? At a genealogical conference a few years ago, I encountered two American women who lived in one of the two oil towns in Saudi Arabia where I grew up (Ras Tanura and Dhahran). They belonged to a thriving genealogy club there, whose members no doubt use some of the techniques described in this book. With the growth of the Internet and E-mail, plus better books on research, long-distance research is a lot easier than it was when I was a child.

People in other circumstances—perhaps living permanently abroad, with no regular trips to the United States—can still do long-distance research in the United States following the techniques described in this book. Keep a few things in mind:

- Repositories, historical and genealogical societies, magazines, etc., generally want payment for documents, memberships, and services in U.S. funds, so identify some way that you can provide such payments.
- Most people in the United States don't send letters overseas and don't realize that postage to Europe, South America, etc., is higher than that within the United States. They'll use the same stamp they'd use to send a letter to Aunt Sally in Tucson. The letter will get there eventually, but very slowly. So arrange to procure some U.S. stamps (a relative or correspondent in the United States will probably be happy to purchase them for you if you send the money), and send a self-addressed, stamped envelope

READ MORE ABOUT IT!

For More Info

When I first started working on my family history, there were only a few books on how to do genealogical research. Now, many more are available. You'll find the following books useful. For full citations, see the bibliography. Look at them at your local library or bookstore, and add some of them to your collection.

Handbooks

- Allen, *First Steps in Genealogy: A Beginner's Guide to Researching Your Family Tree*
- Carmack, *The Genealogy Sourcebook*
- Cerny, *Ancestry's Guide to Research: Case Studies in American Genealogy*
- Croom, *The Genealogist's Companion & Sourcebook*
- Croom, *Unpuzzling Your Past: A Basic Guide to Genealogy*
- Croom, *The Unpuzzling Your Past Workbook: Essential Forms and Letters for All Genealogists*
- Doane and Bell, *Searching for Your Ancestors: The How and Why of Genealogy*
- Greenwood, *The Researcher's Guide to American Genealogy*
- Rose and Ingalls, *The Complete Idiot's Guide to Genealogy*
- Stevenson, *Genealogical Evidence: A Guide to the Standard of Proof Relating to Pedigrees, Ancestry, Heirship, and Family History*
- Stryker-Rodda, *How to Climb Your Family Tree: Genealogy for Beginners*
- Szucs, *Family History Made Easy*
- Willard, *Ancestors* (This is the companion book to a series developed for the Public Broadcasting System in 1997. If you learn well from videos, consider adding this series to your library.)

Books of Essays

- Baxter, *Do's and Don'ts for Ancestor Hunters*
- Heisey, *Genealogy Helps, Hints & Hope*
- Jacobus, *Genealogy as Pastime and Profession*
- Rubincam, *Pitfalls in Genealogical Research*

Address Books

- Bentley, *The Genealogist's Address Book*
- Smith, J.S., *The Ancestry Family Historian's Address Book: A Comprehensive List of Local, State, and Federal Agencies and Institutions and Ethnic and Genealogical Organizations*

Besides a selection of the above books, you should own at least one of the following:

- Eichholz, ed., *Ancestry's Red Book: American State, County & Town Sources*
- Bentley, *County Courthouse Book*
- *The Handy Book for Genealogists*

See appendix B for more information on these three books.

(SASE) when you write. When sending payment for documents or copies, enclose enough extra money to cover the return postage, with very explicit instructions about the cost of overseas postage from the United States.

- My acquaintances from Saudi Arabia said they thought they got so many responses to queries because people were excited to get a letter from so far away.
- Remember that while genealogy is the number one hobby in the United States, stamp collecting is the number two hobby. If the genealogist you write to isn't a stamp collector, he probably knows someone who is. If you're writing from a foreign country, use lots of pretty stamps!

MY AUNTS

Because I had two aunts who helped me a good deal in my early days of researching and delighted in hearing about my finds, I decided to honor them by using their names for the two aunts who appear in this book. However, the reader should understand that any negative qualities attributed to the aunts in this book are purely fictional; I have only positive memories of my aunts and the help they gave me.

CONCLUSION

Now that you've stopped panicking, let's get to work! Before you learn exactly how to go about getting information about your ancestors, you should be familiar with some basics of genealogy. If you're a beginning genealogist, read the next chapter carefully. If you've already started researching, you may find the review helpful and learn something new.

P.S. By the way, in case you're wondering, it turns out that my great-great-great-grandmother was married "only" four times!

Introduction

How Can I Get Information on Ancestors Who Lived Far Away From Me?

While it may at first seem difficult to collect information about ancestors who lived some distance away from where you live, there are several ways to access that information and extend your family lines. These include

- obtaining exact copies of original documents
- collecting information from known family members
- finding copies of original documents (either reproductions, transcriptions, or abstracts) and other family information in books and magazines and on CD-ROM, microfilm, microfiche, and the Internet
- networking to locate distant family members and others who have information about your line
- making a visit to your ancestral area to do research
- hiring a professional genealogist to do research for you

What Are the Formats in Which I Might Get Information From Original Documents?

There are four formats in which you may get information from original documents:

- actual documents
- identical reproductions of documents—made by photocopy, photograph, microfilm, or scanning
- transcriptions of documents—where someone has copied documents word for word by hand or in print
- abstracts of documents—where someone has extracted all useful information (or what that person considered to be all useful information)

Reminder

The best format to use, of course, is the original document, but aside from papers that family members may have, when you're doing long-distance research you may not have access to many of the original documents related to your family.

1

Usually, identical copies of the document are just as good as originals, but they have a few drawbacks. Some reproductions are poorly done and aren't as legible as originals. They may have flaws—such as scratches on microfilm or the image of a piece of dirt that was on the camera lens, photocopy glass, etc.—obscuring information you want to see. And in some cases, a change in ink color may signal to a reader of the original that parts of the document were written at different times; on a black-and-white reproduction, this won't be visible.

A rare problem that some genealogists have encountered with "identical" copies is that occasionally people who wish to prove some point about their lineage falsify documents by changing or adding information. If you have any doubts about a copy of a document that you receive from a source other than the original repository, attempt either to see the original or to get a copy of the document from a trustworthy source.

Transcriptions and abstracts are also useful if you can't get to the original document, but they are prone to problems as well. A person making an "exact" transcription of a document may accidentally skip a line or two (this often occurs when multiple occurrences of the same word or set of words are near each other). The person may misread, say, a name, causing confusion for genealogists who trust the transcription. Or the transcriber may simply copy the information wrong; e.g., transcribers copying from a document with columns sometimes shift the information to the wrong row in a column.

In addition, if you're working with a published transcription, remember that often a document is copied several times between the time of transcription and the time when it is published. Until recently, someone would copy the document by hand and take that copy to a printer, who would typeset it. Or the researcher might take the original transcription home, type it, and then take the typed copy to a printer. Each time a document is copied, errors can creep in. With modern technology, a genealogist can take a laptop computer to a repository and transcribe a document directly into the laptop, creating a file from which the published copy is drawn. However, these transcriptions are a small minority of all that are available, and even in making that one copy, the genealogist may introduce errors.

Abstracts suffer from the same problems as transcriptions, plus one more. The abstractor makes judgments as to what information from the document is important. A person who isn't familiar with the person or family in question may leave out a piece of information that might be very important to researchers.

How Do I Get Copies of Original Documents?

Several kinds of original documents can help you with your research. These include birth, marriage, and death certificates; estate records; land records; censuses; military records; Social Security applications; immigration and naturalization records; religious records; and many others. You or other members of your family may have copies of some of these records that will help you extend your family line. If you don't find them at home, chapters five through eleven of this book will explain how to get them and what sort of information you might find in them. Chapter fifteen discusses how you can determine if an archival repository has material relating to your family.

How Do I Get Information From Family Members?

Information from family members comes in several formats. Family members may have copies of documents that will add to your knowledge about your family. Older family members may be able to give you firsthand information about deceased ancestors or other family members. They may have genealogical information or family histories that were collected by other family members. Chapters three and four discuss what to look for and how to approach family members to draw on their information.

How Can I Find Information in Books and Magazines and on CD-ROM, Microfilm, Microfiche, and the Internet?

While these formats may seem totally different, in many cases they're used to convey the same information. For example, in order to research censuses, genealogists have traditionally requested census microfilm on interlibrary loan from the National Archives. Some genealogists got tired of working with microfilm and began transcribing census records and publishing them as magazine articles or in book format. Recently, various organizations have made both transcriptions and original censuses available on the Internet and in CD-ROM format.

Likewise, consider a book published in the late 1800s. Because the book grew old and fragile, someone, perhaps in the 1960s, might have microfilmed it. A magazine might have reproduced a chapter that discussed something of interest to its readers. More recently, with the growing popularity of CD-ROMs, someone might have put it into this format. One of the growing number of Internet genealogy libraries might make it available to Internet users.

The main difference between these formats is that you can read books and magazines without any special equipment (except maybe glasses), but you need a reader to get information from microfilm or microfiche, or a computer to read CD-ROMs, plus a modem and an Internet provider to access information from the Internet.

All of these formats are useful for genealogists. It may be difficult or impossible to get a copy of an original document (if, for example, the repository charges a large sum to do searches or make copies or if the courthouse burned). If someone has transcribed or extracted the document and published it in one of these media, you can at least discover what's in it. Throughout this book, where relevant, you will learn about records available in these formats. Chapters twelve, thirteen, fourteen, seventeen, and nineteen discuss specifically how you can locate and access these materials, as well as their advantages and disadvantages.

How Do I Locate Other People Who Are Researching My Line?

There are several methods for locating other people, usually distant cousins, who are researching your line. Chapters sixteen and eighteen discuss these avenues.

Visit My Ancestral Area? Hire a Professional Genealogist? How Do I Decide?

After you have explored other avenues of research, you may decide to visit your ancestral area to see what you can find there and/or to hire a genealogist to do research for you there. Chapters twenty and twenty-one discuss considerations in making these decisions and how to proceed if you decide to follow either of these courses.

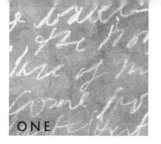

ONE

Some Basics of Genealogy

efore you start your genealogical research, you need to know some basic principles of genealogy. If you're researching already, consider this chapter a review session—maybe you'll even learn something new.

START WITH YOURSELF

The first rule of genealogy is to start with yourself and work backward. It's tempting to choose a famous Revolutionary or Colonial person who shares your surname and try to figure out how, if at all, you descend from him. However, consider that with at least five or six generations between you and him, this person could potentially have thousands of descendants. In the long run, it's easier to identify your ancestors than all those descendants.

Technique

PRIMARY AND SECONDARY SOURCES

Genealogists recognize two kinds of sources: primary and secondary. *Primary sources* are those created by contemporary witnesses, usually eyewitnesses, of an event. These include birth, marriage, and death certificates; baptismal records; deeds; etc. Primary sources are generally very reliable, but they sometimes include incorrect information. A pastor may give the wrong name for the mother of a child in a baptismal record, or a person may lie about his age to get a marriage license or join the military without parental permission.

\di'fin\ *vb*

Definitions

Secondary sources are created by someone other than an eyewitness to an event, sometimes long after the event. They may be based on primary sources, on eyewitness accounts, or on stories passed down through families (and possibly embellished or corrupted in the process). These include sources like published genealogies and county histories. Secondary sources may be correct, but they sometimes include errors, inaccuracies, or pure fantasy.

Some primary sources also include secondary information. For example, a death certificate is a primary source for information about a person's death. But the information it includes regarding the parents and birth of the deceased might have come from his child, who certainly wasn't present at the deceased person's birth and might not have known the deceased's parents.

When looking at sources, especially when you find contradictory information (e.g., two different death dates for the same person) or information that appears to be just plain wrong (a "man" marrying at age eight), consider whether the information comes from primary or secondary sources. Who might have given the information? Would that person have had firsthand knowledge of the facts?

GET EVERY PIECE OF PAPER CREATED BY OR ABOUT YOUR ANCESTORS

Technique

While it's more difficult in long-distance research than in on-site research, **your ultimate goal should be to get a copy of every piece of paper created by or about your ancestors.** The one document you don't see may include that elusive piece of information you really need. Whenever possible, get photocopies of original documents rather than just transcriptions ("exact" duplicates, which, due to transcribing errors, may not be exact) or abstracts (listings of important points in a document, which, because the person doing the abstract is not necessarily familiar with your family, may omit an important fact). If you find a book that includes an abstract of, say, your ancestor's will, also get a copy of the original will. While abstracts and transcriptions include helpful information, they also can contain errors that may mislead you and cause you to waste time chasing false leads.

Reminder

DON'T SKIMP ON PAPERWORK!

When I first started researching, I didn't bother to get the license for the second marriage of my great-grandmother Lovina (Rader) (Reese) West. After all, Andrew West was not *my* ancestor! I was, however, trying to determine the exact death date of Lovina's first husband, Valentine Reese, whom my aunts insisted died in 1916. Finally, I realized that if I knew when Lovina married Andrew, I would at least have a date by which Valentine definitely was dead. When the marriage license arrived, I discovered that it included a space for "Date of death or divorce of previous husband," and there was the elusive date: Despite my aunt's theories, Valentine had died on 29 December 1910.

JUST BECAUSE IT'S IN PRINT DOESN'T MEAN IT'S TRUE!

Just because something is in print (or in a computer or on the Internet) doesn't mean it's true. Many people have published incorrect information, for various reasons. Perhaps they believed it was true (after all, Aunt Sally *said* . . .). Perhaps they wanted it to be true, especially if it connected the line to a famous person or provided eligibility for a lineage society. In some cases, people have intentionally published false information to substantiate famous connections or simply to increase the period between a couple's marriage and the birth of their first child to nine months. Make every attempt to verify in primary sources the information you get from published materials.

Be wary of family stories involving connections to famous people. While famous people are related to *someone*, some people want to attract reflected grandeur to themselves with no real evidence. Just because someone famous has the same surname as one of your ancestors, you can't assume that the celebrity is a relative, especially if the surname is a common one.

COPY MATERIAL EXACTLY AS YOU FIND IT

Whenever possible, photocopy material for your files, whether it's pages from a book, an ancestor's will, or Aunt Nellie's three-page summary of your family's history. If you must transcribe it, copy it exactly as it's written, including abbreviations, misspellings, punctuation, and grammatical mistakes. Don't insert your own comments unless you make it clear that you're doing so. It's better to add comments at the end of the transcription than in the middle; for example, "[note of researcher Hermione Williams: Aunt Nellie spells the name 'Read,' but in his signature, Andrew spelled it 'Reid.']" *Now* you know this is your own comment; write it so that five years later you'll still be able to tell. If someone else were to use the material from your files, confusion might result from unmarked interpolated comments.

READ MORE ABOUT IT!

For more detailed information on citing sources, see Elizabeth Shown Mills's *Evidence! Citation & Analysis for the Family Historian* and Richard Lackey's *Cite Your Sources.*

CITE YOUR SOURCES

To evaluate information, you need to know the source, so note sources of all facts in your genealogical records. For example:
- on a copy of a document, note the courthouse or other repository, file name or number, deed book volumes and pages, etc.
- on a photocopy from a book, note the author, title, place of publication, publisher, date, pages, and the library where you found it
- on a copy of a magazine article, note the author, title, name of magazine, volume, issue number, date, and pages
- on a transcription of an interview with a family member, note the date of the interview and the full name of the person you interviewed
- on a transcription of a census record, note the state, county, town or post office, page, dwelling and family numbers, micropublication number, and microfilm roll number

Make citations specific. If you want to return to the source of a piece of information, it's frustrating to find a citation that simply states the title of a book that has five hundred pages and no index. Make citations clear enough that someone else could look at them and immediately recognize the record to which you're referring. Don't use a code like "file A, source 32." Suppose your documents get shuffled? Suppose your house and your file cabinets burn? Could you reconstruct your sources from something like "file A, source 32"?

Note sources on your records for several reasons:

- For your own reference: Now, when your entire sheaf of papers still fits into one document folder, you know that a deed came from Cocke County, Tennessee. But fifteen years from now, when you've accumulated eight file drawers of material, how will you know that?

- Someone may question where you got a piece of information. It's far better to respond "Indiana County, Pennsylvania, Deed Book 17, page 141" than "I have a copy of a deed I got somewhere."

- If you find conflicting information from two or more sources or an impossible combination of dates in a person's life, knowing your sources enables you to double-check them. Perhaps you'll find that the reason your great-great-grandmother seems to have gotten married at age two is that you transposed her birth year from 1846 to 1864.

- If you publish information on your family, your credibility is greater if you footnote all facts with sources than if you just recite facts.

RESEARCH COLLATERAL LINES, TOO

Often, beginning genealogists say something like, "My goal is to trace my direct line back as far as I can, as fast as I can. Forget those brothers and sisters of ancestors; what good are they?" As genealogists gain experience, they realize that collateral lines (lines of ancestors' brothers and sisters) can yield important clues about their own lines. While your great-grandfather's death certificate may not give his mother's maiden name, perhaps his older brother's death certificate does include this vital information. And living descendants on collateral lines may have family information ranging from Bibles and documents to fascinating stories passed down through their line but not yours. So collect information about siblings of ancestors as well as about ancestors themselves.

SOME NOTES ABOUT NAMES

Names are often a hang-up for the beginning genealogist, who may ignore a particular record because "our family didn't spell the name that way." Seasoned genealogists know that while an *ancestor* didn't spell the name "that way," before modern times it's anyone's guess how the census taker, register of wills or deeds, or other official person might have spelled the name. While this is especially true in dealing with "foreign" (e.g., German or Slavic) names spelled by a person whose first language is English, even simple names often have variant spellings—for example, "Hays" and "Hayes." Standard spelling is a modern invention; in previous centuries, spelling was often phonetic, and people might have spelled their names according to their whim or their own phonetic versions. Even if someone had asked, your ancestor might have been illiterate, with no concept of how the name "ought" to be spelled. Turning up your nose at a record with a variant spelling could mean missing important information.

On the other hand, **beware of the "same name, must be same person" fallacy.** A name you think is unique because the first name, last name, or both are so unusual might belong to more than one person at the same time. Several cousins could have an unusual first name to honor a grandfather; the area where you're researching might be the epicenter for your unusual ancestral surname. Don't attribute data to your ancestor merely on the basis of the name in a record unless (1) other evidence in the record proves it belongs to that person, or (2) you're absolutely certain that your ancestor is the only person of that name in the area.

Warning

Nicknames

Knowledge of nicknames may help you spot information about an ancestor that you might otherwise miss. You probably know that Jim is a nickname for James, and Bob is one for Robert. You might not know that Patsy is a nickname for Martha; Nancy, for Agnes; and Stoffel, for Christopher. Look at a book such as Christine Rose's *Nicknames: Past and Present* for clues about alternative names to watch for while searching for your ancestors.

HANDWRITING

Along with spelling, handwriting can be a problem. In some cases, the problem may simply be legibility; in others, documents may be written in a script, like German Gothic, whose letterforms are quite different from those Americans use today. If you encounter difficulties with handwriting, get help from books such as Kip Sperry's *Reading Early American Handwriting* or Edna M. Bentz's *If I Can, You Can Decipher Germanic Records*, or consult an expert on that style of writing.

DATES

As you research further back on your family lines, you'll need to learn more about dates and dating systems. One important historical event for genealogists is the calendar change in 1752, when the English colonies in North America dropped eleven days from the calendar and changed New Year's Day from 25 March to 1 January. But a little knowledge is a dangerous thing. Once they've learned about this calendar change, some genealogists want to apply it universally. However, in Europe, the calendar changed at different times in different locations (the dates of the change range from 1582 to 1918!). A detailed discussion of this is outside the scope of this book; if you're interested, read the chapters on dates in basic genealogy handbooks or Kenneth Smith's *Genealogical Dates: A User-Friendly Guide*.

In English North America, when New Year's Day fell in March, it was considered the first month of the year. Inexperienced genealogists who find a source which gives a date as "23 1mo 1740" may diligently write in their notes

"23 January 1740," and they will probably be wrong. On the other hand, between about 1700 and 1752, some people used a 1 January start date for the year and began using a system called *double dating*. If you see a date written "28 February 1748/9," it doesn't mean the writer wasn't sure of the year. It means if the year started on 25 March, it was 1748, and if the year started on 1 January, it was 1749. It's best to transcribe nonstandard dates exactly as you find them.

Unless you have a nonstandard date such as the ones discussed above, write it in the genealogically accepted format of "day, month, year"; for example, 6 December 1949. Do not use numbers for months (is 6/12/1949 December sixth or June twelfth?), and use all four digits of a year (did December '49 happen in 1949? 1849? 1749?).

As you collect data on your family, check dates for possible problems. Did someone marry at age five, become a mother at age four or sixty-four, or become a father at ninety? If so, double-check your information! Many genealogical computer programs have an audit function that looks for this sort of problem for you.

COUNTIES HAVE GENEALOGIES, TOO

In the course of investigating your ancestors' genealogy, investigate also the genealogy of their places of residence. In many states, counties were formed from earlier counties, and the state itself might have been formed from another state or territory. One piece of ground might have been in several different counties over the course of its history. For example, an ancestor might have lived successively in Bedford, Westmoreland, and Armstrong Counties, Pennsylvania, without ever moving. To track down records, you must know that although the ancestor sold the land while it was in Armstrong County, he bought it while it was in Westmoreland County, and you'll need to look for the purchase deed there. Appendix B discusses and compares some books you can use to ascertain whether and when the county you're working with was formed from another entity. The maps in William Thorndale and William Dollarhide's *Map Guide to the U.S. Federal Censuses, 1790–1920* show changes in county boundaries between 1790 and 1920.

Important

When you record the location where an event in your ancestor's life took place, use the place names that were in effect at the time. Allentown, Pennsylvania, is in Lehigh County now, but before 1812, Lehigh County was part of Northampton County. So if your ancestor was born there in 1802, give the birthplace as "Allentown, Northampton County, Pennsylvania." To avoid questions, clarify this as "Allentown, Northampton [now Lehigh] County, Pennsylvania." Include the state as well as the county in any location. Many county names occur in more than one state, and you don't want to leave people wondering if the Northampton County you mention is in Pennsylvania, Virginia, or North Carolina.

WHICH ANCESTORS SHOULD YOU RESEARCH?

Some genealogy texts advise you to work on one line at a time, but this can constrict your outlook and slow your research; if you get stuck, you'll have no place to go. It's better to research several lines at a time: if you hit a roadblock on one line, you'll have successes on others to keep up your morale. The amount of research you can do at one time depends on how much time you can devote to genealogy. With long-distance research, you'll find that you write a letter and have to wait a few weeks (or months!) for an answer. Rather than twiddling your thumbs while you wait, work on another line or two or three.

Genealogists who have made some progress on their line like to put their findings into a *fan chart*, a large chart made of concentric circles. Your name and information are in the center circle; the ring around it is divided into two sections for your parents' information; the next ring is divided into four sections for your grandparents' information; the next is divided into eight sections for your great-grandparents' information, and so on. A fan chart of your ancestors may remind you of a spider web, and this is a good metaphor. You're in the center working outward; you can follow one line for a while, and then return to the center and follow another line. If you have three hours every weekend to spend on genealogy and you're only researching one line, you might write two letters and then not use your remaining time. If you're working on all your lines, you'll easily find tasks to fill those three hours and then some.

Genealogical research isn't always a linear pursuit. To continue the spider web analogy, sometimes you'll backtrack in research. You may look at a source and think you've found everything in it relating to your family; six months later, information from another source will prompt you to go back to that source again. In the course of your research, you'll go in and out on the spider web many, many times.

ORGANIZING YOUR RESEARCH

While this book doesn't go into detail about organizing your material, it's important that you begin organizing soon after you start collecting. Wait too long, and organization becomes a daunting task. If you're comfortable with computers, invest in a computer program to keep track of your family. **Having your data in a computer genealogy program can be especially helpful for long-distance research, as you can easily print an up-to-date pedigree chart or family group sheet to send to correspondents.**

Tip

At the very least, use paper pedigree charts and family group sheets. Pedigree charts show all of a person's ancestors, usually for three or four generations back (see Figure 1-1 on page 12). Family group sheets show detailed information on one nuclear family: a married couple and their children, with the children listed in birth order, if you can determine it (see Figure 1-2 on page 13). You can buy printed forms from genealogical publishers (look for ads in genealogical magazines), download forms from the Internet, or photocopy them from genealogy handbooks. These forms help you see what information you have and what you still need to look for. They allow you to see various people in the family in relationship to each other and may highlight problems such as improbable dates.

Many of the basic books listed in the introduction include information on

PEDIGREE CHART #1

Chart of
Faye Irene Thompson

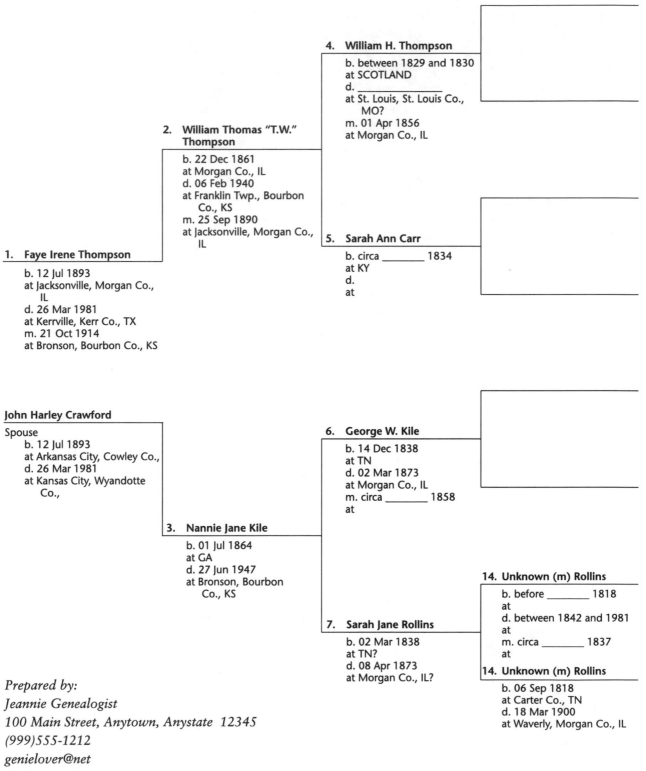

4. **William H. Thompson**

    b. between 1829 and 1830
    at SCOTLAND
    d. _____
    at St. Louis, St. Louis Co.,
       MO?
    m. 01 Apr 1856
    at Morgan Co., IL

2. **William Thomas "T.W."**
    Thompson

    b. 22 Dec 1861
    at Morgan Co., IL
    d. 06 Feb 1940
    at Franklin Twp., Bourbon
       Co., KS
    m. 25 Sep 1890
    at Jacksonville, Morgan Co.,
       IL

5. **Sarah Ann Carr**

    b. circa _____ 1834
    at KY
    d.
    at

1. **Faye Irene Thompson**

    b. 12 Jul 1893
    at Jacksonville, Morgan Co.,
       IL
    d. 26 Mar 1981
    at Kerrville, Kerr Co., TX
    m. 21 Oct 1914
    at Bronson, Bourbon Co., KS

John Harley Crawford

Spouse
    b. 12 Jul 1893
    at Arkansas City, Cowley Co.,
    d. 26 Mar 1981
    at Kansas City, Wyandotte
       Co.,

6. **George W. Kile**

    b. 14 Dec 1838
    at TN
    d. 02 Mar 1873
    at Morgan Co., IL
    m. circa _____ 1858
    at

3. **Nannie Jane Kile**

    b. 01 Jul 1864
    at GA
    d. 27 Jun 1947
    at Bronson, Bourbon
       Co., KS

14. **Unknown (m) Rollins**

    b. before _____ 1818
    at
    d. between 1842 and 1981
    at
    m. circa _____ 1837
    at

7. **Sarah Jane Rollins**

    b. 02 Mar 1838
    at TN?
    d. 08 Apr 1873
    at Morgan Co., IL?

14. **Unknown (m) Rollins**

    b. 06 Sep 1818
    at Carter Co., TN
    d. 18 Mar 1900
    at Waverly, Morgan Co., IL

Prepared by:
Jeannie Genealogist
100 Main Street, Anytown, Anystate 12345
(999)555-1212
genielover@net

Figure 1-1 Sample pedigree chart

FAMILY GROUP SHEET OF
UNKNOWN (M) AND NANCY (ROLLINS) ROLLINS

Husband: Unknown (m) ROLLINS

Born:	bef _____ 1818	
Married:	ca. _____ 1837[1]	TN?
Died:	bet 1842 and 1847[2]	

Father:

Mother:

Wife: Nancy ROLLINS

Born:	6 Sep 1818[3,4]	Carter Co., TN
Died:	18 Mar 1900[3]	Waverly, Morgan Co., IL[3]
Buried:	Youngblood Cemetery[3]	

Father: John Calvin ROLLINS[4]

Mother: Sarah "Sallie" (-?-)[4]

Other Husbands: 2) Enos GREEN[5]; 3) William SMALLING[6]; 4) Benjamin WILSON[7]

Children	Born	Married	Died
Sarah Jane ROLLINS[9]	2 Mar 1838[8,9] TN[9]	ca. 1858[10] TN? George W. KILE[8]	8 Apr 1873[11] Morgan, Co., IL?
Lurinda Caroline ROLLINS[3,9]	8 Aug 1840[9,12,13] Polk Co., TN[13]	6 Feb 1858[14] Bradley Co., TN[14] James T. SMITH[12,13,14]	22 Nov 1940[12] Kansas City, Jackson Co., MO[12]
Martha E. ROLLINS[9]	ca. 1842[8] TN[9]	30 Jun 1861[15] Whitfield Co., GA[15] George W. CLARK[15]	Bet 1870 and 1878?[16]

Notes:

1. Estimated marriage date based on birth of first known child in 1838.
2. Martha E. Rollins born ca. 1842; Nancy's next known child, Margaret Green, born ca. 1847
3. Obituary of Nancy Wilson, *Weekly Illinois Courier*, 21 March 1900, p. 16, for birth and death dates and places.
4. Bible of John Calvin Rollins for birth date and parentage; transcript sent to me by [name]; Bible was in possession of her aunt [name] in 1985.
5. Gravestone of William M. Green, Holmes Cemetery, Morgan County, Illinois, says "son of Enos and Nancy Green."
6. William Smalling household, 1860 U.S. Census, Whitfield County, Georgia, population schedule, Anderson Post Office, page 16, dwelling 59, family 58, National Archives Micropublication M653, Roll 141.
7. Morgan County Marriage Book C:64, County Clerk's Office, Jacksonville, Illinois.
8. Handwritten notes by Effie Eugenia (Thompson) Busby, granddaughter of Sarah Jane (Rollins) Kile.
9. Nancy Green household, 1850 U.S. Census, Polk County, Tennessee, population schedule, 25th Subdivision, 4th Civil District, page 198, dwelling 594, family 600, National Archives Micropublication M432, Roll 892. Note: This census shows "Loucinda C.," age 10, supporting her claim to be 100 years old in 1940 (Lurinda's name is often misinterpreted as "Lucinda").

Figure 1-2 Sample family group sheet

10. Estimated marriage date based on birth of first child in 1859.
11. Petition in probate file of George W. Kile, Morgan County Probate File #1874, County Clerk's Office, Jacksonville, Illinois.
12. Lurinda C. Smith, death certificate 37859, Missouri State Board of Health, Jefferson City, Missouri.
13. Obituary of Lurinda C. Smith, "End to a Centenarian: Mrs. Lurinda C. Smith was 100 in August," probably in a Kansas City newspaper; clipping with no newspaper title or date that I got from my grandmother, Faye Irene (Thompson) Crawford.
14. Handwritten copy of article on 100th birthday of Lurinda C. Smith, "Emporia Woman 100 Years Old—Was Civil War Nurse" (no newspaper title or date indicated), that I got from my grandmother, Faye Irene (Thompson) Crawford (copy sent to her by [name]).
15. Whitfield County Marriage Book A:219–220, Probate Clerk's Office, Dalton, Georgia.
16. Benjamin Wilson household, 1870 U.S. Census, Morgan County, Illinois, population schedule, Wright's Precinct, page 25, dwelling 159, family 159, National Archives Micropublication M593, Roll 263. Household includes housekeeper Nancy Smalling (who married Benjamin in 1871—see note 7) and her daughter Martha Clark, with Martha's daughter Mary A. Clark. There is no further record of Martha Clark in Morgan County: no marriage record and no death record. Either she died between 1870 and the beginning of death records in 1878, or she left the county.

—Prepared by: Jeanie Genealogist, 100 Main Street, Anytown, Anystate 12345

organizing your files. Don't feel compelled to follow one system. Choose a system you like, or choose pieces of several systems. The most important things about your method of organization are that you're comfortable with it and you can find material you want relatively quickly.

RESEARCH LOGS

Many genealogists use a research log to keep track of what they've done and tasks they still need to accomplish (see Figures 1-3 on page 15 and 1-4 on page 16). This is a chart in which you record such things as

- the problem you were trying to solve
- the source you checked (a library book, an index to county deeds, etc.)
- where you found the source (useful if you want to come back to it—you may know now at which library you saw the book, but will you remember ten years from now?)
- the results of your search

Timesaver

A research log can also save time by letting you know that you checked a certain source five years ago. As you work with a research log, you'll think of other fields that you want to add. You can keep this on paper, but it could be helpful to set it up as a computer spreadsheet or database. Experiment to find out what works best for you. You may set up one giant research log or one for each branch of the family or one for each of the surnames you're researching.

You may also want to make charts like the one shown in chapter twenty to keep track of the documents you have located for each ancestor; you can tell at a glance what records you still need for a person.

ANCESTOR SURNAME: KING

Date: 21 Oct 2001
Repository: Anytown Public Library
Call number: 974.888 A739
Source (author, title, publication information): *Armstrong County, Pennsylvania: Her People, Past and Present.* Chicago: J.H. Beers and Co., 1914. Reprint by Windmill Publications, Inc., 1989.
Looking for: biographies for King family
Result: found several on my line; photocopied
File: King

Date: 21 Oct 2001
Repository: Anytown Public Library
Call number: 929 K642
Source (author, title, publication information): King, Wilbur Lewis. *Genealogy of Jacob King (König) and Matheus King (König) of Northampton County, Pennsylvania.* Ann Arbor, Michigan, 1952.
Looking for: information on my King line
Result: has my line back from my mother to the immigrant, Matheus König, but my mother and her sisters are listed as children of their uncle! Photocopied relevant pages.
File: King

Date: 21 Oct 2001
Repository: Anytown Public Library
Call number: 974.888 A717
Source (author, title, publication information): *The Armstrong Democrat and Sentinel published in Kittanning, Armstrong Co., Penna. Genealogical Abstracts, January 1892–December 1984.* Compiled by Nancy Hill Hidinger. Apollo: Closson Press, 1995.
Looking for: any articles on my King family
Result: 22 Dec. 1892: A.C. King's store burned ("the building held heavy insurance . . .") 11 May 1893: A.C. King of Tunnelville appointed postmaster. Photocopied both.
File: King

Figure 1-3 Sample research log

INTERNET OR "INTERNOT"?

This book lists many Internet sources. If you don't have an Internet connection, you may feel left out, but seeing the wealth of information available on the Internet may spur you to figure out a way to use it. If you can't have your own Internet connection, see chapter nineteen for suggestions on how you can get access in other ways.

```
┌─────────────────────────────────────────────────────────────────┐
│              RESEARCH LOG FOR INTERNET SEARCHES                    │
├───────────────────────────────────────────────────────────────────┤
```

Date: 15 October 2001
URL: http://www.familytreemagazine.com/search
Name of site: Family Tree Magazine (search page)
Searched for: Jacob Altman
Result: Seven sites found relating to my Jacob

Date: 15 October 2001
URL: http://www.rootsweb.com/~maillist/surnames/index.html
Name of site: RootsWeb Surname Index
Searched for: Do they have a mailing list for the Altman family?
Result: Yes, they do! Subscribed.

Date: 15 October 2001
URL: http://genforum.familytreemaker.com/
Name of site: GenForum
Searched for: Surname Kile
Result: Yes, they have a forum, with some posts from people for Monroe Co., TN. Need to formulate a query and post it to the list.

Date: 15 October 2001
URL: http://www.familysearch.org/sg/
Name of site: Family History SourceGuide
Searched for: Guide for researching military history
Result: Found *U.S. Military Records Research Outline* and printed it out.

Figure 1-4 Sample research log for Internet searches

CONCLUSION

Long-distance research, like any genealogical research, requires you to start with yourself and work backward. In doing research, you must

- differentiate between primary and secondary sources
- try to get every bit of information you can about your ancestor
- analyze that information
- record the sources of information
- research the siblings of your ancestors
- be aware of the possibility that more than one person might have had your ancestor's name at the same time
- pay attention to dates
- know the history of the area where your ancestor lived
- organize your research so you can find information when you need it
- keep logs of your research

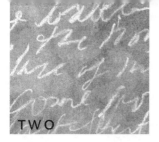

TWO

Some Basics of Letter (and E-Mail) Writing

I n the course of doing long-distance genealogy, you'll write a great many letters. This chapter includes some basic principles to make these letters as effective as possible.

FIRST IMPRESSIONS COUNT

If anything about your letter confuses, frustrates, or angers the person who receives it, that's how the person will remember you. Never demand information; always be polite. Recognize that, hard as it may be to imagine, the person to whom you're writing might possibly have something more important to do than look for your great-grandfather's death certificate. Write letters on white 8½″ × 11″ (21.6cm × 27.9cm) paper when writing to records repositories and when writing your first letter to a potential cousin.

KEEP IT SHORT

Have this engraved on a plaque and hang it over your desk in a prominent place:

Keep your letter short!

Especially if you're writing to a library, historical society, government office, or other official organization, keep it short. Yes, the story of how your great-great-great-grandmother hid the money in the outhouse to keep Sherman's troops from stealing it is interesting, but the person who receives your query has a job to do. This morning's mail brought twenty letters from genealogists; the clerk is doing jobs that five years ago two people handled, and she will really appreciate it if your letter is concise and to the point. She will also appreciate it if you ask for only one or two pieces of information at a time. Even if all eight

Important

Notes

IT'S YOUR DECISION: WRITE TO REQUEST COPIES OF A DOCUMENT OR ORDER MICROFILM?

You may get copies of various documents in several ways, but two of the major ways are (1) write letters requesting a copy or (2) rent microfilm of the documents. Not everyone has access to a Family History Center, but if you do, it may make sense to get microfilm of the documents you want to see, rather than writing to get copies (see chapter thirteen for information on some of the major sources of microfilm, including the Latter-day Saints Family History Library). In some cases the availability of records in CD-ROM format gives a third option.

When making the decision whether to order a paper copy of a document from a repository or rent from a microfilm collection, consider the following:

- Obviously, the first criterion for having to make this choice is that the record actually is available in both formats. Some materials are only available as copies of the original documents from the repository that holds them (most vital records kept on the state level and recent records of most kinds, for example).

- If you rent an index on microfilm to identify your ancestor's record and then write to the repository for a copy of the record (or rent the microfilm that includes it), you may spend more time from the beginning of the process to the end than if you had just written to the repository to request the document.

- If you anticipate that you will only find one or a few of the type of record in question, it may be easier to write to the repository and request it, especially if you can find out the cost ahead of time.

- Some materials are available from a distance only on microfilm or CD-ROM because there is one original, which cannot be copied (census records, for example).

- If it's very expensive to get a copy from the repository, microfilm may be a better choice.

- If you anticipate that you'll be looking for a large number of a particular kind of document (for example, you know that an ancestor had many plots of land, or you have a large number of ancestors who lived in one county), it might make sense to order the indexes for that kind of document to identify citations for the documents relating to your ancestors. Then you can decide whether to rent microfilm of the documents (if film is available) or to write to the repository for copies.

- If you write to a repository and ask the staff to check an index for a document or documents related to your ancestor, they might say nothing is found. If you think they should have found something, you might want to order the index on microfilm to double-check.

Why might a person at a repository not find documents related to your ancestor that actually are in the index? See chapter twelve for a discussion of indexing problems. Beyond those, the following situations can lead to disappointment when someone else is looking something up for you:

- Although at the county or town level, clerks may be more familiar with variant spellings and often have indexes based on phonetic principles to help them, they may miss entries sometimes. The spelling you give for your ancestor's name in your request may have little resemblance to the spelling of the name used in the document and, therefore, in its index. For example, the Swiss name Tscherri might also appear as Scherri, Cherry, and many other spellings, and if you aren't aware of all of them, you might not suggest the one that appears in the index.

- You may ask the repository to check a certain date range. They did so, but documents for your ancestor fall outside that range. Or perhaps there are several indexes, each spanning a different time frame, and they didn't check all that apply to the date range you asked about.

- Sometimes, for unexplainable reasons, people can look at an index and not see something that is right there!

However, if you locate an item in the index when the person at the repository did not, please don't berate the person for not finding it. Workers at these repositories are busy, and most do the best they can.

of your great-grandparents lived in the same county, it's best not to ask for all their death certificates in one request.

Limiting your requests to one per letter may help you get more timely and complete responses. If an item in a multiple-request letter requires special handling, or if the requests require the clerk to search files in widely separated areas (or even separate buildings), the clerk may set aside that letter as future work or answer one question and not the others.

Some of your letters will be to governmental offices and records repositories, but some will be to distant cousins. In the course of doing long-distance genealogy, you'll write to people who don't know you, and you'll want to make a good impression. Someone who has to wade through five rambling pages to find out why you're writing (only to find that a potential common ancestor finally appears on page six) might not bother to write back to you. Yes, it has been quite a struggle for you to get to where you are today on your line, but few people want to hear a blow-by-blow description of the route you followed.

Make your first letter to a potential distant cousin short and concise. One way to keep things concise is to enclose a pedigree chart and/or family group sheet(s) for the family you're asking about. **To save your correspondent some time, highlight the surname(s) of interest on the chart(s).**

Often, two genealogists who are distant cousins find they have much in

Tip

Tip

SALUTATIONS

How do you start a letter to someone you don't know? I used to work in an office with two assistants; most of the time, the people working for me were also female. Periodically, we received a letter that began "Dear Sirs." I always had to repress the urge to return it with a note saying, "Sorry, there are no 'Sirs' here." Because of this, I usually begin letters to bureaucratic offices with the gender-neutral—and, well, *friendly*—salutation "Dear Friends." If you prefer something more formal, you could try "Dear Sir or Madam" (however, the recipient might point out that there are no "Madams" where she works).

If "Dear Friends" is too friendly for you, or if you feel it's too informal for a particular circumstance, try the more formal (and very impersonal) "To Whom It May Concern."

When writing your first letter to a (potential) distant cousin, you may wrestle with whether to call her "Amanda," "Ms. Blake," or "Mrs. Blake." I usually take a chance and use the informal "Amanda." After all, in many cases, I either know or hope that the person is a cousin, however distant; since he or she is family, I feel justified in using the first name.

common and become good friends as well. But in a first letter, refrain from telling the person about your family, your four cats, and your son's scholarship to Yale; save this for later correspondence when (if) you have established your bond.

MAKE YOUR LETTERS LEGIBLE

If possible, type your letters using a computer or typewriter. Use a legible font large enough that your correspondent won't have to squint to read it. If you use a computer, put the key elements of your question in boldface; if you type (and maybe even if you use a computer and set these elements in boldface), use a highlighter to make the information stand out. Then the recipient who reads your letter and puts it in a stack of work will easily be able to see the question when the letter comes to the top of the stack. If you must write by hand, write clearly and legibly; consider printing to make your writing more legible. And again, use highlighter to emphasize the most important words of your query.

INCLUDE FULL CONTACT INFORMATION IN LETTERS

Include your full name and address in all letters, preferably on each page. Don't expect the person answering it to get your address from the envelope (many offices discard envelopes when letters are opened). If the pages of your letter are separated, having your name and address on each page improves your chances of getting what you want. Include your phone number, fax number, and E-mail address as well. Giving people as many contact options as possible will yield more replies.

USE FULL NAMES OF ANCESTORS

If you reply to someone who has sent you information, use full names of the ancestors in question. A letter that says "Do you think John's wife could have been Mary Smith?" can be frustrating if the recipient can't remember which family you were corresponding about or who "John" is.

ASK SPECIFIC QUESTIONS

Beginning genealogists have been known to write to the public library in the ancestral town and say something like, "My third great-grandfather John K. Reid lived in your town. Please send me everything you have on him." Such a letter will probably end up in the trash. Few librarians or courthouse personnel are going to take the time to go through all their material looking for "all" information on John K. Reid, especially if you give no other identifying information! **It's best to ask a specific question or two about your ancestor.** Give any details you have that help to identify him and distinguish him from other men named John K. Reid, such as (approximate, if necessary) dates of birth, marriage, and death; name(s) of spouse(s); names of children; and residence. Even if you have many questions about him, ask a question or two in a letter this month, ask a question or two next month, and so forth. It's unlikely that John K. Reid, dead since 1851, is going anywhere.

State clearly
- the information you need
- the full name of the person (for a marriage record, both people)
- the date or approximate date of the event

Reread the letter. Is it clear? Have you have typed the names and dates correctly?

ENCLOSE A SASE

Is this abbreviation new to you? You'll see it often as you pursue your genealogical research. It stands for "self-addressed, stamped envelope." The envelope should be a business-size envelope (no. 9 or no. 10), not a little bitty one.

Some government agencies may return your stamped envelope and pay postage themselves, but don't assume they all do this. Send a SASE with every query.

OFFER TO PAY FOR PHOTOCOPIES AND POSTAGE

What if the person to whom you wrote has scads of material to send you that won't fit into your SASE? People deal with this in several ways, but it's easier if you've offered in your original letter to pay for photocopies and postage if

Reminder

Tip

FOLDING SASES

Many people have written essays on elaborate ways to fold SASEs to keep the envelope they're in from getting jammed in postal machines. This may be heretical, but I always just fold the envelope in thirds and put it in with the letter. I do put it inside the folds of the letter, which may help to protect it from getting caught in machinery. As far as I know, no envelope that I've sent with a SASE has gotten torn up in transit.

Notes

WHEN SHOULD YOU SEND DONATIONS OR OFFER TO PAY FOR MATERIALS AND WHY?

Government agencies generally charge fees for information. They have, at the very least, a charge for photocopies and maybe a search fee for looking up information. If you want a copy of your grandfather's death certificate, do some research in advance to find out the fee. Sometimes if you specify in your first letter exactly what you want and ask about a fee, the agency will send you the material and a bill. It can be worthwhile to include in your first letter a phrase such as "If the cost of this death certificate is $15 or less, if possible, please send me a copy and bill me."

When writing to a nonprofit institution such as a church or library, it's considerate to send a donation. If you write to them more than once, a donation will make your letter stand out ("Oh, look, here's another letter from that nice lady in Poughkeepsie who sent us twenty dollars a while back, and now she's sent another twenty dollars"). If you aren't a taxpayer in the library's town or a congregant of the church in question, these people are under no obligation to help you; a donation shows that you appreciate the time they're taking to search their records for you.

When writing to a nonprofit institution such as a genealogical or historical society, it's even more important to enclose a donation, although you may find that some societies and libraries charge a fee for research (if they do, they'll let you know). Historical societies are often poorly funded and are grateful for your donation. Also, this type of organization receives many queries in the mail from hopeful genealogists. They have to employ some sort of triage to figure out which ones to answer first. Three things they may take into consideration are

- Is the inquirer a member of the society (see chapter sixteen)?

- Is the question easy to understand and can it be answered quickly?

- Did the inquirer send money?

---

the person can help. To avoid unpleasant surprises, you may want to set a limit on the amount that you're willing to pay. Many people won't ask you to pay, but some genealogists have limited incomes, and even a few dollars for postage or photocopying may be a hardship for them. If someone has a large amount of information, he may use your envelope to send you a letter explaining that he has forty pages of material to send you and the cost of photocopying and postage will be X dollars. Another person might simply use a larger envelope and send you the material. She may specify in her letter the amount she wants you to reimburse her for postage (and photocopies). If she doesn't, use those trusty arithmetic skills from first grade to calculate the reimbursement. Add up the stamps on the envelope and assume that she probably had to pay about ten cents per page for the copies, and reimburse her when you send your thank-you letter. As a matter of courtesy, if you offer to pay and someone sends you materials and asks for reimbursement, send it immediately!

USE ENOUGH POSTAGE

How heavy is that letter? Use a postage scale if you have more than four sheets of paper in your envelope. Causing your correspondent to pay postage due won't endear you to him, especially if he has never heard of you before (first impressions count!).

SEND LETTERS TO THE CORRECT OFFICE

Find out what office keeps the records you need. Sending your letter to the wrong repository will delay your search; it could take them some time to let you know they can't help you, if you hear from them at all!

SEND THANK-YOU LETTERS

You were planning to send a thank-you letter, weren't you? Miss Manners would be very upset if you didn't. After all the work the person went through to search for the information on your ancestors and photocopy it and/or print it out, send a thank-you letter. The next time you write, especially if you want lots more information, your correspondent will remember your courtesy!

DON'T ANTAGONIZE REPOSITORY PERSONNEL

In most cases, people working in courthouses, libraries, etc., will do their best to help you, but sometimes the information just isn't there. It's not the fault of the county clerk that the county didn't record marriages until 1885, thus missing the marriage of your ancestors in 1883. Writing a nasty letter ("They were married in your county; you *must* have a record!") won't help your situation.

PROS AND CONS OF E-MAIL FOR LONG-DISTANCE RESEARCH

E-mail can be very useful to the long-distance genealogist. You can send long messages to distant cousins or potential cousins. You can send large data files without having to worry about postage costs. You can communicate almost instantly with fellow researchers and get a response from them in a few hours, rather than waiting a week or more for a response by mail.

However, **don't fall into E-mail traps.** It's simple to sit down, dash off an E-mail, and send it. It's so simple that some people forget the basic rules of communication. They use sentence fragments, misspell words, run on, change subjects in midstream and come back to the original subject with no warning—and after all this, they forget to proofread. It's so easy to click on "Send"! If

Tip

HOW CAN I SEND MONEY THROUGH THE MAIL?

It's best to send a check or a money order; it's not wise to send cash through the mail. If reimbursing for a small amount of postage, send stamps. The best way to send stamps is to use self-adhesive ones (still on their original backing, of course!).

Important

you use E-mail, think before you write, think while you're writing, and then read through what you have written before you send it to be sure that it's clear and makes sense. If it doesn't, rewrite. Along with this, remember to check your spelling, both with the computer and your eyes.

If you want to send someone a six-generation descendancy chart from your computer genealogy program, you may find it quicker and easier to do so by E-mail than in a letter. But if you include it as part of the text in an E-mail message, the person who receives it may have a problem. Different E-mail readers work differently. As a result, your beautiful six-generation chart may appear to your correspondent as unreadable mishmash. It will be far more readable if you save it as a computer file and send it as an attachment.

On the other hand, some people prefer to have your data on paper, even if you can E-mail it. Recent computer viruses that access a computer through E-mail attachments have made people nervous about any attachment, no matter what its source. Be tolerant of other people's preferences for methods of data exchange.

Definitions

Genealogists often exchange data via E-mail using attached files in a format called GEDCOM (*Genealogical Data Communication*). Most genealogical programs export and import data in this lowest common denominator format. However, in the process of exporting data into the GEDCOM format, you may lose part of your data if your program supports a field that GEDCOM doesn't.

E-MAIL ETIQUETTE

No discussion of E-mail is complete without a discussion of "Netiquette," etiquette for E-mail users.

- End messages with your full name and at least the name of your town and state, if not your full address. People want to know with whom they're corresponding, and "From: genielover@net" with no other "signature" doesn't tell them much.
- DON'T SHOUT!! Writing a message all in capitals is considered boorish and shouting, and it brands you as a Newbie.
- Chech your spellnig (and your grammar). Many E-mail programs have built-in spelling checkers; use yours, and proofread by eye, too. While you're doing that, make sure that your writing makes sense.
- Format your messages for easy reading. Don't run on and on; break your post into paragraphs.
- People reading your E-mail are looking at flat, emotionless words on a computer screen. No visual or tonal cues indicate your tone of voice. If you make a joke, or especially if you make a sarcastic remark, indicate it's a joke with an emoticon—a symbol that uses typed characters to form a sidewise face, like :-) or <grin>, <smile>, or even ROFL (onlinespeak for "rolling on the floor laughing!"). It's best to avoid sarcasm entirely, but if you must use it, precede it with something like, "Excuse my sarcasm, but. . . ."
- Many people set up an E-mail group of good friends to whom they forward

messages (good jokes, really bad jokes, inspirational thoughts). It's so easy to send E-mail to a hundred people at a time this way! Don't add your new genealogical correspondents to this list without checking with them first. They may need to limit the time they spend on E-mail and want to keep it to serious, relevant matters.

- *DON'T* (this is meant to be shouting!) forward junk mail or chain letters, no matter how much good luck they promise the recipient. People hate E-mail chain letters just as much as the ones they get via snail mail.

- Be careful about forwarding files someone has sent you. Recently, many "check out this file, it's cute" messages have resulted in the transmission of computer viruses. Be especially careful with files with a ".exe" extension. Don't open or forward one unless you're absolutely sure what it is.

- Be careful what you say about other people. You have no idea who might be reading over your correspondent's shoulder when he gets the message— or to whom he might forward it!

The above rules apply to all E-mail messages. The following rules apply more specifically to messages you post to an E-mail list (see chapter nineteen for a discussion of E-mail lists):

- Some members of the list may have to pay their Internet provider a fee per message or pay by the minute (or second) for downloading time. Other people have limited time for E-mail and want to get through it as fast as possible. Keep messages short.

- Use a subject line that allows people to whom the post is irrelevant to delete it without reading it. The ideal subject line for a query includes the major surname, a date or date span for the person in question, and a locality. "Searching for my relatives" doesn't tell the reader much; "Schreckengost, 1810, Armstrong County, PA" does. In the body of the post, you have permission to shout in one way: put surnames in capital letters.

- Don't reply to a message simply to say, "I agree," or even, "I agree totally with Jim's post, which is probably the most important thing ever said on this list."

- When you click "Reply" on your E-mail reader, it may provide a reply form that repeats the message to which you're responding. If so, delete all of it except the part relevant to your response to keep the reply short and allow your response to stand out in the post.

- On the other hand, include something in the message that shows what you're responding to so that people who didn't read the original post won't be in the dark.

- Avoid negative or critical statements about others on the list. Sometimes the anonymity of E-mail makes us forget that there's a living, breathing, and maybe bleeding person at the other end of our mail. All members of the list will see your venting of your negative feelings, and you could end up looking worse than the person you criticize.

- Keep on topic. People subscribe to the list to get information on the subject of the list, not to read that joke your best friend sent you, even if it is the funniest joke you've ever heard. You do have permission to post an occasional joke if it relates specifically to genealogy.

ANNOTATE YOUR ADDRESS BOOK

Track as much information as possible about your correspondents. Enter phone numbers, E-mail addresses, and fax numbers in your address book. If a female correspondent tells you her spouse's name, record that, too. You may not need all that information now, but if someone moves and your letter is returned, a phone number or E-mail address may help you to find the person. When answering letters, note or update the year in your address book. In the future, it may be helpful for you to know how recently the person was at that address.

Also make a note in the address book of the lines you have in common with the correspondent. Then if someone sends you a letter that says, "Do you think John could have married Mary Smith?" you can check your address book for clues about which family is involved. Some people keep a separate address book for their genealogical correspondents.

Idea Generator

CORRESPONDENCE LOGS

Some people just send letters and wait for replies, but **you may want to keep a log of letters you've written so you can keep track of what responses you've received** (see Figure 2-1). The log can help you track letters (it may seem as if it's been six weeks since you wrote for a copy of great-grandfather's death certificate, but the log will remind you that it actually has been only ten days). You'll also be able to discover that, while the information in a query looks promising, you wrote to that person before and the line wasn't the same as yours.

You could keep a paper correspondence log, but if you have a computer, you'd do better to use a spreadsheet or database program. You won't have to worry about running out of room in a field. If you want to find out if you've written to a certain person, you can use the computer's ability to sort the spreadsheet alphabetically by any field or to find a specific word in the file to simplify your search.

Date	Addressee/Address	Summary of Question	Date Answer Received
25 September 2001	[Name and address of recipient]	Request for information on the wives of Noah Abraham	15 October 2001
25 September 2001	[Name and address of recipient]	Request for estate papers of Noah Abraham	30 October 2001
2 October 2001	[Name and address of recipient]	Request for estate papers of George W. Kile	

Figure 2-1 A simple correspondence log

What should you include in the correspondence log? You'll definitely want to include

- date of letter
- name and address of correspondent (or institution) you wrote to
- a brief summary of your question or discussion

Also consider including the following fields:

- donation or payments sent
- whether you received an answer
- when you received the answer
- the gist of the answer
- where you filed the answer

Either as part of this log or as a different file, you may also keep a log of letters you've received. Fields for this could include

- the sender of the letter
- date received
- subjects
- where you filed it

PROS AND CONS OF PHONE CALLS

Some people call a repository to ask for, say, a great-grandfather's death certificate, but unless there's some urgency in getting the information, it's better to write. A phone call could interrupt someone in a pressing or important task. She might resent this interruption; further service you receive could reflect this resentment. With a letter, the person can answer at her convenience and give you the best quality service the repository offers.

With potential distant cousins, **make your first contact by mail or E-mail. You have no way of knowing when is a good or bad time to call.** Your call may interrupt dinner preparation or (horrors!) the recipient's favorite TV show, predisposing her not to want to spend time talking to you. Besides, trying to explain your relationship over the phone (with the person on the other end taking hurried and disorganized notes) could be less than satisfying, and if the person misreads those notes, it could cost you vital information on your line.

Tip

In some cases, you'll contact someone on the basis of his having a certain surname. He may or may not be doing family history research. You must approach him politely. Even if you've found a phone number, don't use it—at least not for your first contact. People are very suspicious these days, and if you phone someone out of the blue and tell her you're doing family history research and want to ask some questions about her ancestors, her first reaction may be to wonder what kind of scam you're running.

Under some circumstances, the phone is a better communication tool than a letter. A visually impaired person probably finds it easier to talk on the phone than to read and write letters. An elderly or otherwise infirm person (who has had a stroke, for example) may have trouble writing, and may prefer to use the phone.

CONCLUSION

Since you can't always visit the repositories that hold information about your extended family, you'll often have to depend on letters to find out if this information exists and, if so, how you can access it. You'll also write letters to known relatives and to potential cousins as your research progresses. Write concise and understandable letters with specific questions so you'll get the best possible answers. Enclose a self-addressed stamped envelope with most correspondence, and offer to pay for postage and photocopies. When people help you, send them a thank-you letter. Weigh the pros and cons of using E-mail for genealogical research; if you do use it, follow accepted rules of E-mail etiquette. Also weigh the pros and cons of phone calls for making contact with potential cousins.

Now that you know some basics of making contact with other people, it's time to start your research.

THREE

Long-Distance Research Begins at Home

I f you were building a house, would you begin by constructing the second floor? Of course not! The first thing you need to do is lay the foundation. Likewise, before you can begin the long-distance part of your research, you need to build a foundation of facts for it: names, places, and dates. If you begin distant research without as much knowledge as possible, you might waste time trying to find records in the wrong place or for the wrong name or date. The first place to look for these facts is right in your home. Remember the prime directive for genealogists: Begin with yourself and what you know, and work backward.

WHAT SHOULD I LOOK FOR?

What sources might you already have that would help you get started? The possibilities are endless, but they include

- birth, marriage, divorce, and death certificates
- family Bibles, especially those that have record pages (if there are no register pages, check to see if someone has written records of events elsewhere— on a flyleaf or on some blank or partially blank page)
- published genealogies that include one or more of your family lines
- short handwritten or typed family histories put together by other family members
- birth, graduation, engagement, wedding, and death announcements (individual cards or from newspapers)
- obituaries
- funeral cards
- old letters or diaries
- copies of lineage society application papers (e.g., Daughters of the American Revolution)
- photographs

Sources

- scrapbooks
- books with inscriptions written by the giver or owner
- military records
- copies of legal papers like wills, deeds, or mortgages
- alien registration cards
- naturalization papers or passports
- information on union, professional, or fraternal organization membership
- samplers with family information
- household items with monograms or names
- jewelry with inscriptions

WHAT MIGHT I FIND?

You almost certainly won't find something from every one of these categories, but you probably have something from some of them. Search them all for clues—even if some clues don't have any meaning for you now. Monograms you don't recognize now may later make sense when you learn the names of your great-great-grandparents. A book inscribed "To Lida from her father on her 14th birthday, July 20, 1859," may be the only source for the exact birth date of your great-grandmother, who was listed as being fourteen years old on the 1860 census.

Newspaper clippings can bring both joy and problems. In most cases, the person who clipped the article didn't think ahead to fifty years later when you would find it and didn't bother to mark on it the date, place, and newspaper name. A clipping beginning with a sentence like "John Milliron died Wednesday in this city" could use some context to orient you. But you may find clues to help you narrow down the date and city. Another problem with newspaper clippings is that, until recently, married females were often identified only as "Mrs. John Doe." This may mesh with information you have from other sources (John Milliron refers in his will to his daughter Sarah Doe, so she's probably Mrs. John Doe), but it may add to your list of questions.

How do clippings bring joy to genealogists? Wedding announcements and obituaries often give the names and places of residence of the subject's close relatives, which will advance your research. You may learn of previously unknown siblings or the married names of sisters or daughters. The obituary may tell you the residence of a child whose trail you had lost.

Old photos may be enigmatic, but they may provide clues in two ways. First, someone might have written names on the back of the photos. True, these are often only first names, but even first names may later prove helpful if you don't know now who the people in a picture are, especially if they appear to be a family group. Second, studio portraits often have the name of the studio and the town where it was located printed on their mountings. If a town name occurs with some regularity, especially on photos of several different people, there's a good chance that some of your relatives lived in or near that town, and you'll quite possibly research there.

A postmark tells you when and where a letter was mailed. The postmark on

For More Info

PHOTOGRAPHS CAN PROVIDE MANY CLUES

A good book on how to extract the most information from your family photos and ways you might identify anonymous sitters is Maureen Taylor's *Uncovering Your Ancestry through Family Photographs*. This book includes information not only about analyzing photos, but how to care for your photos.

an old letter may prompt you to start research in a geographical area you hadn't considered previously.

However, the best finds are items that combine names, dates, and/or places of specific events in your ancestors' lives: for example birth, death, or marriage certificates; funeral cards or wedding invitations; or records in a family Bible. Other items may be less formal, such as

- a photograph with a notation like "John Smith on his fifth birthday, April 5, 1898" (it's at this point that you pray you had obsessive-compulsive ancestors!)
- a letter in which a person you can identify says something like, "Grandma Russell was eighty years old when she died" (helpful if you know only Grandma Russell's birth or death date);
- a dated letter from a known person who writes something like, "It is my sad duty to inform you that my dear father passed away last Saturday at 3:00 in the afternoon"

If other relatives live nearby, tell them about your quest for family data, and **ask if they have any family papers, photographs, etc.** In the past, have they shown you anything that might aid you? Remind them of it ("Didn't you say you had Grandma Effie's Bible somewhere and that it had some records in it?"). Don't ask just once. The first time you ask, they may not remember something that could help, so occasionally prompt them, e.g., "Have you thought of anything else you have that could help with my family research?" Mentioning specific items you've found elsewhere may remind them of something that they didn't realize would be useful.

Hidden Treasures

If your home sources include a published genealogy of part of your family, extract the information from it that relates to your line; but remember that just because it's in print, it's not necessarily true. Eventually, attempt to verify this information in primary sources: not only the names, dates, and places, but also (perhaps, especially) the relationships.

STARTING TO SORT IT OUT

Your search at home may turn up much information, or only a little, to help you get started. As you find information, make family group sheets and pedigree charts so you can see your known ancestors and their family members in relationship to each other. As you organize the data, be sure to note the source for each item (the source for the date may be different from that for the place of an event).

You may find that different items give different dates or places for the same event. **Note all the conflicting pieces of information and their sources.** Even if you have information from a primary source document, it may not be correct; documents occasionally have errors. If your two conflicting sources are letters from Aunt Sally and Aunt Nellie, note both pieces of information, even though your experience is that Aunt Nellie has a better memory than Aunt Sally. This might be the one time that Aunt Sally was right. Later in your research, you

Citing Sources

may find conclusive proof that one "fact" or the other is correct, but in some cases you'll never resolve the question of which item is correct.

Beyond the data you've found in your home sources, you can fill in some information from your own knowledge. This might include your own birth and marriage dates and places and those of your siblings; the names of your siblings, parents, and grandparents (and some dates and places for them); and perhaps even information that goes further back.

THE NEXT STEP

Once you've collected and organized data from your home documents and your memory, you're ready to go on to the next step: contacting your known relatives.

FOUR

Collecting Information From Close Relatives

O nce you've found all the information you can at home, your next step is to find out what information about the family your known relatives who don't live near you have. These may be brothers, sisters, parents, aunts, uncles, cousins (first cousins or more distant ones), grandparents, great-aunts, great-uncles, and even great-grandparents. Contact all these people to let them know that you're researching your common family tree (make them feel a part of this operation), and ask if they have information that could help you.

BEGIN WITH LETTERS AND CHARTS

To start, write letters to these relatives telling them of your interest, and ask if they can help (see Figure 4-1). With each letter, enclose a copy of the pedigree chart and at least some of the family group sheets related to their portion of the line (be prepared to explain these charts in case relatives don't follow them at first). You'll get varying responses. Some relatives may write long letters with lots of information; others may say, "Sorry, I don't know anything about the family"; others may not respond at all. You can predict most of their responses based on previous experience, but you may be surprised: Aunt Marge, who has never written you more than two lines on a Christmas card each year, may stun you with a fourteen-page essay on the family. Family history has always fascinated her, but she didn't think anyone else cared and now is ecstatic that someone else is interested.

WHAT IF THEY DON'T RESPOND?

The relatives who don't respond to letters may have information, and it's your job to figure out how to get it from them. If you both have E-mail and you know they respond to that, your route is clear. For the rest, phone calls may

[Your postal address, phone number, and E-mail address]

[date]

[address of recipient]

Dear Aunt Nell,

I have recently become interested in the history of our family, and I am hoping that you will help me in my quest to learn more about our ancestors.

I did some research in papers that Mother had and have come up with some basic information about some of our ancestors. I'm enclosing a pedigree chart that shows you how far back I've gotten. Can you fill in any of the blanks for me? I'm especially interested in finding out when your grandfather Valentine Reese died, or at least in getting any information that will help me narrow down his date of death.

I'll be grateful for any help you can give me in this. I enclose a self-addressed, stamped envelope for your convenience in replying. If you would rather discuss this on the phone, drop me a note and let me know when it would be convenient for me to call you.

Love,

[your name]

> "Our family"—make her feel a part of this.

> Don't overwhelm her.

> Ask one or two specific questions.

> Even for close relatives, send a SASE (although she'll probably tell you that you shouldn't have!).

> So *you* pay the phone bill!

Figure 4-1 Letter to a known close relative asking for help on your line.

be the answer. Make two calls: one to set up a convenient time for them to talk, and one actually to get the information. If you call out of the blue to ask for information, it may be a bad time, and they might just tell you they can't help. Setting up an appointment to call will allow them to look for family papers and recall family stories, as well as ensure that you will have sufficient time to discuss this information.

PLAN A FAMILY REUNION!

Do several of your relatives get together on some occasion, such as Christmas? If so, bring your pedigree charts and family group sheets, and see if they can fill in any blanks. If there isn't a time when far-flung members of the family get together, consider organizing a family reunion. This has two benefits: you'll see relatives who may be able to help your quest, and a reunion is just plain fun! Make it up as you go along, or read books like Tom Ninkovich's *Family Reunion Handbook: A Complete Guide to Planning and Enjoying Family Reunions* or the *Reunions Workbook & Catalog* from *Reunions Magazine* (see appendix A for information on contacting *Reunions Magazine*). If you decide to hold regular reunions, consider subscribing to *Reunions Magazine* and/or *TRNEWS*, The Reunion Network's quarterly newsletter. The Reunion Network holds inexpensive seminars to help people with reunion planning.

INTERVIEWING TECHNIQUES

Have pedigree charts and family group sheets in front of you when interviewing. They'll help you keep your ancestors straight (especially if several had the same or similar names), and you can check to see if dates and places that your informants suggest are plausible. Make notes on the appropriate person's sheet (but don't try to make formal entries at this time; these should be work sheets only!). When taking information over the phone, try to keep your notes legible and organized, and transcribe them immediately after the phone call while you can still interpret them. Call back with follow-up questions if you aren't sure about something you wrote.

When interviewing, don't overwhelm your informant with questions. Allow lots of time for Uncle Vern to answer, and don't make him feel pressured; if he does, he might try to come up with some answer—any answer, not necessarily the right answer—just to please you. Be sensitive: an older relative may become tired, and spending time thinking about loved ones who are now dead may bring back painful or overwhelming memories. Interviews should be kept to about an hour at a time.

When interviewing relatives by mail, don't send huge lists of questions. While you want to find out all the answers at once, remember that a letter with some news and two or three questions may stimulate them to reply. A letter with fifty-four questions may intimidate them so much that they'll just put it away unanswered.

Besides asking people what they know about the family, ask if they have any old family papers or photos. Look for the same things you looked for at home (see list in chapter three).

Has someone previously unknown to the family contacted a relative looking for genealogical information on the family? Even if the relative didn't answer the letter, she might have saved it.

Problems You May Encounter While Collecting Information From Your Relatives

One problem you'll have to deal with is imprecision. You'd really like to get a definite date for an event, but your informants may only be able to give you a certain time frame. If they don't have exact information, ask questions like "Did Grandma Thompson die before or after Grandpa Thompson?" This may give you at least a date range for an event. Once you've interviewed a few

MISPLACED RELATIVES?

Sometimes people "misplace" relatives. In the course of your interviews, someone may mention a cousin, second cousin, etc., with whom she has lost contact. For various reasons, you might want to try to locate him. If so, read Kathleen Hinckley's *Locating Lost Family Members & Friends*, which details techniques for locating misplaced people who are quite possibly still alive.

Oral History

people, you'll have information to help relate events to each other. If Aunt Sally is at a loss to remember when Grandma Thompson died, mention that Aunt Nellie knew it was sometime in the fall of 1922, because it was soon after she started first grade. This may jog Aunt Sally's memory that it was between Halloween and Thanksgiving, thus narrowing the time frame a bit more.

Different relatives may give you contradictory information. Aunt Sally says that your grandmother died on 26 March 1956, while Aunt Nellie says she died on 28 March 1956. At this point, don't argue with them. If they're together at the time, try to be conciliatory: "I'll put down both of these dates, and I'll see if I can find any information to help sort this out." **If someone gives you a date or place that differs from the one you currently have on your sheet, don't assume he's wrong.** Make a note of it, with the source, and look for a source that will conclusively prove which is right. Or, if you already have the information from a primary source, let the contradictory information from your relative slide. You don't want to antagonize him, and this might be one of those rare times when a primary source is wrong. Think of this as opening a new door for searching: is Great-Grandma West's death date behind door number one, door number two, or door number three?

Important

Unfortunately, another problem is relatives giving you event dates, time frames, or ancestor names that are just plain wrong. While it's frustrating to discover this, don't hold it against them. Chances are they were doing their best to give you an answer.

On the other hand, someone *may* try to sabotage your efforts. In most cases, sabotage is an attempt to keep you from learning information that someone thinks would cast aspersions on the family honor: Uncle William went to jail for embezzling; Aunt Susie took laudanum; Grandma Emma was born five months after her parents' marriage. Naming certain illnesses, such as cancer or syphilis, as causes of death may be considered taboo. If you discover the truth, don't hold it against them. Especially when dealing with older people, realize that they don't want to rake up old scandals.

CONCLUSION

There are many ways to collect information from the relatives you know at the beginning of your search. These include letters, phone calls, and E-mail. A family gathering can give you an opportunity to search the collective memories of your relatives, although individual encounters may prove more productive. During interviews, keep pedigree charts and family group sheets handy to help avoid confusion, like mistaking one ancestor for another of the same name. Be forewarned: your relatives may not have answers to all your questions, and some of their answers may be incorrect. Use the information they give you as a foundation on which to base more formal research.

FIVE

Vital Records: Birth, Marriage, Death

O nce you've collected home data and interviewed relatives, you've laid the foundation that will allow you to branch out to look at some primary sources, and vital records are the ones with which to start. According to Webster, *vital* means "recording data relating to lives" but also "of utmost importance." This is definitely true for genealogists, because vital records often contain data that's crucial to family history research: dates and places of events; names of parents and spouses.

Obtain copies of any vital records that exist for all of your ancestors, even the people you know and the people you think you have full information on. You may find surprises!

Research Tip

WHAT SORT OF INFORMATION MIGHT I FIND IN THESE RECORDS?

There are three types of vital records. Depending on the time period and location, they include varying pieces of information. Don't expect to find all the types of information listed in the paragraphs below on all certificates you get. Generally, the earlier the record, the less specific the data you will find in it.

Birth records usually contain the name, date, and place of birth; the child's sex; whether this was a multiple birth; names, residences, races, and occupations of parents; ages of parents at the time of the child's birth; and whether the birth is legitimate. They may include the number of children born alive to this mother and the number stillborn to the mother.

Marriage records usually, but not always, include at least two parts: the license application and the return of the license. A license application (which might not have been required in the time and place of your ancestors' marriage) doesn't prove that two people married; it proves that they applied for a license to do so. The return, filed by the person who officiated at the ceremony, proves that the marriage actually took place. The license application includes information such as the names, races, ages, occupations, birth dates, birth places, and ages of the applicants. The relationship of the applicants to each other and prior marriages of the couple may also appear. The more recent the license, the more likely it is to include the couple's parents' names. The return of the license includes, at least, the date and place of the ceremony and who performed the marriage.

Death records include two types of information. *Personal information* may include the name of the deceased; the deceased's race, sex, marital status, date of birth, age at death, occupation, birthplace, and residence; names and birthplaces of the deceased's parents; name of the surviving spouse; the deceased's citizenship and highest grade of education completed; whether the person served in the armed forces; the name of the informant for this information; and the informant's relationship to the deceased (this may help you judge the accuracy of that information). *Information specific to the death* includes place, date, time, and cause of death; attending physician; place of interment; and undertaker. Recent death certificates (after 1937) may include the deceased's Social Security number (see chapter nine for more information on Social Security). One major reason genealogists request death certificates is to find the names and birthplaces of the deceased's parents. Unfortunately, Murphy's Law often applies here. If you already know the names of the deceased's parents, they will probably be on the death certificate. If you ordered the death certificate in hopes of learning the names of the parents, Murphy's Law says that the names won't be there. Cross your fingers when you order!

For More Info

READ MORE ABOUT IT!

For an in-depth look at death records, see Carolyn Billingsley and Desmond Allen's book *How to Get the Most Out of Death Certificates.*

WHY SHOULD I GET COPIES OF VITAL RECORDS?

If these records exist for your ancestors, they'll give you concrete and usually correct information to help you to trace your line further back. A death certificate may give you the name of the cemetery where the person was buried; you can go there or search for a published reading of the cemetery to find out who's buried near the ancestor and whether other people of the same surname were buried there. Now that you have an exact date of death, you can search for an obituary that may contain useful information about your family. A marriage license may include the unexpected news that an ancestor had a previous marriage, and documents relating to that marriage may aid your search.

WHERE CAN I FIND VITAL RECORDS?

Locations of vital records vary by state and by time period. In many states these records began relatively recently. For example, Pennsylvania kept vital records sporadically in the early 1850s, then didn't require them again until the late 1800s; New York kept vital statistics from 1847 to 1852, then began again in 1880. In some cases, specific areas (especially large cities) kept vital records before the state required them. If your ancestor was born before birth registrations were required but was alive and working for an employer after 1937, he

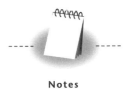

THESE RECORDS AREN'T FREE

Expect to pay a fee to obtain copies of vital records. Often you'll have a choice between certified and uncertified copies. A certified copy has a stamp or emboss-ment that makes it an official copy for various uses. If you want a copy of a record purely for the information in it, an uncertified copy (which is cheaper) is fine. If you're applying for membership in a lineage society, you may need a certified copy.

You can find out the exact fee for a record in several ways:

- Write or call the repository to get the fee for a specific record. Many repositor-ies have automated phone systems that include recorded messages about their fees.

- Check online sources; some repositories have Internet pages that give infor-mation about fees.

- If you're in a hurry to obtain the record and can't readily get information from the repository about the cost, send a check (at least ten or fifteen dollars) with your request and hope that the amount is sufficient.

Although a few repositories won't accept checks and ask for a money order, unless you know otherwise, assume that they will accept a check. Never send cash to a repository.

---

might have filed a delayed birth certificate to prove his birth date so that he could apply for Social Security.

Locating vital records in large cities like New York City and Philadelphia can be complex, as records from different time periods may be stored in different offices. If you write to the wrong office in a large city, they often send you the correct address to which to write for the record.

Usually, when they were first legally mandated, records were kept at the local (town or county) level, but later, registration shifted to the state level. **Appendix C gives information on more recent vital records kept at the state level, including the dates for which records are available at that level.**

Some records continue on the local level as well. The books mentioned in appendix B tell you where to find vital records kept at the county and town levels, the dates for which each jurisdiction holds records, and addresses to which to write for the information.

When consulting the books listed in appendix B, read not just the information on your ancestral county or town but also the introductory material about the state, to be sure that you know which records are kept where for what time periods. Pay attention to the date when your ancestral county was created in relation to the date of the event in question (do you need to look for records in a parent county as well?).

HOW DO I REQUEST VITAL RECORDS?

To request vital records, send a letter to the office that should hold the record, giving as much of the following information as you know:

- **Birth records:** full name of person (maiden name if a woman); sex and race; date and place of birth; names of parents; purpose for which you are requesting the record; your relationship to the person whose record you are requesting (see Figure 5-1)

[Your postal address, phone number, and E-mail address]

[date]

Registrar of Births
[address of recipient]

Specify relationship.

Give full name, place and date of birth, and names of parents (or as much of this as you know).

To Whom It May Concern:

I would like a copy of the **birth certificate** of my husband's grandmother:

Margaret Anna Roos (white female)
Born: Newtown, New York
24 October 1876
Parents: Martin and Anna Mary (-?-) Roos

State purpose for which you need the record.

State type of copy needed.

I do not need a certified copy. I am requesting this record for genealogical purposes and would like a photocopy of the original record. I enclose a check for $15, which I understand is your fee for a birth certificate.

Find out fee and enclose it.

My husband, a direct descendant of Margaret Anna Roos, has signed this request.

Be prepared, in case they're really strict, i.e., they send copies only to direct descendants.

Thank you for your help in this matter. I enclose a self-addressed, stamped envelope for your convenience in replying.

Sincerely,

Always send a SASE.

[your name]

[your husband's name]

Figure 5-1 Request for a birth record

- **Marriage records:** full names of the bride and groom; their ages; date and place of marriage; names of parents; purpose for which you are requesting the record; your relationship to the couple whose record you are requesting (see Figures 5-2 on page 41 and 5-3 on page 42)

[Your postal address, phone number, and E-mail address]

[date]

Morgan County Clerk
[address of recipient]

To Whom It May Concern:

I would like to get a copy of the **marriage license application and return** of my great-grandparents: —— Specify relationship.

William Thomas Thompson (may also be listed as
Thomas William or T. W. Thompson), age 28
Parents: William H. Thompson and Sarah Ann Carr
Nannie Jane Kile (may also be spelled Kyle), age 26
Parents: George W. Kile and Sarah Jane Rollins
Married: 25 September 1890
Morgan County, Illinois

Can you please tell me what the fee will be for this record? I do not need a certified copy, but I would like a photocopy of the original, as this is for genealogical purposes.

If the cost is under $10 and you are able to send the photocopy and a bill, I would appreciate it if you would do so. Otherwise, I will send a second request with a check for the fee after you let me know what it is.

Thank you for your help. I enclose a self-addressed, stamped envelope for your convenience in replying.

Sincerely,

[your name]

Callout boxes:
- Ask for both documents.
- Give full names—and possible variant spellings—and ages.
- Give names of parents, if known.
- Give date and place when known.
- Specify type of copy needed so they can quote the correct fee.
- Make a polite request for a bill and immediate gratification.
- Always send a SASE.

Figure 5-2 Request for a marriage record (date known)

- **Death records:** name of person (married surname if a married woman); sex and race; date and place of death; names of parents; purpose for which you are requesting the record; your relationship to the person whose record you are requesting (see Figures 5-4 and 5-5)

In some cases, you will request a certificate to find it out some piece of this information that you don't know. If so, give as much information about the person as possible to help the office identify the correct certificate. If you don't

[Your postal address, phone number, and E-mail address]

[date]

Armstrong County Clerk
[address of recipient]

Dear Friends:

I would like a copy of the **marriage license application and return** of my great-grandparents:

Give names of parents, if known.

Give full names.

Andrew West
Parents: not known
Lovina Catherine (Rader) Reese
Parents: _____ Rader and Mary Ann (Milliron) (Rader) Gould
Married: between 1912 and 1920
Armstrong County, Pennsylvania

Give a date range to decrease the number of indexes the clerk may have to check.

Enclose the proper fee.

I enclose a check for $7, which I understand is the fee you charge for marriage records. If there is a charge for searching the marriage indexes, please let me know. I do not need a certified copy, but I would like a photocopy of the original record, as this is for genealogical purposes.

Specify type of copy needed.

Thank you for your help with this request. I enclose a self-addressed, stamped envelope for your convenience in replying.

Sincerely,

[your name]

Figure 5-3 Request for a marriage record (date not known)

Warning

know the exact date of the event, you may have to pay a fee for the clerk to search records in a date range you specify. Fees may be for a time span as small as three months and could add up quickly, so do as much homework as possible to narrow the potential date range.

State in your request that you want the record for genealogical purposes and you want a photocopy of the original record. You may still get a transcription or a computer-generated version of an old record. But if you get a computer-generated record requested for genealogical purposes, it may include more information than if you hadn't stated that this was why you needed it.

Some offices allow you to order certificates by phone, but be cautious about this. You may spell the name very carefully, but many letters can sound alike over the phone. You may get a response that no record was found for your ancestor

[Your postal address, phone number, and E-mail address]

[date]

[State] Division of Vital Records
[address of recipient]

To Whom It May Concern:

I would like a copy of the **death certificate** of my great-grandfather:

Aaron Calvin King (white male)
Parents: George and Mary Ann (Fiscus) King
Died: 23 October 1925, age 71
Armstrong County, Pennsylvania

I am requesting this record for genealogical purposes and would like a photocopy of the original record. I enclose a check for $15, which I understand is your fee for a death certificate copy.

Thank you for your help. I enclose a self-addressed, stamped envelope for your convenience in replying.

Sincerely,

[your name]

| Specify relationship. |

| Give full name of person and parents, and give date and place of death. |

| State that request is for genealogical purposes in order to get a copy of the original. |

| Find out fee and enclose it. |

| Always send a SASE. |

Figure 5-4 Request for a death record (date known)

Jacob *Sitler*, while you had requested a record for Jacob *Fitler*. Your credit card will still have a charge for this search, which the office carried out in good faith because they mistook your *F* for an *S*.

What Problems Might I Encounter in My Quest for Vital Records?

In some counties, employees won't search indexes for genealogists in response to mail requests, although they will generally make a photocopy if you give them an exact citation for a record. You may have to try to find a microfilm index to rent or hire a researcher to look for your records for you.

Most states have closed recent vital records to protect the privacy of living people. For example, many states restrict access to birth certificates less than seventy-five years old. This means you must be either the person whose record you're requesting or a close relative or legal agent of that person. If the record you're requesting isn't yours, state your relationship to the person in question, even if you're requesting a record from before the time when records are closed.

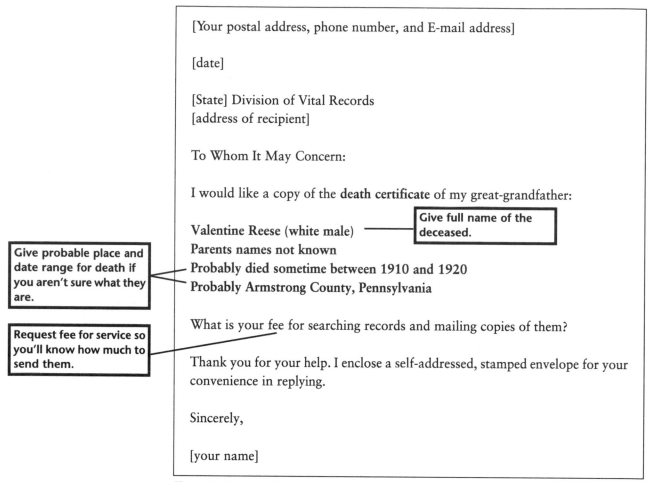

[Your postal address, phone number, and E-mail address]

[date]

[State] Division of Vital Records
[address of recipient]

To Whom It May Concern:

I would like a copy of the **death certificate** of my great-grandfather:

Valentine Reese (white male) — **Give full name of the deceased.**
Parents names not known
Probably died sometime between 1910 and 1920
Probably Armstrong County, Pennsylvania

Give probable place and date range for death if you aren't sure what they are.

What is your fee for searching records and mailing copies of them?

Request fee for service so you'll know how much to send them.

Thank you for your help. I enclose a self-addressed, stamped envelope for your convenience in replying.

Sincerely,

[your name]

Figure 5-5 Request for a death record (date not known)

When you request the record of your spouse or another close relative and have their consent to get the record, write the letter in that person's name and have the person sign it.

County clerks and other county employees are paid with taxes to provide services for taxpayers in their county; they aren't usually mandated to help genealogists. Don't expect that they'll drop everything to work on your request. It may take a while from the time you request the record until you get it. Some agencies will respond immediately; some will take several weeks. For a few weeks before and after Election Day, town and county clerks are very busy, so requests may pile up. It's best not to send requests at this time.

As was previously mentioned, not all blanks are filled in on all records, or information may be disappointing. Initials may appear rather than full names; birthplaces may be given as the state or country when you hoped to find a specific town. You may request a record in hopes of finding the parents' names only to discover that at the time of the event, that question wasn't on the application or the informant didn't know the parents' names. Perhaps even worse, the information you wanted may be on the form, but due to problems with handwriting or faded ink, it may be illegible.

Does the marriage license application include the woman's parents' names? If not, the surname she gave on the application might not be her maiden name. Especially if she was older than about twenty-three at the time of marriage, it could be the surname of a previous husband. The marriage license might include information on whether either member of the couple was previously married; that will help resolve such questions.

Information is only as good as the people who gave it. Often the informant for a death certificate is a child of the deceased. At a very stressful time, that child was trying to remember the names of grandparents who might have died before he was born or his parent's birth date and place, which he never bothered to clarify.

Some states no longer include the cause of death on death certificates because of privacy concerns (a movement that started soon after recognition of the AIDS epidemic). If you have requested a death certificate to learn the cause of death because you're tracing family health history, you may be disappointed. If a cause of death does appear on the death certificate, it may be given in antiquated language that means nothing to you. Also, remember that in earlier days, doctors had fewer sophisticated tests and the cause of death may not be accurate.

Reminder

What If I Write to a Repository That Should Have a Record and They Don't Find It?

There are two possibilities: either the record doesn't exist, or the person searching didn't find it. Review your request. Did you give correct information? Possibly you think of your ancestor by her maiden name, and you requested her death certificate under this name without providing her married surname. If you did give the correct information, let this request sit for a while. Unless there's some urgency in your obtaining the certificate, wait a few months, then submit the request again. Perhaps a different person will find the record just where it ought to be.

Even if registration was required during a certain time period, there's no guarantee that a given record actually exists. Some events, for whatever reason, never made it into the appropriate record books. In some localities, record books for some time periods have been destroyed in fires, floods, and other disasters.

OTHER SOURCES FOR VITAL RECORDS

You can use several other sources in your search for vital records:

Sources

- Some county Web pages in the USGenWeb project have indexes or abstracts of vital records for their county. See chapter nineteen for more information about the USGenWeb.
- In some colonies, especially those that are now the New England states (and especially Massachusetts), laws were passed requiring town or county clerks to keep vital records. Many of these have been transcribed and published. Check library catalogs for these records. If you do obtain published vital records, remember the possibility of transcription errors. See chapter twelve for more details on locating information about library holdings.

- Many genealogical societies publish abstracts of vital records in their journals or as pamphlets or books. These usually include the information you need to order a copy of the actual record, such as marriage book number and page. See the "Indexes to Genealogical Periodicals" section in chapter seventeen for sources to help you identify periodical articles. Check library catalogs for books of transcriptions of vital records.
- Check the Family History Library Catalog at a Family History Center or on the Internet at <http://www.familysearch.com> (see chapter thirteen for information on locating a Family History Center) to see if microfilm of vital records for your ancestor's county or state is available.
- Global Data has published some marriage records on CD-ROM, and Brøderbund has published some marriage record indexes on CD-ROM. When purchasing these CDs, read the description carefully to be sure the CD covers your locality and time period of interest. Some titles can mislead you into believing you're getting records for the entire state, when the CD only includes a few counties. Brøderbund has also published some collections of mixed types of vital records for some states. See the publishers' catalogs or Web sites for more information on what's available.

CONCLUSION

Vital records abstracts in genealogical periodicals and books can be helpful if you don't know the date of an event for your ancestor. However, since locating vital records is usually a straightforward proposition, it's best to begin by writing to the office that should hold the record. You may also be able to get copies of vital records on microfilm, but because of privacy considerations, many vital records are not available on film. Searching secondary sources should be a backup strategy, since most secondary sources involve transcriptions, which may contain errors. Vital records will give you concrete, usually correct, information about your ancestors that will allow you to look for other sources to flesh out your picture of them.

SIX

Estate Files: Not Just Wills

O ften, beginning genealogists think of estate records solely in terms of a will; they say "I tried to get my ancestor's will, but he didn't leave one, so I couldn't find out anything about him." In fact, although wills sometimes include many details about the deceased's family, estate files contain many other documents. The estate file of a person who didn't leave a will often contains more family information than the file of someone who did.

WHO WOULD HAVE AN ESTATE FILE?

Until somewhat recently, men were more likely than women to have estate files, but under some circumstances, women might have had estate files, so always check for them as well. It's better to be disappointed up front than to find out later that a woman left an estate file that included the very piece of information

Definitions

SOME DEFINITIONS

In working with estate files, you may encounter some terms you aren't familiar with.

An **estate file** or **estate packet** is a collection of papers related to the settlement of the estate of one person. This may also be referred to as a **probate file** or **probate packet**. Technically, *probate* refers to the settlement of the estate of a person who left a will, so probate files are one type of estate file.

A person who died **testate** left a valid will when he died; a person who died **intestate** left either no will or an invalid will.

you'd been seeking for ten years. Women who married more than once often had estate files because they had written a will to preserve the rights of their children from a prior marriage to their father's land or other possessions.

WHAT MIGHT I FIND IN AN ESTATE FILE?

The many types of documents you may find in an estate file include

- letters of administration (naming an intestate person's close relatives and/ or friends who petitioned to administer the estate)
- an estate inventory (that, by the number and type of items listed, gives you some idea of your ancestor's relative wealth and may give you clues about the person's occupation)
- a list of who bought what at the estate sale (relations of the deceased often buy at estate sales)
- a final account of the estate (who got how much money; in some cases you can deduce relationships from the proportionate amounts various people received)
- petitions (which may state the relationship of one or more heirs to the deceased)
- receipts from anyone who received money from the estate
- petitions for guardianship of minor children (that may give an age range or the exact ages of the children)
- a list of the deceased's heirs, including their relationship to that person

In some cases a man's estate might not be fully settled until after his widow's death. In earlier times, before death certificates, a document from an estate might be the only clue you have to the exact date of the widow's death, or at least a date by which she had died. Some estates weren't settled until all children had reached their majority, so the date of settlement may help to establish approximate ages of one or more children.

HOW CAN I ACCESS MY ANCESTOR'S ESTATE FILE?

See Also

Access estate files in the same way you did birth, marriage, and death records. **See appendix B** for some books that give the jurisdictions that hold estate files and the dates for which they hold them. Write to the office for the area where your ancestor lived to find out how to obtain information on your ancestor's estate, and give the person's full name and date and place of death (see Figure 6-1 on page 49). Note: If your ancestor died while away from home, the estate would have been probated in the place where he or she lived. Be sure to specify that you want *all papers* related to the estate file, and ask for the cost of getting copies of these papers.

At this point, things may get interesting. While some agencies charge a small fee per page for copying estate materials, other agencies may charge a relatively high fee (say, seventy dollars) just to look in their index to see if your ancestor had an estate file. Even if the fee per page is low, some estate files may include

[Your postal address, phone number, and E-mail address]

[date]

Clerk of Probate Court
[address of recipient]

Dear Friends:

Specify relationship.

I am interested in getting copies of the **papers in the estate file** (of my great-grandfather):

Give full name and date and place of death.

John H. Crawford
Died: 27 October 1892
Cowley County, Kansas

List the types of papers you want.

These papers may include items such as
- a will
- letters of administration
- bonds
- inventory
- sale list
- account/settlement
- distribution
- receipts from heirs and creditors
- petitions
- guardianship papers

Request the cost for photocopying and mailing the papers.

Can you please tell me what the cost would be to obtain copies of any of the above papers that exist in John H. Crawford's estate file?

Always send a SASE.

Thank you for your help. I enclose a self-addressed, stamped envelope for your convenience in replying.

Sincerely,

[your name]

Figure 6-1 Request for cost of copies of papers from an estate file

hundreds of pages of documents. If the cost is high, weigh the relative merits of
- paying the fee to get the materials now
- hiring a genealogist to abstract and/or copy the estate papers for you (see chapter twenty-one)
- going to the area at some future time to research these papers yourself (see chapter twenty)

[Your postal address, phone number, and E-mail address]

[date]

Clerk of Probate Court
[address of recipient]

Dear Friends:

Thank you for your response to my letter requesting the cost of getting **copies of the papers in the estate file** of my great-grandfather:

John H. Crawford
Died: 27 October 1892
Cowley County, Kansas

These papers would include items such as a will, letters of administration, bonds, inventory, sale list, account/settlement, distribution, receipts from heirs and creditors, petitions, guardianship papers, etc.

As I stated in my previous letter, I would like copies of all papers related to this estate. I enclose a check for $15 as quoted by you, to cover the cost. Thank you for your help with this request.

Sincerely,

[your name]

> **Your letter may go to a different person this time, so state again the name, date and place of death of the person.**

> **State again the types of papers you want.**

> **Send a check for the amount they quoted you.**

> **This time you *don't* need to send a SASE, because there could be many papers involved and they will have taken postage into consideration in their price quote.**

Figure 6-2 Request for copies of papers from an estate file based on a response to a request for cost

If there's a large packet of materials and you opt to have the repository photocopy them for you, ask them to copy the whole packet (see Figure 6-2). Don't skimp and say something like, "Just copy the important papers." The people in this repository aren't familiar with your family and might not recognize the importance of some document that's exactly what you need to solve a particular problem.

Most courts transcribe documents such as administration bonds, wills, and petitions related to estates into books, and the photocopies you receive may be made from these books. Since these are transcriptions, errors might have crept in. If you get a copy of a transcription, write to find out if the agency still has the original document. If so, request a copy of it to ensure that you have the best copy of the information.

ADDITIONAL RESEARCH STRATEGIES FOR ESTATE RECORDS

Consider looking for estate files of collateral relatives as well as ancestors. Estate files of ancestors' siblings may contain useful information, especially if the sibling was unmarried. An unmarried person's will may name brothers, sisters, nieces, and nephews. If an unmarried person died intestate, the estate was divided among the person's siblings; if any of them had predeceased him, their share was divided among their children. Such an estate file can be a rich source of information on the family.

Research Tip

While estate files were usually created immediately after a person's death, under some circumstances, they may have been created much later. For example, in Armstrong County, Pennsylvania, the estate file for Henry Rader, who died as a Civil War soldier in 1865, wasn't created until 1871, apparently to provide a vehicle for his children's guardian to render a final account of the pension money paid to them.

Likewise, Peter Shellhammer died in Westmoreland County, Pennsylvania, in 1829. An estate file for him was created in Armstrong County, Pennsylvania, almost one hundred years later. Peter had owned land in Armstrong County that he willed to his children; it was passed down through inheritance. The Armstrong County estate file apparently was created to satisfy some legal technicality to enable sale of the land. So if there's no estate file for your ancestor at the time of his death, but you find an estate file for someone with the same name as your ancestor, created sometime after his death, take a look at it. It might be the estate file of a descendant named for the ancestor, but it might be a file for the ancestor.

If your ancestor owned land in a county other than the one he lived in, check to see if an estate file was created for him there, as one was for Peter Shellhammer.

If your ancestor died at about the time that a new county that included his land was formed, inquire about his estate in both the old and new counties. If it took a few years for a new county to get its court system set up, or if his estate settlement was prolonged, both counties may have files relating to his estate.

OTHER SOURCES FOR ESTATE INFORMATION

Sources

If you have problems in obtaining estate records (for example, the repository charges an exorbitant fee), some other sources can provide estate information.

- Many genealogical societies publish abstracts of wills, administration bonds, etc., in their journals or as pamphlets or books. These usually include the information you need, such as a file number, to order the papers from the actual estate file. See the "Indexes to Genealogical Periodicals" section in chapter seventeen for sources to help you identify periodical articles. Check library catalogs for books of transcriptions of estate information.

- Check the Family History Library Catalog at a Family History Center or on the Internet at <http://www.familysearch.com> (see chapter thirteen for information on locating a Family History Center) to see if microfilm of will books or other estate materials for your ancestor's county is available.
- A few CD-ROM vendors, including Brøderbund, Heritage Books, and Palladium, have issued CDs of will abstracts for some areas. Check their catalogs or Web sites to see if they've published a CD that includes your ancestral area.

CONCLUSION

While materials from estate records may be abstracted in genealogical periodicals and books, locating the actual records is usually easy if you know the county where your ancestor died. It's best to begin by writing to that county for copies of the documents rather than trying to search out periodical articles with the information—especially since most of the sources listed in the section above involve transcriptions of the information, which may contain errors. Estate files may include many types of documents that may give you few or many details on an ancestor and that person's heirs.

SEVEN

Land Records

lthough they can seem dull and boring, land records can contain many interesting facts about your ancestors. Try to get a copy of every land record your ancestor created for grant, purchase, or sale of property.

WHAT MIGHT I FIND IN A DEED?

Some deeds may simply include information that fleshes out your knowledge of your ancestor's life, such as names of trees used for markers at the corners of the land, creeks or other natural features used as boundaries or corner markers, improvements to the property (houses, barns, mills, and other structures), or your ancestor's occupation.

Deeds may include other pieces of information that can aid your genealogical research:

- If your ancestor bought land prior to moving to an area, the deed might list his previous residence.
- Neighbors might be relatives: if the surname is the same as your ancestor's, the neighbor might be a father, uncle, or brother. If the surname is different, the neighbor of your ancestor (or of his father) might be the father or brother of the ancestor's wife whose surname you are seeking.
- Your ancestor might be one of a group of people buying land as trustees for a church. If so, search for that church's records to see if they mention him or other members of his family.
- Deeds may include information about a kinship between the buyer and seller, although lack of such information in a deed doesn't mean no such relationship existed. If land is sold in the course of settling an estate, the deed often lists all the heirs, including their places of residence, which can help you fill spaces on a family group sheet or locate family members who moved away.
- In more recent years, people purchased cemetery lots; such a deed may help you locate your ancestor's grave.

Notes

- The chain of title in a deed may identify your ancestor's father—and even ancestors further back if the land was in the family for several generations.
- It's sometimes difficult to find the first name of a man's wife, especially before 1850. If he sold land, depending on the state (or colony) and time period, she may be a party to the sale; if so, her first name will be on the deed.
- In rare cases, a deed may include information such as the death date of the previous owner of a piece of land or the marriage date of a man purchasing land.

Warning

Witnesses to deeds may be relatives, but in the past several years, many genealogical magazines have published the fallacious "information" that witnesses to deeds absolutely always are related to the husband and wife selling the land. An interesting article which attempted to trace the "genealogy" of this assertion is "Just Because It's in Print Doesn't Make It So," by Desmond Walls Allen in the Federation of Genealogical Societies *Forum*, Winter 1991, pages 3–5. After you've located several deeds for ancestors whose family you know, see for yourself that witnesses are often no relation to the couple; they are merely people who happened to be handy.

METHODS OF ACQUIRING LAND

Generally, people acquired land in the United States and its parent colonies in one of four ways:

- original purchase or grant in state-land states
- original purchase or grant in public-domain states
- purchase from nongovernmental entities (usually other people, but sometimes land companies or corporations)
- inheritance

For More Info

READ MORE ABOUT IT!

To learn more about land records, read
- Hone, *Land & Property Research in the United States*
- Hawkins, *Research in the Land Entry Files of the General Land Office*
- Salmon, *Women and the Law of Property in Early America*

DID HE OWN LAND AT ALL?

Did your ancestor own land? The 1850, 1860, 1870, 1900, 1910, and 1920 federal censuses have questions about real estate that may help to answer this. If you're still not sure, check land records in case he did.

PRIVATE LAND TRANSACTIONS

When searching for land records for an ancestor, the first place to search (because it's the easiest) is in records for private land sales. Other than for the original purchase of land, deeds are generally registered on the county level; in Connecticut, Rhode Island, and Vermont, they are registered at the town level. You have two alternatives in researching private land transactions: investigate whether land records from your ancestor's area have been microfilmed and work with the microfilm (see chapter thirteen for sources for renting microfilm), or contact the offices in the area that hold the deeds (to identify the office, see appendix B for books that list the offices of counties and towns and the dates for which they hold deeds).

To begin your search, write to the Registrar of Deeds or equivalent office in the jurisdiction where your ancestor lived. If your ancestor lived there before the current county (or town) was formed, also write to the Registrar of Deeds in the parent county (and if necessary, that county's parent county, and so forth) to investigate earlier records (see Figure 7-1 below).

[Your postal address, phone number, and E-mail address]

[date]

Registrar of Deeds
[recipient's address]

Dear Friends:

I would like a photocopy of all the listings in your

Grantor and Grantee Indexes
For the name Robert Walker
Between 1813 and 1913

> State which indexes you want checked.

> Give full name of person in question.

> Give a hundred-year range of dates starting when the person was eighteen years old.

I enclose a check for $5 to cover the cost of the copies. If this is not enough, please let me know.

> There probably won't be many pages, so unless they charge a search fee, five dollars should cover the photocopying cost.

Also, please let me know what the cost will be to get a copy of any of these deeds.

Thank you for your help. I enclose a self-addressed, stamped envelope for your convenience in replying.

> Always send a SASE.

Sincerely,

[your name]

Figure 7-1 Request for information from deed indexes

Ask the office to photocopy the pages from the grantor index and the grantee index for your ancestor's name for a hundred-year period starting with the year when your ancestor was eighteen years old. If more than one ancestor of the same surname lived in the county, request copies of all pages from the indexes for that surname. Offer to pay for the photocopies. Don't cut off your request at the date of your ancestor's death; sales might be registered under his name (as "estate of [ancestor]") after his death if

---

SPECIAL TERMINOLOGY FOR LAND RECORDS

Admr(s): Short for *administrator(s)* (of an estate).

Et al.: Abbreviation for the Latin *et alii*, meaning "and others," indicating that more people were party to the sale than just the person listed in the index. Deeds with this notation are often deeds made by several heirs to an estate and can be very useful.

Et ux. or **et uxor**: Latin for "and wife."

Exr(s).: Short for *executor(s)* (of an estate).

Grantee: A person who buys land.

Grantor: A person who sells land.

Lots: A term for (usually) square or rectangular pieces of land in cities or towns.

Metes and bounds: The system for describing land boundaries used in state land states. These plots are often irregularly shaped; descriptions use unfamiliar measurements such as chains, links, rods, poles, and perches. The plot's angles and boundaries are often marked with natural features such as trees, stumps, rocks, and creeks or rivers, with the direction of each piece of the boundary from one feature to the next given in compass bearings. Descriptions usually name the owner of each piece of land contiguous to the one being described.

Public-domain states: States in which the original seller or grantor of land was either the federal government or the previous owner of the territory (e.g., France or Spain).

Rectangular survey system: The system used to identify a piece of land in a public domain land state. Plots of land are described by their relationship to imaginary lines on the map called "principal meridians." Descriptions use three terms of measurement:

- *section*: The basic unit of the system, a square tract of land one mile by one mile containing 640 acres. Sections are subdivided into halves, quarters, etc. Natural features in the landscape can make for uneven divisions in sections.

- *township*: In the rectangular survey system, thirty-six sections arranged in a six by six square.

- *range*: Described by imaginary north-south lines, six miles apart, on the boundaries of townships; a tier of townships.

Townships are north or south of baselines and east or west of principal meridians. For example, T2N, R8W 3rd PM is the second township north of the baseline in the eighth range west of the third principal meridian (the

---

meridian in question is often not named in records, as the county and state location show which one is meant). Townships can be divided into sections and fractions of sections. For example, SE1/4 of Section 31, T2N, R7W, 3rd PM is the southeast quarter of section 31 in the second township north of the baseline in the seventh range west of the third principle meridian. Generally, these land descriptions contain less information on boundaries, neighbors, etc., than you find in land described with the metes and bounds system because the township/range description pinpoints the land exactly, so there's no need to include other detail.

State-land states: States in which the original seller or grantor of land was the colony, territory, or state.

- land was sold in settling his estate
- he bequeathed land to an heir and that person or subsequent heirs later sold the land (land might be passed down by inheritance several times before it is sold)

Step By Step

WHAT DO I DO NOW THAT I HAVE THE INDEX PAGES?

Basically, there are four possible results from your request:
1. You'll find a few listings for your ancestor in either the grantor or grantee listings or both
2. If he had a common surname, like Smith, there may be huge numbers of listings for his name
3. You may find no listings at all
4. Some courthouses won't research deeds by mail; these usually send you a list of people who do research for hire

In situations 2 and 4, check the Family History Library Catalog at your local Family History Center to see if land records for your ancestor's area are available on microfilm. If not, you may need to consider hiring a genealogist residing in the ancestral area to research the land records for you.

If you find only a few listings for your ancestor, write again and order copies of these deeds (see Figure 7-2 on page 58). Once you get them, match up the deeds for purchase of land with deeds for sale of land. Are there deeds for purchase of land for which there are no sale deeds? If so, did the ancestor bequeath the land to someone in his will? If he didn't, you may want to investigate more to find out what happened to the land. For example, the land might have been sold as part of a bankruptcy proceeding; if so, it might be registered in a different set of books, or the sheriff, rather than your ancestor, might be listed in the index as the grantor. Alternatively, the sale might be indexed under the name of the administrator of the ancestor's estate.

If you have a deed for sale of land with no matching purchase deed at the county or town level, is there a chain of title that gives clues as to whether your

[Your postal address, phone number, and E-mail address]

[date]

Registrar of Deeds
[recipient's address]

Dear Friends:

Thank you for sending me copies of the grantee and grantor deed index listings for **Robert Walker**. Based on these listings, I would like **copies of the following deeds:**

Deed Book 7, p. 132–end: Alexander Walker to Robert Walker
Deed Book 8, p. 150–end: John King to Robert Walker
Deed Book 9, p. 3–end: George Crownover to Robert Walker
Deed Book 17, p. 46–end: Robert Walker to James Altman
Deed Book 19, p. 27–end: Robert Walker to John Walker

As the cost per deed is $2, I enclose a check for $10 to cover the cost of the copies of these five deeds.

Thank you for your help in this matter.

Sincerely,

[your name]

State the name of the person again.

Give full citations for the deeds: There might be more than one deed on a page, so you need to give the names of grantors and grantees.

Send money based on the cost they have quoted you.

Figure 7-2 Request for copies of deeds

ancestor bought the land from the state or the federal government or inherited it? If so, your next step is to investigate the records that the chain of title suggests. If the chain of title says he purchased it from an individual, investigate the grantor index under the name of that individual.

Have you found a will for your ancestor? If he bequeathed land, he might mention its provenance in the will.

What if you find no land records at all on the county or town level for your ancestor, but you know he had land (for example, he bequeathed land in his will)? He might have acquired the land in one of two other ways: inheritance or original purchase from a colony, territory, state, or the federal government.

ACQUISITION OF LAND BY INHERITANCE

The most likely sources of land inheritance are your ancestor's father, father-in-law, grandparents, siblings, and siblings of parents. Investigate their estates to find out whether they might be the source of the land.

Land acquired by inheritance generally isn't recorded in land record books, but if your ancestor later sold the land, the deed may include a chain of title showing from whom he inherited it. In a more complex scenario, this land might have passed by inheritance to one or more generations of heirs. If you aren't sure how he obtained the land, follow the trail of inheritance to the point where one of his heirs finally sold the land; the deed for this sale might include a chain of title that shows how your ancestor got it.

FINDING RECORDS OF ORIGINAL PURCHASES OR GRANTS OF LAND IN STATE-LAND STATES

State-land states are those in which, depending on the time frame, the original seller or grantor of land was the colony, territory, or state. If your ancestor obtained land as the original purchaser, consider getting copies of the documents related to this purchase. These may include

- application: a request to purchase land, including information describing the land and its boundaries
- warrant for survey: an authorization for a surveyor to survey the land
- survey: a formal description of the land recorded in the land office (a map of the property, which might include the names of neighbors, often accompanied these descriptions)
- patent: the official title to the property, giving the purchaser possession of the land

When writing to state offices about these documents, state the full name of the purchaser/grantee, and the county where the land was granted (if applicable, the name of the county where the land was at the time of purchase, not the current county where the land is). (See Figure 7-3 on page 61.)

If you believe your ancestor was an original purchaser or grantee of land in a state-land state (for example, you know he was an early settler), you may be able to get a head start on your research into original land grants by studying published lists of grantees for those states. To identify such lists, look at

- the "Land Records" section in the article on your ancestral state in *Ancestry's Red Book*
- chapter eight, "Research in Land and Tax Records," in *The Source*
- periodical indexes, for articles on early land records for the state (see the "Indexes to Genealogical Periodicals" section in chapter seventeen)
- the bibliography on pages 85–88 of Hone's *Land & Property Research in the United States*

FINDING RECORDS OF ORIGINAL PURCHASES OF LAND IN PUBLIC-DOMAIN STATES

The remaining states (public-domain states) are those in which the original seller or grantor of land was either the federal government or the previous owner of the territory (e.g., France or Spain). Records of sales before the United States owned a territory are beyond the scope of this book. See E. Wade Hone's

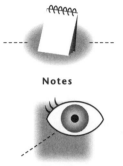

Notes

See Also

STATE-LAND STATES

To obtain information on original purchase of land in state-land states, write to the offices listed below. **See appendix E for their addresses.** For states where land records are kept at the county or town level, **see appendix B for books that list repositories to contact and their addresses.**

- **Connecticut**: Records were kept at the town level from the beginning.

- **Delaware**: Delaware State Archives.

- **Georgia**: Georgia Surveyor General Department, Floor 2V, Georgia Department of Archives and History.

- **Hawaii**: Bureau of Conveyances, 403 Queen Street, Honolulu, Hawaii 96913.

- **Kentucky**: Secretary of State's Office, Room 148, Capitol Building, Frankfort, Kentucky 40601.

- **Maine**: Records may be in the Massachusetts State Archives for earlier purchases or in the Maine State Archives for later purchases.

- **Maryland**: Maryland State Archives.

- **Massachusetts**: First land records may be at the county or town level; try the county first.

- **New Hampshire**: New Hampshire Division of Records and Archives (purchases before 1771) or the county (purchases after 1771).

- **New Jersey**: New Jersey State Archives.

- **New York**: New York State Archives.

- **North Carolina**: Land Grant Office, Office of the Secretary of State, 300 North Salisbury Street, Raleigh, North Carolina 27603.

- **Pennsylvania**: Land Records Office, Pennsylvania State Archives.

- **Rhode Island**: Records were kept at the town level from the beginning.

- **South Carolina**: South Carolina Department of Archives and History.

- **Tennessee**: Public Services Section, Tennessee State Library and Archives.

- **Texas**: General Land Office, 1700 North Congress Avenue, Austin, Texas 78701. State grants are also usually recorded in county records.

- **Vermont**: Records were kept at the town level from the beginning.

- **Virginia**: Library of Virginia, 800 East Broad Street, Richmond, Virginia 23219-8000.

- **West Virginia**: Office of State Auditor, Capitol Building, West Wing 231, Charleston, West Virginia 25305.

[Your postal address, phone number, and E-mail address]

[date]

State Land Records Office
[recipient's address]

Dear Friends:

I believe that my ancestor

Peter Shellhammer (born ca. 1755, died 1829)

purchased **land from the government of [state] in Westmoreland County** during his lifetime. Can you please tell me what is the procedure for finding out whether he made such a purchase and getting copies of the paperwork involved in the purchase? What are the related fees?

Thank you for your help. I enclose a self-addressed, stamped envelope for your convenience in replying.

Sincerely,

[your name]

> **Give your ancestor's name when you first write; some offices may check their indexes and let you know if they find anything.**

> **The procedure in each state is different. Most have handouts that explain the papers involved in the purchase, and what you must do to get copies. These handouts also list the fees involved.**

> **Always send a SASE.**

Figure 7-3 Request for information on getting papers related to an original purchase of land from a state-land state

Land & Property Research in the United States for information on Spanish and French records. These records are in foreign languages and may be in a handwriting style quite different from any to which you are accustomed.

Your ancestor might have received land from the federal government as bounty land in return for military service. To learn more about getting information about bounty land grants, see the "Military Records" section in chapter nine.

The process of purchasing land from the federal government generated several documents that might include useful information about your ancestors. These were
1. an application
2. a receipt for payment
3. a warrant for survey
4. a survey, recorded in the township plat books
5. information registered in tract books
6. land entry case files at the General Land Office
7. a final certificate for the patent issued to the applicant
8. a patent, given by the General Land Office

Case files also exist for rejected, revoked, contested, or cancelled claims, and these may contain more information than a routine claim that proceeded with no problems.

The later your ancestor acquired land from the federal government, the more information the paperwork contains. Case files for land acquired after 1862 under the Homestead Act often include paperwork with extensive genealogical information.

If your ancestor purchased land from the federal government, you need the following pieces of information to get the records:

- purchaser's full name
- state where the land is located
- (before 1908) legal description of the land (section, township, range,) or the name of the land office, type of file, and land entry file number
- (after 1908) the certificate or serial patent number

Internet Source

Land records for several states are indexed, and you may be able to check an index for your ancestor's name to find the information you need to request the records. Indexes for land sales prior to 1908 in public-domain states are available on the Internet from the **General Land Office at <http://www.glorecords .blm.gov>**. At this site, you can search federal land patent databases by the name of the purchaser, view the image of the land patent, and if you wish, order a certified copy for a small fee. The indexes for some of these states are also available from the Government Printing Office on CD-ROM (request information from the Superintendent of Documents, P.O. Box 371954, Pittsburgh, Pennsylvania 15250-7954).

CD Source

Make every attempt to access either the CD-ROM or Internet index for your ancestor's state (see chapter nineteen for ways to access the Internet if you don't have a personal account). If you absolutely can't get to these indexes, you must go through a multistep process to get copies of your ancestor's federal land records.

First, you need an exact description of the land (section, township, range, etc.). You may have it already from a deed. If not, you may have to look at tract books for the area where your ancestor lived. These are microfilmed and available for loan (see chapter thirteen for sources for renting microfilm). Tract book entries should indicate the final certificate or patent number.

Second, you need to identify the land office that served that area (sometimes identified in the tract book). Hone's *Land & Property Research in the United States* has maps showing areas each land office covered.

Once you've gotten the information needed to request your ancestor's land records, request a copy of NATF Form 84, the official form for requesting land entry files from the National Archives, from

National Archives and Records Administration
Old Military and Civil Records (NWCTB), Room 11E
Washington, DC 20408

LAND RECORDS ON CD-ROM

Brøderbund, the U.S. Bureau of Land Management (BLM), Global Data, and Palladium have issued CD-ROMs containing land records for selected states. Most of these CD-ROMs contain BLM records, although a few contain deed abstracts. Contact the publishers or see their Web pages to find out what records are available.

Fill in the form (see Figure 7-4 on page 64) and return it. Ask for copies of *all papers* in the file. If you include credit card information with your order, the National Archives will charge that account for the cost of photocopies and send them to you. Otherwise, they'll send you a form telling you the charge for photocopying the papers in question, then send the copies after you send payment.

CONCLUSION

Land records may seem boring, but in the midst of the dry legal language, you may find a wealth of information to add to your family knowledge. If ancestors had land, they may have acquired it by purchase or grant from their colony or state; purchase or grant from the federal government; purchase from private individuals; or inheritance. Attempt to get copies of all land records for your ancestors, both as grantor and grantee, to be sure you don't miss any records that give details about their life and family.

National Archives Trust Fund Board NATF Form 84 (8-97)

OMB Control No. 3095-0033 Expires 02-28-2000

NATIONAL ARCHIVES
ORDER FOR COPIES OF LAND ENTRY FILES
(See Instructions page before completing this form)

DATE RECEIVED IN NWDT1

INDICATE BELOW THE TYPE OF FILE DESIRED AND THE METHOD OF PAYMENT PREFERRED.

1. FILE TO BE SEARCHED *(Check one box only)*

☒ GENERAL LAND ENTRY FILES

☐ BOUNTY-LAND WARRANT FILES

Please refer to instructions for descriptions of these types of land entry files.

2. PAYMENT METHOD *(Check one box only)*

☐ **CREDIT CARD** *for IMMEDIATE SHIPMENT of copies (see instructions for credit cards we can accept).*

Exp. Date:

Signature:

Daytime Phone:

☒ **BILL ME** *(No Credit Card)*

REQUIRED MINIMUM IDENTIFICATION OF LAND FILE - MUST BE COMPLETED OR YOUR ORDER CANNOT BE SERVICED

3. NAME OF ENTRYMAN *(Give last, first, and middle names)*	4. LAND LOCATED IN STATE OF	5. APPROXIMATE DATE OF ENTRY *(Exact date, if known)*
DICKSON, JOSEPH	ILLINOIS	24 APRIL 1820

PLEASE PROVIDE THE FOLLOWING ADDITIONAL INFORMATION FOR GENERAL LAND ENTRY FILES

PRE-1908 GENERAL LAND ENTRY FILES

6. LEGAL DESCRIPTION OF LAND

SECTION NUMBER	TOWNSHIP NUMBER	RANGE NUMBER
29	14 N	4 W

7. TYPE OF GENERAL LAND ENTRY *(Check one)*

☐ CREDIT ☑ CASH ☐ HOMESTEAD ACT

If other, specify:

8. PATENT, FINAL CERTIFICATE, OR DOCUMENT NUMBER	9. NAME OF LAND OFFICE
436	SPRINGFIELD

POST-1908 GENERAL LAND ENTRY FILES

10. SERIAL PATENT NUMBER

PLEASE PROVIDE THE FOLLOWING ADDITIONAL INFORMATION FOR MILITARY BOUNTY LAND WARRANTS

11. YEAR OF ACT AUTHORIZING WARRANT	12. NUMBER OF ACRES	13. WARRANT NUMBER

If available, please attach one copy of the original land patent, tract book pages, or Bureau of Land Management GLOARS listing for this land entry.

DO NOT WRITE BELOW - SPACE IS FOR OUR REPLY TO YOU

☐ **NO–We were unable to locate the file you requested above. No payment is required.**

DATE SEARCHED	SEARCHER

☐ REQUIRED MINIMUM IDENTIFICATION OF LAND FILE WAS NOT PROVIDED. Please complete blocks 3 (give full name), 4, and 5 and resubmit your order.

☐ A SEARCH WAS MADE BUT THE FILE YOU REQUESTED ABOVE WAS NOT FOUND.

☐ See attached forms, leaflets, or information sheets.

☐ **YES–We located the file you requested above. We have made copies from the file for you. The cost for these copies is $10.**

DATE SEARCHED	SEARCHER
FILE DESIGNATION	

Make your check or money order payable to NATIONAL ARCHIVES TRUST FUND. Do not send cash. Return this form and your payment in the enclosed envelope to:

NATIONAL ARCHIVES TRUST FUND
P.O. BOX 100221
ATLANTA, GA 30384-0221

PLEASE NOTE: We will hold these copies awaiting receipt of payment for only 45 days from the date completed, which is stamped below. After that time, you must submit another form to obtain photocopies of the file.

THIS IS YOUR MAILING LABEL.

PRESS FIRMLY.

NAME (Last, First, MI) GENEALOGIST, JEANIE

STREET 100 MAINST

CITY, STATE ANYTOWN, ANYSTATE *ZIP CODE* 12345

E183556

INVOICE/REPLY COPY - DO NOT DETACH

Figure 7-4 NATF Form 84, for requesting copies of land entry files from the National Archives

EIGHT

Censuses

FEDERAL CENSUS RECORDS

The federal government took its first census in 1790 and has taken one every ten years since then. The government keeps census data confidential for seventy-two years after the census, so the most recent census records aren't available for researchers except in special cases. Most of the 1890 census no longer exists, having been destroyed after it was damaged in a fire in 1921 (for a full account of the sordid details, see the article "First in the Path of the Firemen: the Fate of the 1890 Population Census" in the spring 1996 issue of NARA's magazine *Prologue*, or the same article on the Internet at <http://www.nara.gov/publicati ons/prologue/1980cen1.html>).

Population Schedules

Of the several types of federal census records, genealogists use the population schedules most. The first six population censuses, from 1790 to 1840, list by name only the head of each household. In 1790, the sole concern was whether white males in the household were over or under age sixteen (i.e., whether they were old enough to join the military); the other categories were "free white females," "all other free persons," and "slaves." In subsequent censuses, more age divisions and questions were added (such as the number of people in the household over age twenty-one who couldn't read or write), giving you a little more information on the family.

Although the earlier censuses name only the head of household, you can often put together the data about other members of the household with other information you have about the people in the family to draw some conclusions about them. By correlating age ranges of an ancestor on sequential early censuses, you can narrow the possible age of someone whose birth date you don't know. If you're trying to identify an ancestor's father by looking at households where the head of household has your ancestor's surname, not finding a child in the appropriate age range for your ancestor can suggest ruling out that person as a potential

For More Info

READ MORE ABOUT IT!

- The National Archives genealogy Web site at <http://www.nara.gov/geneal ogy/#guides> has links to several pages of information about the federal census.

- William Dollarhide's *The Census Book* gives an in-depth look at the federal census through the years, detailing what censuses are available for each state and/or county and listing many published census indexes (book and CD-ROM formats). It includes a CD-ROM with the text of the book and forms to use when extracting census information.

- For each census taken in each state between 1790 and 1920, Thorndale and Dollarhide's *Map Guide to the U.S. Federal Censuses, 1790–1920* has a map showing current county boundaries and the county boundaries in effect at the time of the census. This may help you to pinpoint the county in which you should look for your ancestor.

- *Using the Census Soundex* is a free brochure available from Product Development and Distribution Staff (NWCP), National Archives and Records Administration, Room G-7, 700 Pennsylvania Avenue NW, Washington, D.C. 20408 (telephone (202) 501-5235 or (800) 234-8861). To order via E-mail, send your request to <inquire@nara.gov> (include your name, postal address, and "GIL 55 please").

---

father. Some listings may raise more questions than they answer. For example, you may find more people listed in an age and sex category than you can account for in other records. Who were they? If elderly people were in the household of a middle-aged ancestor, were they parents of the husband or wife, or perhaps a maiden aunt and unmarried uncle? Raising these questions may stimulate you to do further research, and the answers you find will help to fill in your family tree.

In 1850, for the first time, the census listed the names of all free persons in each household and specific details of age, sex, race, birthplace, etc., for each. However, the exact relationship to the head of household wasn't stated until the 1880 census; before then, be careful about jumping to the conclusion that all children in the household were born to the head of household. Gradually the government added more and more questions, so that in 1880, for example, enumerators asked for the place of birth of both parents. Unfortunately, in most cases, enumerators followed instructions and listed the place of birth only as a state or foreign country, not a city; occasionally, they gave more detail than they were required to. In 1900, women were asked how many children they had borne and how many of these were living; answers to this question can help in determining the makeup of a family. For example, if the wife said she had borne six children, five of whom were living, and eight children in the household were listed as sons or daughters of the head of household, that wife was probably at least a second wife.

Beginning genealogists may find an ancestor on one census and think they've finished their census research for that person. But **it's important to locate** *all* **census records for your ancestor and compare them.** From 1850 forward, looking at all censuses will help to ensure you don't miss a record of a child who died young. Or you may find, for example, that in one census, the age given for a person varies more or less than ten years from the age in each census before and after (e.g., ages in three sequential censuses given as thirty, thirty-five, and fifty). You might guess that in the aberrant census, information came from someone who didn't know how old the person was. If you had looked only at this census, you might have been led astray. On the other hand, it's possible that the seemingly "aberrant" census is correct and the others are wrong.

This brings up an important point. While censuses are primary records, and while you know the name of the person who recorded the information, you rarely can tell who gave the information to the enumerator. Especially in rural districts, where enumeration involved a lot of travel, the person making the record wouldn't have wanted to retrace his steps if the head of the household, or even the whole family, hadn't been home. He might have collected information from a neighbor in order to avoid having to make a return trip. So if another primary source doesn't agree with census information, the other primary source is quite possibly correct.

What Census Should I Look At? Census Indexes are Available in Many Formats

Before you look at the census, you need to determine which microfilm to order. Do you know in what county your ancestor lived during the census year? If not, do you at least know in what state? In the worst case, you may only be able to narrow the location down to several states.

Finding information about an ancestor from a census used to involve sitting down with the census microfilm for the county where you thought your ancestor lived, crossing your fingers, and reading through the census page by page, name by name, to find (you hoped!) your ancestor's listing. However, in the past twenty years, many census indexes have been published. These indexes can tell you where a person (or people) with your ancestor's name lived in a state and save you time by allowing you to go directly to the entry (or entries) in the microfilm. An index tells you the exact microfilm you need to borrow, which could save you money on rental fees.

If your ancestor's name is common, you may find more than one listing for it in the indexes, and you need to check them all to be sure you've found your ancestor's record. The census record may include enough details that you can be certain you have the right person, but with the earlier censuses, you may not be sure.

Index Options That Include the Actual Census

Most census indexes include listings only of the heads of household, not of every person in every household. Remember that if you work with a transcription of a census, you should view it only as a guide to lead you to the original.

MY ANCESTOR'S NOT IN THE CENSUS!

See chapter twelve for a general discussion of problems in indexes. Beyond those problems, census indexes can present special problems for the genealogist:

- If your ancestor moved around a lot, it's possible that he wasn't where you think he ought to have been. Even if he seemed to have stayed put, he might, for some reason, have moved away at the time of one census and later returned.

- Your ancestor might not have moved, but the boundaries of his county or other jurisdiction might have moved. Research the genealogy of his location to be sure you're looking in the right jurisdiction for that time period.

- It's not uncommon to find someone using a first name on one census and a middle name on another. Some census takers used only initials, especially for people with long last names.

- More than one index may be available for a particular census; if so, check others to see if you can find your ancestor's name.

- If none of these solutions work, you're back to doing it the old-fashioned way: reading through the census name by name and hoping that the census taker didn't miss your ancestor entirely.

- As a last resort, if you didn't find your ancestor by reading through the census, go through again and read the *first* names of everyone on the census; look for your ancestor's first name or, if the census is 1850 or later, the first names of the people you expect to find in the household. If the census taker really mangled the spelling of the last name or had atrocious handwriting, you might have missed the surname even if it was there.

The Government Printing Office published transcriptions of the 1790 census in a series of books called *Heads of Families at the First Census of the United States Taken in the Year 1790, [name of state]*, including Connecticut, Maine, Maryland, Massachusetts, New Hampshire, New York, North Carolina, Pennsylvania, Virginia, Rhode Island, South Carolina, and Vermont. Census returns for Delaware, Georgia, Kentucky, New Jersey, Tennessee, and Virginia were destroyed in a fire in 1814. For Virginia, the series substitutes the incomplete state enumerations of 1782, 1783, 1784, and 1785. These books have every-name indexes. If your library doesn't have the book for the state you need, try to get it on interlibrary loan. If it isn't available on interlibrary loan, you can probably get at least a copy of the page from the index that includes your ancestor's name, and then request the page(s) with listings for people with that name.

A subscription Internet site, <http://GenealogyLibrary.com/> has mounted scanned copies of some censuses and plans to put up others. The site also includes indexes of these censuses; search for your name of interest, and if you get any matches, click on the entry to go directly to an image of the census for your ancestor.

Several vendors, including AllCensus, Brøderbund, Census View, Heritage Quest, and S-K Publications, sell CD-ROMs containing full images of censuses. Not all vendors have all censuses available; check their catalogs or Internet sites, and compare prices (which vary widely) before you buy. Also verify whether the CDs are indexed; some aren't, and it's worthwhile to pay more for an indexed version. If you're researching many families in a location, you may want to purchase these CDs. The CDs are only as good as the original census, so they include the same faint and/or illegible handwriting that you may struggle with on the microfilm.

Historical or genealogical societies often publish as a book or magazine article transcriptions of complete copies of a census for a county or township (the 1790 and 1850 censuses are the most popular for this). Contact the historical and genealogical societies for your county of interest, and check genealogical periodical indexes and library catalogs to find out what's available.

At least one vendor, S-K Publications, has published books that are photocopies of the census for some specific counties and years.

On the Internet, USGenWeb has begun a project to transcribe and mount census data; check the site for your county to see if it includes the censuses you need, or search the USGenWeb's Census Project site at <http://www.usgenweb.org/census/>. You get files of census transcriptions from this site by FTP (file transfer protocol). If you're not familiar with it, don't worry about the technicalities of this process. You'll actually download a file into your computer; your computer and the Internet site handle the details. This transcription project is going slowly since it relies on volunteers, and most of the censuses available so far are pre-1850 censuses.

Index Options That Don't Include the Actual Census

Accelerated Indexing Systems (AIS) published large numbers of census indexes in book format in the 1970s and 1980s, mainly indexing censuses for 1790 through 1850. Precision Indexing has also published book and microfiche indexes of some censuses. These are available in many libraries. If your library doesn't have the index for the state and year you need, try to get a copy on interlibrary loan. Since most libraries consider these reference books, you might not be able to get the entire index on loan. In that case, ask your librarian to request through interlibrary loan a photocopy of the page(s) that should include your ancestor's name.

When you can't pinpoint where your ancestor lived, the *AIS Microfiche Indexes of U.S. Census and Other Records* is a good starting place. This microfiche includes the AIS census indexes for the 1790 through 1850 censuses, plus some other records in nine indexes. Major Family History Centers and large genealogical libraries hold this microfiche set. For more information about this microfiche set, see the Family History SourceGuide "Accelerated Indexing Systems, U.S. Census Indexes (on Microfiche)" at a Family History Center or on the Internet at <http://www.familysearch.org/sg/> (listed toward the bottom of the list of source guides under "United States").

The contents of the AIS census indexes have been transferred to CD-ROMs that Brøderbund sells. Heritage Quest has also issued some CD-ROM census indexes.

Check the Internet at <http://www.censuslinks.com/> to see if someone has mounted a free index for an area you're interested in. This site also includes links to tax records and military records.

Recently, the Ancestry Web site mounted the AIS state and federal census indexes from 1790 to 1870 at <http://www.ancestry.com/census/> as a subscription database. Search for a name in all the indexes available, or limit your search by state. These indexes include federal and state population censuses plus some special federal censuses, and even censuses for some parts of Canada. You can also view a complete list of indexes available for each state. To give you an idea of what is available, the list for Pennsylvania includes the federal census indexes for the 1790 through 1870 censuses; a 1772 tax list for Northampton County; the 1840 pensioners list; the 1842 and 1857 Chester County "census indexes" (apparently actually tax lists, as there's no such thing as a Chester County, Pennsylvania, census for these years); and the 1890 naval veterans schedule. Although this is a subscription database, you can do the first part of the search free: enter your ancestor's name and search to see where someone of that name is indexed. If you limit your search to one state, you'll get a number of hits or a message that no one of that name was found. If you don't limit the search, you'll get a breakdown of hits by state (giving the total number of hits in all indexes for the state, but no information about which index or indexes for the state actually contained the name). **The computer only searches for the name as you typed it at the search screen.** If your ancestor is in the index, but you've entered a different spelling of the name, the computer won't find the person (see the "My Ancestor's Not in the Index!" section in chapter twelve for a discussion of the problems of finding a specific name in indexes).

Warning

Sometimes genealogical societies publish indexes to censuses for the area they cover. Search for them in periodical indexes (see the "Indexes to Genealogical Periodicals" section in chapter seventeen) or check with societies in your ancestral area. Indexes produced by a local historical or genealogical society have an advantage over indexes produced by a national company: the indexer is more likely to be familiar with unusual names in the area and to have transcribed them correctly.

Historical and genealogical societies sometimes have one unpublished copy of an index of a census for the area they cover. If you can't locate an index you need among the indexes mentioned above, write to the local historical or genealogical society or library for your area of interest to ask if they have one.

Check the catalog at your local Family History Center to see if it lists an index that will help you. On the Internet, check the catalogs of the Library of Congress, the National Genealogical Society, and other libraries with strong genealogical holdings to see if they list indexes that you need (see chapter twelve for a discussion of such libraries).

Soundex Indexes

The Works Projects Administration produced indexes or partial indexes to the censuses from 1880 through 1930, mainly to help people who were eligible for Social Security benefits prove their age. Organizations that rent census microfilm have these indexes available for rent. However, rather than using a straight alphabetical index, these indexes use a system called Soundex.

Soundex was developed to help government employees, but it's useful for genealogists as well, since census takers often wrote what they heard and didn't bother to ask for the correct spelling of a name. However, some errors may lead to a name being given a Soundex code different from the one for the correct spelling, so Soundex may not be the final answer to your problems.

If formulating a Soundex code for your ancestral surname seems confusing (see pages 72 and 73), take heart! The National Archives has mounted "The Soundex Machine," which provides automatic Soundex coding, on the Internet at <http://www.nara.gov/genealogy/soundex/soundex.html>. Many genealogical computer programs also can automatically generate the Soundex code for a name.

The following Soundex indexes are available:

- The Soundex for the 1880 census indexes *only* households that included children ten years of age or under.
- The good news is that, theoretically, the 1900 and 1920 Soundex indexes include all households in all states.
- Soundex indexes for 1910 are available for only twenty-one states: Alabama, Arkansas, California, Florida, Georgia, Illinois, Kansas, Kentucky, Louisiana, Michigan, Mississippi, Missouri, North Carolina, Ohio, Oklahoma, Pennsylvania, South Carolina, Tennessee, Texas, Virginia, and West Virginia.
- The 1930 Soundex indexes cover Alabama, Arkansas, Florida, Georgia, Louisiana, Mississippi, North Carolina, South Carolina, Tennessee, and Virginia. Seven counties are indexed for both Kentucky (Bell, Floyd, Harlan, Kenton, Muhlenberg, Perry, and Pike) and for West Virginia (Fayette, Harrison, Kanasha, Logan, McDowell, Mercer, and Raleigh).
- For the 1910 census, there are street indexes to thirty-nine cities; for the 1930 census, four cities. These can help you decide where to begin your search. These indexes are available on loan from the Family History Library through Family History Centers (see chapter twelve for information on borrowing from the Family History Library).

How to Get Copies of Census Records

If you live near a large library or a National Archives branch you may have access to microfilm copies of the censuses you need to trace your ancestors. The central library in a large metropolitan area may own out-of-state censuses.

If no local collection includes the censuses you need, you have several options. Ask the reference librarian at your public library if they order census microfilm on interlibrary loan for patrons. If your library isn't doing this already, perhaps you can convince them to start.

Notes

THE SOUNDEX SYSTEM

On their Web page at <http://www.nara.gov/genealogy/coding.html> the National Archives gives the following explanation of how Soundex works:

Basic Soundex Coding Rule

Every Soundex code consists of a letter and three numbers, such as W-252. The letter is always the first letter of the surname. The numbers are assigned to the remaining letters of the surname according to the Soundex guide shown below. Zeroes are added at the end if necessary to produce a four-character code. Additional letters are disregarded.

For example, Washington is coded W-252 (W, 2 for the S, 5 for the N, 2 for the G, remaining letters disregarded). For example, Lee is coded L-000 (L 000 added).

Soundex Coding Guide

THE NUMBER	REPRESENTS THE FOLLOWING LETTERS
1	B, F, P, V
2	C, G, J, K, Q, S, X, Z
3	D, T
4	L
5	M, N
6	R

Disregard the letters A, E, I, O, U, H, W, and Y.

Additional Soundex Coding Rules

1. *Names With Double Letters*

   If the surname has any double letters, they should be treated as one letter.

   For example, Gutierrez is coded G-362 (G, 3 for the T, 6 for the first R, second R ignored, 2 for the Z).

2. *Names With Letters Side by Side That Have the Same Soundex Code Number*

   If the surname has different letters side by side that have the same number in the Soundex coding guide, they should be treated as one letter.

   For example, Pfister is coded as P-236 (P, F ignored, 2 for the S, 3 for the T, 6 for the R).

   For example, Jackson is coded as J-250 (J, 2 for the C, K ignored, S ignored, 5 for the N, 0 added).

3. *Names With Prefixes*

   If a surname has a prefix, such as Van, Con, De, Di, La, or Le, code both with and without the prefix because the surname might be listed under either code. Note, however, that Mc and Mac are not considered prefixes.

continued

> For example, VanDeusen might be coded two ways:
> V-532 (V, 5 for N, 3 for D, 2 for S)
>
> or
>
> D-250 (D, 2 for the S, 5 for the N, 0 added).
>
> [Many surnames that do not necessarily sound alike may receive the same Soundex code.]

See chapter thirteen for information on vendors who rent and sell census microfilm directly to genealogists. If you have many ancestors in the same county in a given census year, consider purchasing the census microfilm or CD-ROM.

If all else fails, but you've been able to identify a citation for the census record of your ancestor, you can request a copy of the record from the National Archives with NATF Form 82 (see Figure 8-1 on page 74).

See Also

Census Records for the Past Seventy-Two Years

Under certain circumstances, the National Archives will research census records not yet open to the public and release information about a person to that person or the person's heirs or legal representatives. The information you can get will include the person's name, relationship to head of household, age at the time of the census, and state of birth. Note that this information does not include the name of the head of household. The search is expensive (check with the Census Bureau for current fees). For full information on requesting such a search, see the U.S. Census Bureau Web site at <http://www.census.gov/geneal ogy/www/agesearch.html> or contact them at

U.S. Census Bureau, National Processing Center
1201 E. 10th St.
Jeffersonville, IN 47132
(812) 218-3046

Recording the Information You Find

Before looking for ancestors on the census, get forms for organizing census information. These are available as loose forms from some genealogical publishing companies (look for ads in genealogical magazines) and as forms you can download from the Internet or photocopy from some genealogy handbooks. They simplify extraction by providing the headings from the census columns, and they may prompt you to extract information you might otherwise have missed. Two types of forms are available: those for collecting information about one family from all censuses on which it appears, and those for collecting information about several families from one specific census.

Forms for recording census data also have spaces that prompt you to list full source information about the census record. Whether you use the forms or not, write down the name of the head of household; the year of the census; county

Timesaver

NATIONAL ARCHIVES
ORDER FOR COPIES OF CENSUS RECORDS
(See Instructions page before completing this form)

DATE RECEIVED IN NNRG

INDICATE BELOW THE METHOD OF PAYMENT PREFERRED

☐ CREDIT CARD *(VISA or MasterCard)* for IMMEDIATE SHIPMENT of copies
Account Number:

Exp. Date: Signature

Daytime Phone:

☒ **BILL ME** *(No credit card)*

REQUIRED MINIMUM IDENTIFICATION OF ENTRY MUST BE COMPLETED OR YOUR ORDER CANNOT BE SERVICED

1. CENSUS YEAR	2. STATE OR TERRITORY	3. COUNTY
1910	PENNSYLVANIA	ARMSTRONG

4. TOWNSHIP OR OTHER SUBDIVISION	5. NAME OF HEAD OF HOUSEHOLD	6. PAGE NO.	7. ENUMERATION DISTRICT *(for 1880, 1900, 1910, and 1920 only)*
WICK BORO	VALENTINE S. REESE	5	051

PLEASE PROVIDE THE FOLLOWING ADDITIONAL INFORMATION IF KNOWN

	NAME	AGE	SEX	NAME	AGE	SEX
8. MEMBERS OF HOUSEHOLD	VALENTINE S REESE	56	M	MARY	18	F
	LOVINA	49	F	FREDERICK	15	M
	SAMUEL	25	M			
	WARREN	21	M			

NATIONAL ARCHIVES TRUST FUND BOARD   NATF Form 82 (rev. 10–93)

DO NOT WRITE BELOW – SPACE IS FOR OUR REPLY TO YOU

☐ **NO--We were unable to locate the entry you requested above. No payment is required.**

SEARCHER	DATE SEARCHED

☐ REQUIRED MINIMUM IDENTIFICATION OF ENTRY WAS NOT PROVIDED. Please complete blocks 1, 2, 3, 4, 5, 6, and 7 and resubmit your order.

☐ Due to the poor quality of the microfilm, the pages you requested cannot be reproduced clearly on our equipment.

☐ The microfilm roll for the State and county for which you requested copies is missing and will take 1 to 2 months to replace.

☐ OTHER:

_____

_____

_____

☐ **YES--We located the entry you requested above. We have made copies of the entry for you. The cost for these copies is $6.**

CENSUS YEAR	STATE OR TERRITORY
COUNTY	
MICROFILM PUBLICATION	ROLL	PAGE NO.
SEARCHER	DATE SEARCHED

Make your check or money order payable to NATIONAL ARCHIVES TRUST FUND. Do not send cash. Return this form and your payment in the enclosed envelope to:

NATIONAL ARCHIVES TRUST FUND
P.O. BOX 100221
ATLANTA, GA   30384-0221

PLEASE NOTE: We will hold these copies awaiting receipt of payment for only 45 days from the date completed, which is stamped below. After that time, you must submit another form to obtain photocopies of the record.

THIS IS YOUR MAILING LABEL. PRESS FIRMLY.

C212016

STREET
100 MAIN ST

CITY, STATE
ANYTOWN, ANYSTATE

INVOICE/REPLY COPY – DO NOT DETACH

Figure 8-1 NATF Form 82, for requesting copies of census records from the National Archives

and state; post office; page, dwelling, and family numbers; and National Archives micropublication and reel numbers. For the censuses from 1880 on, you also need the enumeration district and supervisor's district numbers. This information is important so you can refer to the original record again or tell someone else where it is.

Other Federal Schedules

At some point, you may also investigate the other federal schedules: agriculture, industry/manufacturing, mortality, slave, and union veterans (1890). Of these, the most useful to genealogists are the mortality schedules, taken only in the census years of 1850 through 1880. The census taker was instructed to ask who in the household had died between June 1 of the year before the census year (1849, 1859, 1869, and 1879) and May 31 of the census year (1850, 1860, 1870, 1880). He recorded the age at death, cause of death, month of death, place of birth (usually state or foreign country, not city), and other information. These schedules are especially interesting if you're researching family health history. Even if you aren't, if some of your ancestors were considerate enough to die during the time periods these schedules cover, you may find an approximate death date for someone who died before death certificates were issued.

Sources

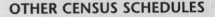

Notes

OTHER CENSUS SCHEDULES

Agriculture schedules are available for the 1850 through 1880 censuses. For each farm, these list the name of the owner or manager; number of acres (improved and unimproved); value of the farm, machinery, and livestock (many enumerated by type); amount of various products produced during the preceding year, etc.

The schedules variously called "manufacturing" (1820 and 1880) and "industry" (1850 through 1870) include the name of the manufacturer, the type of business or product, amount of capital invested, information on raw materials used and products, kind of power used, number of men and women employed, etc.

Slave schedules were taken in 1850 and 1860. If you're researching an African-American family, don't expect too much from these schedules, as they usually don't list the names of the slaves. They include only the owner's name and the age, sex, and color of each of his slaves. Other columns are "Fugitives from the State," "Number manumitted," and "Deaf & dumb, blind, insane, or idiotic."

While these other schedules provide little information that's strictly genealogical, they may give you details of your ancestor's life that you might not find anywhere else. In some cases, information in these schedules may work with other information to help you solve genealogical puzzles. Most, if not all, of them are available on loan from Heritage Quest and other sources for microfilm loan (see appendix D for more information).

Most of the 1890 census has been lost; if one of your ancestors was a Civil War veteran of the Union Army and either he or his wife was still alive in 1890, the Union Veterans Schedule for 1890 may help you. The only such enumerations that survive are about half of the enumeration for Kentucky and the information from all states subsequent to Kentucky in alphabetical order (including Washington, D.C.). The entries include the name of the veteran or widow, the veteran's rank and military unit or vessel, his dates of enlistment and discharge, his length of service, any disability, and general remarks. While these censuses were supposed to enumerate only Union veterans, some include information on Confederate veterans as well (usually crossed out, but readable). If you're having trouble identifying your veteran ancestor's military unit in order to pursue military service or pension records, this schedule may help you.

Clues From the Census for Further Research

Census records include many clues that can lead you to other records:

- Different birth states for children in a family give clues about the migration route of the family. If children were older than ten years old at the time of the census, this provides one or more other states to research on previous censuses.
- If a census shows an ancestor owned property, look for land records and/ or an estate file for him.
- The 1900 census gives the month and year of each person's birth. Although this information may not be correct, send for the birth certificate if the birth date is within the time frame when the state where the person was born issued birth certificates.
- If census indexes lead you to your ancestor in a county or state other than where you expected, search for other records for the ancestor in that locality.
- The 1900, 1910, 1920, and 1930 censuses show an immigrant's immigration year and naturalization status; this can be a clue to seek naturalization papers.

STATE CENSUSES AND CENSUS SUBSTITUTES

Wow! The states took censuses, too? There's information to supplement the federal census? Don't get too excited; for many states, surviving state censuses and census substitutes (voter rolls, city directories, etc.) are few and far between. Those that survive may not include the whole state or area you need; indeed, only a few counties may survive from a given state census. No state censuses exist at all for Connecticut, Idaho, Kentucky, Montana, New Hampshire, Ohio, Pennsylvania, and Vermont. Early state censuses that survive usually follow the pattern of early federal censuses, listing only the name of the head of household, with the rest of the household represented only by a count of various age groups.

However, **state censuses were usually taken in years other than those of the federal censuses and sometimes include information other than that in federal censuses.** If a state census that enumerates an ancestral family does survive, it may

Reminder

add to your family information, narrow the date of arrival or departure of a family in an area, or fill in information about the family in the period between 1880 and 1900. Also, you may find recent census information from a few states that took censuses within the last seventy-two years that are open to the public, while federal censuses from that time period are not available. As with the federal census, state enumerators sometimes added information and comments beyond what was required that may help you. Remember, get every available record relating to your ancestors. If a state census exists that might include one of your ancestral families, make every effort to look at it.

It's not practical to list all the available state censuses here. The best source for this information is Ann Lainhart's *State Census Records*. This book has a short section (one to five pages) for each state for which she has identified existing state censuses or substitutes (there are no sections for Connecticut, Idaho, Kentucky, New Hampshire, Pennsylvania, or Vermont). These discuss what's available for the state (including territorial enumerations), what repository holds the originals, whether any of the information has been published (with citations), and whether (or under what conditions) the holding repository will search the census for information on your ancestor.

In *Ancestry's Red Book*, the chapter for each state includes a section on censuses that discusses federal, state, and territorial censuses and census substitutes. The only states for which nothing but federal censuses are discussed are the District of Columbia, Idaho, and West Virginia.

The Source, revised edition, pages 134–135, includes a list of state censuses that gives only the year of the census and whether it's full or partial. None are listed for Connecticut, Idaho, Kentucky, Montana, New Hampshire, Ohio, Pennsylvania, Vermont, or West Virginia.

Many state censuses are available on microfilm from the Family History Library. Some state libraries, state archives, and state historical societies lend census microfilm. Some individual state censuses (or portions thereof) have been transcribed and published. Often these appear as an article in a historical or genealogical magazine. If you don't have access to Lainhart's *State Census Records*, check genealogical periodical indexes for citations for state census transcriptions.

CONCLUSION

Genealogists find census records useful because they give detailed information about all the people in one household, including, in later censuses, information on how these people are related to each other. The amount of detail in census records varies greatly depending on their date; earlier censuses are much less specific than later ones. Genealogists should attempt to look at every listing in the population schedules that includes their families. The many census indexes available can make the process of locating an ancestor on the census relatively simple, but if an ancestor proves elusive, be alert for the possibility of spelling variations or misspellings of the name. In some cases, genealogists may be able to find state census records for their ancestors.

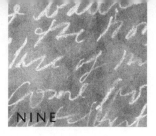

NINE

Other Federal Government Records

T he National Archives and Records Admininstration (NARA) and other U.S. government agencies have immense collections of records of inter-actions between people and the federal government. Besides census records and land records, genealogists find Social Security applications, military records (especially pension and bounty land records), immigration records, and naturalization records most useful.

For a brief general overview of records at the National Archives, request a copy of their free pamphlet *Using Records in the National Archives for Genea-logical Research* (specify "GIL 5") from

Product Development and Distribution Staff (NWCP)
National Archives and Records Administration, Room G-7
700 Pennsylvania Ave. NW
Washington, DC 20408
(202) 501-5235 or (800) 234-8861

Alternatively, request it via E-mail from inquire@nara.gov.

For in-depth information about research in the National Archives, read the U.S. National Archives and Records Administration's book *Guide to Genealog-ical Research in the National Archives.*

SOCIAL SECURITY APPLICATIONS

The Social Security Administration, not surprisingly, keeps Social Security ap-plications. If your ancestor worked for another person (i.e., wasn't self-employed) after 1937, that ancestor probably had a Social Security number. To get the number, the person had to complete Form SS-5, which included the following information:

- full name
- full name at birth, including maiden name
- present mailing address
- age at last birthday
- date of birth
- place of birth (city, county, and state)
- father's full name
- mother's full name, including maiden name
- sex
- race (the applicant chose what to put in this space)
- whether the applicant had applied for Social Security or Railroad Retirement before
- current employer's name and address
- date signed
- applicant's signature

If there's any chance your ancestor might have applied for a Social Security number, send for the application. You may have this information from other sources, but they may be secondary sources. Your ancestor personally supplied the information on the SS-5.

What If I Don't Have My Ancestor's Social Security Number?

A copy of an SS-5 costs more if you don't have the person's Social Security number (SSN). However, there are several ways to get a person's SSN:

Money Saver

- If you're requesting the form with the consent of a living person, that person may supply the SSN.
- If you're requesting the form of a deceased person, you'll need a copy of the death certificate (which you should get anyway) to prove the death. Death certificates from most, if not all, states include the SSN.
- Family papers such as insurance policies, bank statements, or military records may include the SSN.
- Many genealogy Web sites offer searches of the Social Security Death Index (SSDI), which gives information on some deceased persons who had a Social Security number. This database has two limitations: most of these deaths occurred after 1962, and the person's death must have been reported to the Social Security Administration (usually when the family applied for Social Security death benefits). Information for those who are listed includes the Social Security number; date of birth; state from which the person applied for the Social Security number (not necessarily the state of birth); state of death; date of death; city, state, and zip code of the person's last known residence; and zip code where the final payment was sent. Sites that offer the database include RootsWeb at <http://ssdi.genealo gy.rootsweb.com/cgi-bin/ssdi.cgi> and Ancestry.
- The Ancestry Web site at <http://www.ancestry.com> makes applying for a copy of the SS-5 even easier for you. If you find a listing for someone in the SSDI on their site, you can follow a link to a page that automatically

generates a letter requesting the person's SS-5. Just print out the letter, fill in your name and address, write a check for the correct amount, and mail it to the Social Security Administration.

Your public library or local Family History Center may have the Social Security Death Index on CD-ROM (available from Brøderbund), or you can buy it yourself.

How Do I Get an SS-5?

To request a copy of your ancestor's Form SS-5, write to

Social Security Administration
Office of Central Records Operations

[Your postal address, phone number, and E-mail address]

[date]

Social Security Administration
Office of Central Records Operations
FOIA Workgroup
P.O. Box 33022
300 N. Greene Street
Baltimore, MD 21290

Dear Friends:

I would like a copy of the SS-5 for my grandfather:

Give full name of the person.

John Sylvester Doe
Give Social Security number.
SSN 123-45-6789
Born 13 April 1910, Butte, Montana
Died 29 February 1964, Butte, Montana

Give birth and death dates and places to differentiate him from others of the same name.

He is listed in the Social Security Death Index.

Give evidence of his death.

I enclose a check for $7, which I understand is the cost of this document when the requestor supplies the SSN.

Enclose a check for the correct amount.

Thank you for your help in this matter.

Sincerely,

[your name]

Figure 9-1 Request for an SS-5 from the Social Security Administration (SSN known)

FOIA Workgroup
P.O. Box 33022
300 N. Greene St.
Baltimore, MD 21290

Your inquiry should include:
- your request for a copy of Form SS-5
- the person's name
- evidence of the person's death (possibly, the fact that he's listed in the

---

[Your postal address, phone number, and E-mail address]

[date]

Social Security Administration
Office of Central Records Operations
FOIA Workgroup
P.O. Box 33022
300 N. Greene Street
Baltimore, MD 21290

Dear Friends:

I would like a copy of the SS-5 for my grandfather:

Richard Sylvester Roe ── | **Give full name of the person.** |

Born 19 April 1890, Butte, Montana
Died 21 January 1940, Butte, Montana ──── | **Give birth and death dates and places and names of parents to differentiate him from others of the same name.** |
Father: William Roe
Mother: Jane (-?-)

I enclose a copy of his death certificate as proof of his death. ──── | **Give evidence of his death.** |

I have not been able to find his Social Security number.

I enclose a check for $16.50, which I understand is the cost of this document when the requestor does not know the SSN. ──── | **Enclose a check for the correct amount.** |

Thank you for your help in this matter.

Sincerely,

[your name]

Figure 9-2 Request for an SS-5 from the Social Security Administration (SSN not known)

Social Security Death Index) or, if the person is still alive, a statement signed by the person giving permission for you to get a copy of his SS-5
- the person's Social Security number (see Figure 9-1 on page 80)

If you don't have the Social Security number, you also must include:
- the person's date and place of birth
- names of the person's parents (see Figure 9-2 on page 81)

If you're making the request to find out birth and/or parental information, give whatever information you do have, and state that you're making the request to obtain more information on the person.

How Much Will I Have to Pay?

For information on current fees, consult the National Archives and Records Administration Social Security Records Web page at <http://www.nara.gov/genealogy/socsec.html> or call the Social Security Administration at (800) 772-1213.

Alternatively, send your request without payment and ask them to let you know what the cost of the copy is.

My Ancestor Didn't Have a Social Security Number, and I'm Stuck on His Line!

If a recent ancestor didn't have a Social Security number, perhaps deceased siblings did. The sibling's SS-5 should include information about your ancestor's parents.

For More Info

READ MORE ABOUT IT!

For more information on Social Security applications, see the pamphlet *Social Security Applications: A Genealogical Resource,* by Allen and Billingsley.

MILITARY RECORDS

If one of your ancestors served in the American military, a wealth of genealogical information may await you in the files at the National Archives. This could include the maiden name of a man's wife (or wives) and their marriage date; the names and dates of birth of at least some children; and death information for the veteran, the spouse, and possibly some of the children. There's generally more information for veterans of later wars than for those of the American Revolution.

The names of the parents of the ancestor or the spouse *could* appear in the pension file, but no forms request this information. However, you may find information that will help you to identify parents; for example, the place of marriage might be close to the home of the family of one or both spouses.

I'm Not Sure If My Ancestor Served in the Military

Many sources list people who served in the military. Some major ones include
- *Index of Revolutionary War Pension Applications in the National Archives* (lists those who served in Continental forces and received pensions)
- *DAR Patriot Index* (lists soldiers whose descendants have joined the Daughters of the American Revolution)

WAS HE OF MILITARY AGE BETWEEN 1861 AND 1865?

On the 1870 census, the family of William Henderson Crawford had a child born in 1861 and the next child born in 1865. This four-year gap between children could have been because a child born between the two died young. However, without even being sure that William *was* in the Army, I made an educated guess that the gap occurred because he was away fighting in the Civil War, so I sent a form to the National Archives requesting a pension record for him. There *was* a pension record, and I vastly expanded my information about his family with it. The moral of this story: If your ancestor was between ages eighteen and forty-five around 1861 to 1865, request a military record for him even if you have no evidence that he fought.

- The U.S. Census Bureau's *A Census of Pensioners for Revolutionary or Military Services* (lists information about pensioners for Revolutionary or military service from the 1840 U.S. Census)
- The U.S. Pension Bureau's *List of Pensioners on the Roll January 1, 1883* (lists all pensioners alive at that date)
- the only surviving portion of the 1890 census (part of the census of Union veterans and their widows—half for the state of Kentucky and all for states that fall alphabetically after Kentucky)
- county histories that include lists of people from the county who fought in the Civil War, including their units (Usually these lists give only a name and rank, but they may at least help you to ascertain that a person with your ancestor's name fought in the Civil War.)
- *General Index to Pension Files 1861–1934* (NARA Microfilm Publication T288; 544 rolls of film)
- Brøderbund CD-ROMs of military records, mostly dating from the early history of the United States (You can purchase these, or you can access them through a subscription at the Family Tree Maker Web site at <http://familytreemaker.com>.)

What Military Records Aren't at the National Archives?

If your ancestor was in a state militia unit or other local unit during the American Revolution rather than in the Continental forces, the National Archives may have no records for him. In that case, contact the state archives of the state from which he served (see appendix E for addresses).

During the Civil War, some soldiers from the South served in state militia units rather than the Confederate States Army. Records for these units, if they survive, are at the state level, often in the state archives. Some southern states paid pensions to Confederate veterans; again, these records are at the state level.

For More Info

READ MORE ABOUT IT!

- See the NARA genealogy Web site at <http://www.nara.gov/genealogy/> for links to NARA Web pages about military records from various time periods.
- James C. Neagles's *U.S. Military Records: A Guide to Federal and State Sources, Colonial America to the Present* gives an in-depth look at what military records are available and what they contain.

\di'fin\ *vb*

Definitions

What Military Records Are at the National Archives?

The National Archives holds service records up to the early part of the 1900s. General Information Leaflet 7, *Military Service Records in the National Archives of the United States*, available from NARA, includes more detailed information on these holdings. Later records are at the National Personnel Records Center (NPRC), 9700 Page Boulevard, St. Louis, MO 63132. Release of information from these records is severely restricted.

What Kind of Military Records Does NARA Have?

Military service for the United States has produced three basic kinds of records:

- **Military service records** give information on the person's service in the armed forces. Personal details in these records may include name, place of birth, age at enlistment, date and place of enlistment, regiment or company, and brief physical description. They also contain information on the date and reason for termination of service: death, desertion, discharge, illness, or disability. If the person received a pension, much of this information is also in the pension file. However, if your ancestor had no pension file, or even if there is one, consider ordering the military file to compare information between the two files.
- You can expect to find **bounty land warrant application files** only for soldiers who served in wartime between 1775 and 3 March 1855, but only if the soldier actually applied for a warrant. These files include material similar to that in pension files, but generally with less detail. However, if your ancestor had a bounty land warrant application file, it is worth ordering it to see what is in it.
- **Pension files** contain various information depending on the circumstances of the application. These files can be a gold mine of genealogical information. To get a pension, the soldier had to prove that he was in service. Especially for earlier time periods, files may include testimony from comrades in arms or from the soldier himself describing his service and naming officers and fellow soldiers. If pension money was requested for a wife (or widow) and/or children, there will be affidavits to prove the couple was married that give the exact date and place of the wedding. Pension files may be the only source for a marriage date during times when marriage registration wasn't required. Likewise, there often is a list of some or all children, especially minor children, with dates of birth. If the soldier was wounded or had contracted a chronic ailment, such as dysentery, while in the service, especially if he was applying for an invalid pension, files include testimony from doctors about the effects of these wounds or ailments on the soldier's ability to work.

Pension files may include unexpected gifts from our ancestors or insights into their lives. You have no guarantee that you will find anything like this in the files you get, but some pension files contain items such as the record pages torn from a family Bible sent in as proof of the applicant's marriage or children. Even the letters and affidavits in files may bring you closer to your ancestors.

Although much of the information in the files is on standardized forms, some files contain letters from the soldier or other members of the family. These may be the only documents you ever find that the ancestor personally wrote; they may help you get to know him a little better.

Some information may merely give you a close-up look at the life of your ancestors. Details of the economic condition of an ancestor might describe specifically how he earned his income. A letter explaining why he couldn't work might include a testimonial stating that when he could work, he was a good worker. Testimony justifying the monetary need for a pension might include details of crops planted and harvested or other items your ancestor produced and their value.

Confederate States Records

NARA's collection includes some records of men who served in the Confederate States Army. These are military records only (no pension records) and have little genealogical information, but they can help if you're trying to prove (to join a lineage society, for example) that an ancestor had Confederate service. Some of the southern states paid pensions to their soldiers, and getting information on an ancestor's service can help you if you want to see if there is a pension record.

How Do I Access Military Files?

Write to

> General Reference Branch (NNRG)
> National Archives and Records Administration
> Washington, DC 20408

Or E-mail them at inquire@nara.gov. (Remember to include your name and postal address in the E-mail!)

Ask for NATF Form 80 (they will send only three copies of the form at a time). A cover sheet on the form gives detailed instructions for completing and submitting it. Use a separate form to request each type of record, even for the same person.

You must supply at least
- the soldier's full name
- the war in which he served or dates of service
- the state from which he served
- for the Civil War, whether he served in the Union or Confederate army

Other information, such as the military unit, is optional, so don't panic if you don't know it. Give whatever information you do have. However, if you can't give enough specific information about your ancestor, you may receive the file of another person of the same name. (See Figure 9-3 on page 86.)

Expect to wait six to eight weeks for a response to your request. If NARA has records on your soldier, they'll send you a notice telling you the cost of

OMB Control No. 3095-0032 Expires 9-30-96

NATIONAL ARCHIVES
ORDER FOR COPIES OF VETERANS RECORDS
(See Instructions page before completing this form)

DATE RECEIVED IN NWDT1

INDICATE BELOW THE TYPE OF FILE DESIRED AND THE METHOD OF PAYMENT PREFERRED.

1. FILE TO BE SEARCHED
(Check one box only)
- ☒ PENSION
- ☐ BOUNTY-LAND WARRANT APPLICATION *(Service before 1856 only)*
- ☐ MILITARY

2. PAYMENT METHOD *(Check one box only)*
- ☐ CREDIT CARD for *IMMEDIATE SHIPMENT* of copies *(see Instructions for credit cards we can accept)* .

Signature: Exp. Date: Daytime Phone:

☒ **BILL ME** *(No Credit Card)*

REQUIRED MINIMUM IDENTIFICATION OF VETERAN - MUST BE COMPLETED OR YOUR ORDER CANNOT BE SERVICED

3. VETERAN *(Give last, first, and middle names)*
CRAWFORD, WILLIAM HENDERSON

4. BRANCH OF SERVICE IN WHICH HE SERVED
- ☒ ARMY
- ☐ NAVY
- ☐ MARINE CORPS

5. STATE FROM WHICH HE SERVED
OHIO

6. WAR IN WHICH, OR DATES BETWEEN WHICH, HE SERVED
CIVIL

7. IF SERVICE WAS CIVIL WAR,
- ☒ UNION
- ☐ CONFEDERATE

PLEASE PROVIDE THE FOLLOWING ADDITIONAL INFORMATION, IF KNOWN

8. UNIT IN WHICH HE SERVED *(Name of regiment or number, company, etc, name of ship)*

9. IF SERVICE WAS ARMY, ARM IN WHICH HE SERVED
- ☐ INFANTRY
- ☐ CAVALRY
- ☐ ARTILLERY

If other, specify:

Rank
- ☐ OFFICER
- ☐ ENLISTED

10. KIND OF SERVICE
- ☐ VOLUNTEERS
- ☐ REGULARS

11. PENSION/BOUNTY-LAND FILE NO.

12. IF VETERAN LIVED IN A HOME FOR SOLDIERS, *GIVE LOCATION (City and State)*

13. PLACE(S) VETERAN LIVED AFTER SERVICE
MUSKINGUM CO, OHIO

14. DATE OF BIRTH
Ca. 1830

15. PLACE OF BIRTH *(City, County, State, etc.)*
OHIO

18. NAME OF WIDOW OR OTHER CLAIMANT
ELIZABETH WILSON CRAWFORD

16. DATE OF DEATH

17. PLACE OF DEATH *(City, County, State, etc.)*

NATIONAL ARCHIVES TRUST FUND BOARD   NATF Form 80 (rev. 8-97)

DO NOT WRITE BELOW - SPACE IS FOR OUR REPLY TO YOU

☐ **NO—We were unable to locate the file you requested above. No payment is required.**

DATE SEARCHED	SEARCHER

☐ **REQUIRED MINIMUM IDENTIFICATION OF VETERAN WAS NOT PROVIDED.** Please complete blocks 3 (give full name), 4, 5, 6, and 7 and resubmit your order.

☐ **A SEARCH WAS MADE BUT THE FILE YOU REQUESTED ABOVE WAS NOT FOUND.** When we do not find a record for a veteran, this does not mean that he did not serve. You may be able to obtain information about him from the archives of the State from which he served.

☐ See attached forms, leaflets, or information sheets.

☐ **YES—We located the file you requested above. We have made copies from the file for you. The cost for these copies is $10.**

DATE SEARCHED	SEARCHER

FILE DESIGNATION

Make your check or money order payable to NATIONAL ARCHIVES TRUST FUND. Do not send cash. Return this form and your payment in the enclosed envelope to:

NATIONAL ARCHIVES TRUST FUND
P.O. BOX 100221
ATLANTA, GA 30384-0221

PLEASE NOTE: We will hold these copies awaiting receipt of payment for only 45 days from the date completed, which is stamped below. After that time, you must submit another form to obtain photocopies of the file.

THIS IS YOUR MAILING LABEL. PRESS FIRMLY.

SEND TO:

NAME *(Last, First, MI)*
GENEALOGIST, JEANIE

STREET
100 MAIN ST.

CITY, STATE
ANYTOWN ANYSTATE

ZIP CODE
12345

A382689

INVOICE/REPLY COPY - DO NOT DETACH

Figure 9-3 NATF Form 80, for requesting copies of military records from the National Archives

getting the records (if you marked "Bill me"), or they'll charge your credit card and send you the copies immediately (if you included a credit card number). Upon receipt of the money (if you opted to be billed), they'll send you photocopies of some of the papers (selected for genealogical content) from the files. Some files are quite thick. If you have reason to suspect that there's more information in the file that would be useful to you (for example, a letter in the file refers to some item of which you didn't receive a copy), submit a new request to NARA asking for a quote of the cost of all records in the file.

Other Sources for Military Records

Revolutionary War service, pension, and bounty land application files are available through the NARA Microfilm Rental Program and other sources for microfilm rental. See chapter thirteen for information on renting microfilm.

These microfilms are also available at National Archives regional facilities (see the listing of these in appendix D).

Sources

IMMIGRATION RECORDS

Passenger lists can help genealogists, but there are some problems associated with them:

- few passenger lists survive for earlier ships coming to the colonies and this country
- some passenger lists that do exist aren't indexed

From the Colonial Period to 1820

Few official immigration lists survive from before 1820. One major exception is the records Pennsylvania kept, published in Ralph Beaver Strassburger and William John Hinke's *Pennsylvania German Pioneers: A Publication of the Original Lists of Arrivals in the Port of Philadelphia From 1727 to 1808.* However, these include only immigrants who weren't British subjects; your German ancestor may appear on them, but your English, Irish, Scottish, or Welsh ancestor won't.

Substitutes for passenger lists in the early period of the colonies and the United States include newspaper testimonials from satisfied passengers; ads placed by recent arrivals looking for friends and relatives; and diaries, journals, and narratives of immigrants. In some cases, researchers have compiled "synthetic" passenger lists: speculations as to which people were on what ship based on other records. Periodical indexes and library catalogs will help you to locate some of these items (see the "Indexes to Genealogical Periodicals" section in chapter seventeen).

Some colonies (especially Virginia and Maryland) granted to immigrants headrights: a certain amount of land to the immigrant and each of his family members and servants. Records of these can show that your ancestor was an immigrant and give you a date by which the person was in the colony, but they won't tell you the exact date of immigration or the ship.

From 1820 to the 1950s

If your ancestor arrived during a time for which passenger lists exist, you still may face problems in locating the name on a list. While immigration now is funneled through certain specific ports of entry, in earlier times ships might have landed at any of forty or so ports. Immigrants might have found it cheaper to take a ship to Canada and travel from there to the United States. Few of the records of people who crossed into the United States from Canada or Mexico (kept only from 1895 to 1952) are indexed. In addition, **not all passenger lists for the United States are indexed:** most notably, those for the port of New York, a major entry point, aren't indexed between 1846 and 1897. At least one group is working on an index of later lists, but it isn't available at this writing. Even if a list was made during the early period in which they were mandated, there's no guarantee that it has survived. However, if the record of your ancestor's immigration has survived, you'll learn ways to find it later in this chapter.

Reminder

From the 1950s to the Present

If you're dealing with a recent immigrant, the person may or may not still be around to tell you about the immigrant experience. If your immigrant arrived in the 1950s or later, he or she might have arrived by airplane; there are very few lists of plane passengers.

What Might I Find on a Passenger List?

Like many other records, information on passenger lists varies over the years. Early lists may or be just that: lists of the names of the people who sailed on a particular vessel. These lists may include other identifying information, such as age. After 1820, lists were supposed to include the name, age, sex, occupation, country of origin, and country of destination of all passengers. After 1893, if the person was going to join a relative, lists include the name and address of that person, which might help expand your genealogical research. After 1907, lists include the name and address of the nearest relative of the immigrant in the place of origin.

How Can I Locate Passenger Lists?

If any of your immigrant ancestors came to this country within the past hundred years, investigate whether anyone in your family has information that might help you identify the ship they sailed on and the date of arrival. **Immigration was a momentous experience, and people often treasured mementos, such as tickets, travel papers, letters related to the voyage, etc.** If your ancestor became a citizen after 1906, naturalization records may include information about the ship and date of arrival. The 1900, 1910, 1920, and 1930 censuses asked what year an immigrant came to the United States, which, assuming your ancestor remembered the year correctly, will help pin down an arrival date.

Hidden Treasures

How do you proceed if there's no such information in your family? The good news is that all passenger lists from 1820 forward have been microfilmed, so you have a chance to look at the ones that may include your ancestor even if you can't leave home. Several sources can help you narrow down the possibilities. See chapter thirteen for information on renting microfilm of passenger lists and their indexes.

Indexes to Passenger Lists

NARA has microfilm indexes for many passenger lists after 1820. See their microfilm catalogs for lists of these indexes. Chapter thirteen of this book gives information on ordering this microfilm.

Internet Source

IMMIGRANT SHIPS TRANSCRIBERS GUILD ON THE NET

The Immigrant Ships Transcribers Guild (ISTG) is transcribing ship passenger lists and mounting them on the Internet at <http://istg.rootsweb.com/>. Since this is a volunteer operation, the lists mounted are only a small fraction of those available. You can search the site by date of travel, ship's name, port of arrival or departure, captain's name, or surname of passenger. However, the surname index may not be complete. Names of some passengers on the voyage of the *Phoenix* to Pennsylvania in 1749, whose list is posted on the site, weren't in the surname index. This may be because this list was "off-site," i.e., linked to, but not part of, the ISTG Web site.

Sources

There are many published indexes to passenger lists. *Passenger and Immigration Lists Index: A Guide to Published Arrival Records of About 500,000 Passengers Who Came to the United States and Canada in the Seventeenth, Eighteenth, and Nineteenth Centuries* (P. William Filby, ed.) attempts to index all listings of passengers to the thirteen colonies and the United States in the earlier years. Beyond the original work published in 1981, Filby and his collaborators have published yearly supplements. Like any such work, it will never be complete, but it's a good starting place for researching earlier arrivals. This book is now available on CD-ROM from Brøderbund.

For More Info

READ MORE ABOUT IT!

To learn more about passenger lists, read Colletta's *They Came in Ships* and Tepper's *American Passenger Arrival Records*. These include extensive listings of published indexes to passenger lists and more information on how to use them.

The National Archives has an informative Web page on immigration records at <http://www.nara.gov/genealogy/immigration/immigrat.html>.

The U.S. Immigration and Naturalization Service has a Web page about immigration arrival records at <http://www.ins.usdoj.gov/graphics/aboutins/history/ImmRecs/ImmRec.htm>.

Some published indexes of passenger lists contain names of passengers who came to a specific port or region. Others index passengers of a specific ethnic group—for example, Ira A. Glazier and P. William Filby's series *Germans to America: Lists of Passengers Arriving at U.S. Ports* (Wilmington, Del.: Scholarly Resources, Inc., 1988–) and *Italians to America: Lists of Passengers Arriving at U.S. Ports, 1880–1899* (Wilmington, Del.: Scholarly Resources, Inc., 1992–). Read the introductions to such works to find out what ports and dates they cover.

Problems in Passenger Lists

Usually an employee of the ship or shipping line wrote the passenger lists, so the spelling of your ancestor's name may only vaguely resemble the way the family actually spelled it. Women in some European countries use their maiden name on legal documents even after marriage, so if you're looking for a married female ancestor, check for her maiden name as well. In general, look for the original name of the immigrant, not an Anglicized form of the name that the family assumed after arrival in the United States. Occasionally you will find that your immigrant ancestor came to the United States, lived here long enough to start using an Anglicized form of the name, went back to Europe, and then returned to the United States. In these rare cases, the returning ancestor may be listed under the Anglicized form of the name.

Once you have obtained a copy of the passenger list, beware of the "same name, must be same person" problem. Look for identifying details to prove that you really have found your ancestor.

How Can I Get a Copy of an Actual Passenger List?

Passenger lists are kept confidential for thirty years after the arrival of the vessel. You can request a search of passenger list indexes from the National Archives; use NATF Form 81, available from

Attn: NWCTB
National Archives and Records Administration
700 Pennsylvania Ave. NW
Washington, DC 20408-0001

The form must include the full name of the person, the port of arrival, and the month and year of arrival (see Figure 9-4 on page 91). To request information from a time and port when lists weren't indexed, include either an exact date of arrival or the name of the ship. If NARA locates your ancestor, they'll photocopy the page(s) on which the person or family appears for a small charge.

See chapter thirteen for information on borrowing microfilm of passenger lists. NARA has copies at its service centers in Washington, D.C.; its regional records services facilities have some, but not all, immigration records.

Two CD-ROM vendors—Brøderbund and Palladium—**have published some passenger lists on CDs.** Check their catalogs or Web sites to see what they have available.

CD Source

OMB Control No. 3095-0031 Expires 9-30-98

NATIONAL ARCHIVES ORDER FOR COPIES OF SHIP PASSENGER ARRIVAL RECORDS

(See Instructions page before completing this form)

DATE RECEIVED IN NWDT1

INDICATE BELOW THE METHOD OF PAYMENT PREFERRED.

☐ **CREDIT CARD** for IMMEDIATE SHIPMENT of copies *(see Instructions for credit cards we can accept).*

Exp. Date: *Signature:* *Daytime Phone:*

☒ **BILL ME** *(No credit card)*

IDENTIFICATION OF ENTRY

DATE OF ARRIVAL	FULL NAME OF PASSENGER *(Give last, first, and middle names)*	AGE	SEX
27 MARCH 1883	PHILIP BERGMANN	39	M
PORT OF ENTRY: NEW YORK	NAMES OF MEMBERS OF IMMIGRANT FAMILY		
WHERE NATURALIZED *(if known)*			
SHIP NAME *(or Carrier Line)*: SS WESTPHALIA			
PASSENGER'S COUNTRY OF ORIGIN: GERMANY			

NATIONAL ARCHIVES TRUST FUND BOARD NATF Form 81 (rev. 8-97)

DO NOT WRITE BELOW - SPACE IS FOR OUR REPLY TO YOU

☐ **NO--We were unable to locate the record you requested above. No payment is required.**

MICROFILM PUBLICATION	ROLL	PAGE
RECORDS SEARCHED		SEARCHER
		DATE SEARCHED

☐ A SEARCH WAS NOT MADE because the records you requested are not documented in our ship passenger arrival list records. Please see the reverse of this form. Also, please see the enclosed pamphlet for further information about our holdings.

☐ A SEARCH WAS NOT MADE because insufficient information was supplied. Please see the reverse of this form.

☐ A SEARCH WAS MADE BUT THE RECORD YOU REQUESTED ABOVE WAS NOT FOUND. Please see the reverse of this form.

☐ A SEARCH WAS MADE BUT THE EXACT RECORD YOU REQUESTED ABOVE WAS NOT FOUND. We found a record that may be the one you seek. Please see the reverse of this form.

☐ **YES--We located the record you requested above. We have made copies from the record for you. The cost for these copies is $10.**

MICROFILM PUBLICATION	ROLL	PAGE
SEARCHER		DATE SEARCHED
ARRIVAL DATE		
PORT		
SHIP		

Make your check or money order payable to NATIONAL ARCHIVES TRUST FUND. Do not send cash. Return this form and your payment in the enclosed envelope to:

NATIONAL ARCHIVES TRUST FUND
P.O. BOX 100221
ATLANTA, GA 30384-0221

PLEASE NOTE: We will hold these copies awaiting receipt of payment for only 45 days from the date completed, which is stamped below. After that time, you must submit another form to obtain photocopies of the record.

SEND TO:

THIS IS YOUR MAILING LABEL. PRESS FIRMLY.

NAME (Last, First, MI): GENEALOGIST, JEANIE	
STREET: 100 MAIN ST.	
CITY, STATE: ANYTOWN, ANYSTATE	*ZIP CODE*: 12345

B555214

INVOICE/REPLY COPY - DO NOT DETACH

Figure 9-4 NATF Form 81, for requesting copies of ship passenger arrival records from the National Archives

The American Family Immigration History Center at Ellis Island is working on a project to computerize immigration records of people who entered the United States through Ellis Island between 1892 and 1924. A Web site, <http://www.ellisisland.org/history.html>, describes the project. The Center expects to complete the first phase of the project in 2001, making printouts of information available at Ellis Island. Later, information will be available through the Internet, and more ports and dates will be added. If your ancestor entered the United States through Ellis Island, keep an eye on this project.

NATURALIZATION RECORDS

Although the United States passed its first naturalization act in 1790, naturalization records weren't standardized until 1906. Before 1906, an alien could seek naturalization in any court: town, county, state, federal, or other. This makes it difficult for the genealogist to search for an ancestor's naturalization papers, as they might be filed in one of many places. Furthermore, earlier naturalization papers often contain little material of genealogical interest. However, following the dictum of seeking all papers related to an ancestor, the diligent researcher should try to locate naturalization papers, even early ones.

What Kinds of Records Might I Find?

Definitions

The process of naturalization in the United States includes several sets of papers:
- **Declaration of Intention** ("first papers"; an immigrant could file these as soon as he arrived in the United States; after 1862, aliens who had served in the U.S. Army—and after 1894, those who had served in the Navy or Marine Corps—could apply for citizenship without filing a Declaration)
- **Petition** ("second" or "final papers"; an alien filed these papers after meeting the residence requirement [usually five years; after 1862, an immigrant who had served in the U.S. Army could apply for citizenship after only one year's residence])
- **Naturalization Oaths**
- **Certificate of Naturalization** (which the new citizen kept)
- **Naturalization Certificate Stubs** (kept by the court)

Naturalizations in the Colonial Era

At various times, the colonies required arriving aliens (i.e., people who weren't subjects of the King of Great Britain and Ireland) to take an oath of allegiance. The individual colonies kept these; most of them don't survive.

All people of European descent who lived in the new United States at the end of the Revolutionary War automatically became citizens of the country, so they have no naturalization records unless they were previously naturalized. Likewise, people of European descent who resided in a territory—such as the Louisiana Purchase, Texas, etc.—when the United States purchased or otherwise annexed it automatically became citizens and didn't go through the naturalization process.

Naturalizations Between 1790 and 1906

Naturalization laws changed some during this time period, but many things remained constant. Usually, only adult men applied for naturalization; their wives and minor children gained citizenship along with them. Between 1855 and 1922, an alien woman could also gain citizenship by marrying a citizen. Few people know that between 1866 and 1922, a native-born American woman might *lose* her citizenship if she were married to an alien, even if she never left the United States, and she could only regain her citizenship when and if her husband was naturalized.

Naturalization papers were important documents, so if your ancestors are more recent immigrants, someone in the family may still have them. If your ancestors came to the United States during an earlier time period, you may have an interesting

For More Info

READ MORE ABOUT IT!

- If you can make a relatively good guess as to where your ancestor lived when he was naturalized, investigate whether naturalization records from that area have been published or indexed. Schaefer's *Guide to Naturalization Records of the United States* is a useful guide to availability of naturalization records. It gives a detailed listing, by state and county, of which courts hold what naturalization information, with a discussion of the available indexes. However, given the huge number of courts in which a person could be naturalized in earlier times, it's probable that these lists aren't complete. The book also includes citations for some published lists of naturalizations and gives the Family History Library microfilm number for both publications and records which have been microfilmed. Finally, it gives a brief bibliography, slanted towards court and naturalization records, for genealogical research in each state.

- *They Became Americans: Finding Naturalization Records and Ethnic Origins* by Loretto Dennis Szucs also includes much useful information on locating naturalization records, including a listing by state explaining which National Archives branch services the state and what records from that state, by date, are at the branch.

- For a detailed discussion of the changes in naturalization laws and procedures in the United States over the years, read Newman's *American Naturalization Records, 1790–1990: What They Are and How to Use Them.*

- The National Archives has a Web site with information about naturalization records at <http://www.nara.gov/genealogy/natural.html>.

- The U.S. Immigration and Naturalization Service has a Web page about naturalization records at <http://www.ins.usdoj.gov/graphics/aboutins/history/NatzRec/NATREC.htm>.

search ahead of you. Because naturalization papers can be difficult to locate, if you don't find them in the courthouse(s) near where the person lived, you may want to delay hunting for them until relatively late in your search. Because of the residence requirement, the aspiring citizen who moved around might have filed different papers in courts that were widely separated geographically, and you may have to do some detective work to locate them.

Step By Step

To track down your ancestor's naturalization papers, begin by writing to the county court(s) in the area(s) where you know he lived. See appendix B for books which give the addresses of these courts. If he stayed in one place and went to the county court to be naturalized your search may be somewhat simple. If not, you may have to research potential courts where he might have been naturalized and write letters to all of them. Also, while your ancestor was presumably happy to have gotten to America, he might have been reluctant to give up his birth nationality. He might have delayed the citizenship process, or he might never have become a citizen.

Another fact may hinder your search: it wasn't necessary for a person to reside in the area of the court where he was naturalized. So even if he went to a county court, if the courthouse of the county next to the one he lived in was more convenient, he might have gone there to be naturalized.

Regional Records Service Facilities of the National Archives have compiled indexes of some or all of the earlier naturalizations in their region. If you're having trouble finding your ancestor's naturalization papers, write to the Regional Records Service Facility for the area where your ancestor lived and ask them to search their index (see Figure 9-5 on page 95). Give the date of immigration and/or naturalization if you have been able to locate this information (through the census, for example).

Check the Family History Library Catalog at your local Family History Center under your county of interest for naturalization records. If the actual records haven't been filmed, maybe the index has been (but remember the potential for problems with indexes, especially with long foreign names!). Brøderbund has issued some CD-ROMs of naturalization records for selected areas. If your ancestor lived in one of these areas, consider purchasing the CD-ROM.

Genealogical periodical indexes include listings of published naturalization abstracts and indexes that have appeared in magazines. See the "Indexes to Genealogical Periodicals" section in chapter seventeen for a listing of the major indexes.

Some counties with USGenWeb Internet sites have loaded indexes of naturalizations at the county level onto their sites. Check the site for your ancestor's county to see if such an index is available (see chapter nineteen for information on the USGenWeb project).

Reminder

The censuses of 1900, 1910, 1920 and 1930, might give clues about your ancestor's naturalization status. These censuses asked for year of immigration and citizenship status. The status was indicated as *al* for "alien," *pa* ("papers") for aliens who had begun the naturalization process, and *na* for "naturalized." However, from 1900 to 1920, the naturalization question applied only to foreign-born *males over the age of twenty-one.* You won't find this information for females or minor children. In 1930, the naturalization question applied to all foreign-born people,

[Your postal address, phone number, and E-mail address]

[date]

[recipient's address]

Dear Friends:

Can you please check your **index of naturalization papers** to see if there is a listing for my husband's great-grandfather:

> **Give person's name and date and place of birth.**

Leo Oppenheimer
Born 24 August 1848, Germany
Came to United States ca. 1865
Naturalized before 1876

> **Give details such as date of immigration that will help to narrow the date of naturalization. If you have established the year of naturalization from other records, give it.**

Thank you for your help in this matter. I enclose a self-addressed, stamped envelope for your convenience in replying.

Sincerely,

[your name]

Figure 9-5 Request for a search of a naturalization index

male or female, of any age. Finding a status of *na* for a female doesn't mean that you'll find naturalization papers for her, although you should check. She might have gained derivative citizenship before 1922 through her father or husband.

The 1920 census also asked for the year of immigration, whether the person was naturalized, and the year of naturalization. If you can pin down where your ancestor lived at this time, this should aid your search for his papers.

Depending on the time and state of issue, a death certificate may also indicate whether the person was a citizen of the United States. If it says he wasn't, don't bother to hunt for naturalization papers for him unless some other source clearly indicates that he *was* naturalized.

People who received land under the Homestead Act of 1862 had to have at least started the naturalization process by filing a declaration of intention. If they were immigrants who had already been naturalized, their files include a statement to that effect, which should indicate where and when they were naturalized. See chapter seven for more information on getting Homestead Act files.

Naturalizations After 1906

Naturalization papers filed after 1906 are much easier to locate, since courts were required to file duplicate copies of them with the Bureau of Immigration and Naturalization. (See Figure 9-6 on page 96.) With standardization of the

[Your postal address, phone number, and E-mail address]

[date]

Immigration and Naturalization Service
FOIA/PA
2nd Floor ULLB
425 I St. NW
Washington, DC 20536

Dear Friends:

I would like a copy of the **naturalization papers** of my husband's great-grandfather:

Eliphalet Smith
Born 10 June 1848, England
Naturalized in 1908

Thank you for your help in this matter. I enclose a self-addressed, stamped envelope for your convenience in replying.

Sincerely,

[your name]

Give full name, date and place of birth, and any information to narrow down the naturalization date.

Figure 9-6 Request for naturalization papers granted after 1906

process, the alien had to fill out forms that included much genealogically useful information, including place of birth; age or date of birth; nationality; marital status; names, ages, and places of birth of spouse and children; etc.

To obtain copies of these papers for genealogical use, send a request to

Immigration and Naturalization Service
FOIA/PA
2nd Floor ULLB
425 I St. NW
Washington, DC 20536

State that you're requesting naturalization papers, and include the alien's full name (give alternate spellings if you think the name may be misspelled) and date and place of birth. NARA will notify you of the cost of photocopying whatever records they find.

For more information, check out the Immigration and Naturalization Service (INS) Web site at <http://www.ins.usdoj.gov/>.

Special Cases

- A person born overseas to American parents was automatically a citizen.
- Until 1922, a married alien woman couldn't become a citizen unless her spouse was a citizen.
- Before 1922, a female citizen of the United States who married an alien *might* lose her U.S. citizenship. Between 1866 and 1907, she lost her citizenship only if she left the United States.
- Until 1940, children under age twenty-one automatically became citizens when their father was naturalized.
- Until 1929, a certificate of citizenship was issued only to the person who was actually naturalized. A wife or child who became a citizen as a result of the naturalization of a husband or father didn't receive a certificate, although some were issued retroactively.
- Former slaves became citizens through legislation in 1868.
- Native Americans became citizens through laws passed in 1887 and 1924.
- Aliens from many Asian countries weren't allowed to apply for citizenship between 1882 and 1943.

Notes

CONCLUSION

Social Security, military, immigration, and naturalization records may include a wealth of genealogical information; it's worth tracking them down to find out. If immigration and naturalization records prove elusive, wait until the end of your search to pursue them, since you may have found clues that will help you locate them.

TEN

Other Sources of Information

S ome other useful sources of genealogical information include church records, cemetery records, and funeral home records. Once you start looking for such records, consider acquiring a telephone book for the area where your ancestors lived (conveniently, many phone books now cover full counties). You may want to consult the yellow pages to identify these and other institutions in the area.

RELIGIOUS RECORDS

Religious records may include records of baptisms, confirmations, bar and bat mitzvahs, marriages, deaths, and burials. In times past when Communion wasn't available every Sunday, as it is now in many churches, some churches made lists of those who attended Communion on a given Sunday. Unfortunately, there's no guarantee that the records from your ancestor's time have survived. If they have, church records of baptisms, marriages, and deaths will give you information to fill in birth, marriage, and death dates on your pedigree charts. In some cases, a baptismal record gives a birth date; in some cases, only the date of baptism, which at least establishes that the person was born on or before that date (in the case of an adult baptism, way before!). Confirmation records often include the age of the confirmand and may include the names of father and mother, allowing you to place the person into a family group. Communion records may group members of a family together, although in some cases, the list of communicants is divided by sex. Marriage records may reveal a female ancestor's maiden name.

How Do I Know My Ancestor's Religion?

The first thing you need to know to locate religious records pertaining to your ancestors is their religious affiliation. However, in very early periods of an area's settlement, a church of their denomination might not have existed, and a religious ancestor might have used the services of whatever pastor was available for essential sacraments such as baptism, marriage, and burial.

Many sources can yield clues about your ancestors' religious preferences. First, there's family tradition, although you must be careful with this. Aunt Nellie is a staunch Lutheran, so she assumes that her great-great-grandfather must have been one, too. Or, a family story may describe the apostasy of some ancestor who strayed from the family's accepted religion ("and that's why we attend the Episcopal church and not the Baptist church"). Published family histories sometimes include information on people's religious affiliation.

Your search through family papers may reveal baptismal, confirmation, or marriage certificates or notations in a family Bible that show the family's religious affiliation. These may mention the exact church where an event happened.

Hidden Treasures

Biographical articles in county histories and obituaries often mention a person's denomination and may name the person's congregational affiliation. A county history may also include information on a church's history; for example, "In 1825, Alexander Walker started to construct a meetinghouse," or "The original members of the church were twenty-four, namely. . . ." Since the history of the church tells you when it started, for records before that date look for other churches of that denomination in the area. A church's history may say that the people who started it were originally members of another congregation, but left because of a doctrinal dispute (adding an interesting footnote to your information about your ancestor). Or perhaps the congregation became too large for its building, and members who lived in a distant area built a new church.

If your ancestor was an officer of his church (e.g., vestry member), and the church bought land, his name may be on the purchase deed.

How Do I Locate Churches in the Area Where My Ancestor Lived?

There are several ways to locate churches in the area where your ancestor lived. County histories often list at least the earlier churches, with some history, which will help you to pin down a given congregation's starting date. There's no sense in trying to locate records for your ancestor at a church that didn't exist until after his death.

Many denominations issue a directory of all churches in the denomination. If you know your ancestor's religious affiliation, contact the local church of that denomination and ask if it has a directory you can consult. The directory may list the dates when churches were founded, allowing you to know whether a church existed when your ancestor lived in the area.

Check the listings in the yellow pages for your ancestral area under "Churches." These may not list the date a church was founded, but if you know your ancestor belonged to a certain denomination which has only one listing in the yellow pages, consider contacting that church for information.

How Do I Locate Religious Records for My Ancestor?

First, a warning: Locating the church your ancestors might have attended doesn't guarantee locating its records. In some cases, especially in the early days, churches didn't keep records. Paper was scarce and was saved for other things. Some denominations were more scrupulous than others about keeping records. Even if the pastor did keep records, he might have taken his record book with him when he moved on to another church.

Learn about the practices of the denomination to which your ancestor belonged. Don't search for baptismal records for children if the group practiced only adult baptism.

Because genealogists find religious records so useful, many genealogical and historical societies sponsor projects to transcribe them. They may be published in genealogical or historical magazines or as books. Check periodical indexes (see the "Indexes to Genealogical Periodicals" section in chapter seventeen) for listings to see if such records for the area where your family lived have been published in periodicals. Check library catalogs to see if any have been published as books (see chapter twelve for information on accessing library catalogs via the Internet).

Check the Family History Library Catalog at your local Family History Center (or on the Internet at <http://familysearch.org>) to see if it includes listings for religious records for your ancestral area on microfilm that you can order from the Family History Library.

Some societies and individuals have mounted transcriptions of church records on the Internet, often at the USGenWeb site for the county in question. See chapter nineteen for information on the USGenWeb.

Some church records or abstracts of records are available on CD-ROM. Major vendors who have published such CDs include Brøderbund and Palladium. Check their catalogs or Web sites to see if any of their church record CDs cover your ancestral area.

A genealogical society might transcribe records to save the information, but might not be able to afford to publish the transcriptions. Write to the genealogical society for the area to ask if they have any transcribed records which might help you or know the location of any (see chapter sixteen for information on locating the genealogical society in your ancestral area).

Finally, if you're relatively certain which church your ancestor attended, you can write directly to the church to see if they have any records that might help you.

What Do I Say in My Request for Information From a Church?

The church your ancestor attended doesn't owe you any service, and may have a small staff that's stretched to the limit. Your letter should be friendly and shouldn't make too many requests (you can always write to them again). (See Figure 10-1 on page 101 and Figure 10-2 on page 102.) When you first write to the church,

- ask if they have records of the type and for the time frame in which you're interested
- if the information you need will require much research (e.g., searching for baptismal records for your ancestor's sixteen children), ask if they can recommend a local researcher to search the records

[Your postal address, phone number, and E-mail address]

[date]

Blessed Virgin Mary Help of Christians Church
[recipient's address]

Dear Friends:

I have recently learned that my husband's great-grandparents were married in your church. I would like a copy of this marriage record:

Martin Roos
Anna Mary Kallenbach
Married 23 July 1876

> State full names of couple if known.

> State date of marriage.

Can you please tell me if you still have the **record book for marriages** from this time period? If so, would it be possible for you to send me a copy of this record?

> Ask if the record is available and if they are able to copy it.

If you no longer have this record book, can you tell me where it is?

> Older records might have been sent to a central archive.

Thank you for your help. I enclose a self-addressed, stamped envelope for your convenience in replying, as well as a donation of $10 for your church.

> Enclose a donation (and of course, a SASE).

Sincerely,

[your name]

Figure 10-1 Request to a church for a search of records (one event, date known)

If you specify exactly what you're looking for and pin the event down to a relatively narrow time frame ("the marriage record of my ancestors John King and Susannah Heilman, sometime between 1809 and 1810"), you leave the door open for the church to either go ahead and do the research for you or recommend a researcher. Alternatively, the church may inform you that although it was started in 1800, they have no records before 1840, so they can't help you. You may hear anecdotes about a church that believed its early records were lost, but these records were discovered—maybe in a locked closet in the basement no one had thought to check. However, if the church says its early records are lost, they probably are. Don't write and pester them to "please look again."

When you first write to a church for help, enclose a small donation (five to ten dollars). If they write back with information from their records, it's worthwhile to send another small donation. You may want to write to them again for more records, and you want to make a good impression on them. If you're a member

Tip

[Your postal address, phone number, and E-mail address]

[date]

Blessed Virgin Mary Help of Christians Church
[recipient's address]

Dear Friends:

Some time ago you sent me a copy of the marriage record for my husband's great-grandparents:

Martin Roos
Anna Mary Kallenbach
Married 23 July 1876
(therefore, children born ca. 1876–1900)

> **State full names of people involved in the records.**

> **Give date(s) or date range for the event(s).**

I am interested in finding out if **any of their children were baptized in your church.** Can you recommend a researcher in your area who is familiar with your records and might undertake this search for me?

> **For multiple records, ask for information on potential researchers (but if they do the research for you, that's fine, too!).**

Thank you for your help. I enclose a self-addressed, stamped envelope for your convenience in replying, as well as a donation of $10 for your church.

> **Enclose a donation (and of course, a SASE).**

Sincerely,

[your name]

Figure 10-2 Request to a church for a search of records (date[s] not known)

of the same denomination as that of the church, it's a good idea to mention this in your letter.

Church Archives

If the church your ancestor attended no longer has its older records or is no longer in existence, the records might have been transferred to a regional archive center. Elizabeth Petty Bentley's *The Genealogist's Address Book* and Juliana Szucs Smith's *The Ancestry Family Historian's Address Book* list addresses for the archives of many religious groups.

Gospel Truth?

Once you've located a church record dealing with your ancestors, you might find something in it that disagrees with your other sources. Pastors, like census takers, didn't always bother to ask about the spelling of a name or might have been unsure of a name. ("Hmmm, was the mother of that child I just baptized

Maria Barbara or Anna Barbara?") Like other records, church records aren't always totally correct.

CEMETERIES

Cemeteries can help you in several ways:

- Your ancestor's gravestone usually shows at least a death date and may show a birth date (or a death date and the age at death, from which you can calculate the birth date).
- Your ancestor's gravestone may include information beyond birth and death dates, such as parents' names, a woman's maiden name, place of birth—even the number of children the person had.
- Other people buried around your ancestor may have the same surname or the ancestor's spouse's surname. Try to find out who these people are, as they may be siblings or parents of ancestors.
- You may find a tombstone for a child whom you hadn't previously known about because the child was born and died between two censuses.

How Do I Locate the Cemetery Where My Ancestor Might Be Buried?

Locating your ancestor's burial site can be difficult, if not impossible. In early times, people were buried in a plot on the family land under a small wooden marker (long since rotted away), a stone marker with little or no inscription on it, or no marker at all. If you locate such a family plot and are able to visit it, you may see some marked graves and some indentations in the ground that are obviously graves with no markers.

If your ancestor died at a time when death certificates were issued, start with the death certificate, which often includes the cemetery's name. Obituaries may also name the cemetery (the more recent the obituary, the more likely it is to give this information). If you've located the church where your ancestor worshipped, find out if it had a cemetery and whether the cemetery records have been published or you can request a search of them.

Research Tip

You may identify the cemetery of your ancestor's burial only to discover that at some later time, the graves were moved to make way for a road or shopping center or reservoir. If so, you'll have to do some detective work to track down the current location of the graves; also, investigate whether someone made a reading of the stones before the graves were moved.

You might assume that a person would have been buried in the area where the death occurred. However, once railroads spanned the country, it wasn't uncommon for a person's body to be shipped far from the place of death for burial in a family plot or next to a spouse who had died earlier. An obituary or death certificate may mention this, but you may not identify such a burial until you've traced other members of the family to discover that, for example, your grandfather is buried next to his parents, three states away from where he died.

Internet Source

TOMBSTONES ON THE WEB

USGenWeb sponsors The Tombstone Transcription Project, whose goal is to do readings of cemeteries and mount them on the Internet. Check out their site at <http://www.roots web.com/~cemetery/> to see if transcriptions of stones in cemeteries in your ancestral area are available. And do a favor for some other long-distance researcher: Volunteer to transcribe a cemetery in your area!

How Do I Locate Published Readings of Cemeteries?

Search for published readings of cemeteries (transcriptions of information from tombstones) in much the same way you searched for transcriptions of church records. Check periodical indexes and library card catalogs for published readings of stones. Write to the local historical or genealogical society to see if they have unpublished transcriptions. Check the USGenWeb Web page for the county to see if it includes any cemetery readings. Some DAR chapters have collected inscriptions from cemeteries; they deposit these readings in their state library and the DAR library in Washington, D.C. Contact the state library in your ancestral state to see if they have information from relevant cemeteries.

What Do I Say in My Letter to a Cemetery Office?

Many cemeteries don't have offices (the burial plot on the family farm, for example), so you can't write to them. If a cemetery is associated with a church, write to the church for help (see the section above on churches for information on locating them).

Churches may not have records of burials in their graveyards, especially older burials. It's possible that, to answer your request, someone would have to go to the graveyard and locate the grave, which could be difficult in a large graveyard. The person at the church who answers your letter may also be put off if you ask for information on a large number of tombstones. Be sensitive to this if you write to a church for gravestone information, and offer to pay for their services. In any event, enclose a donation, and send another donation if they send you a reading of the stone or stones in question.

More modern cemeteries, which operate as businesses, are listed in the yellow pages under "Cemeteries," allowing you to find their mailing address. You may also find a directory of cemeteries at your public library. These cemeteries are better able to help you, as they generally have kept records of all burials in their cemetery. Their records may include the name, age/birth date, death date, interment date, cause of death, location of grave, and the undertaker's name. What's more important is that, generally, everyone buried in a plot has some relationship to the plot's owner. Cemetery records usually list all the people buried in the plot.

When writing to a cemetery, state your relationship to the person in question, since many cemeteries won't answer queries without this information. (See Figure 10-3 on page 105.) Ask the cemetery to send you copies of the records for all people buried in the plot with your ancestor(s). These may hold some surprises! If nothing else, you may find people you had "misplaced."

Problems With Transcriptions of Tombstones

Once you've found a transcription, you may think you have it made; but **remember, transcriptions may not always be accurate.** Occasionally, a reader may decide that the information on a stone is incorrect and "correct" it in the written version. Some gravestone transcribers insert notes about the person into readings based only on something they believe is correct, with no solid documentation. You can't always tell from a published reading whether the information

Warning

[Your postal address, phone number, and E-mail address]

[date]

Evergreen Cemetery
[recipient's address]

Dear Friends:

| State relationship. |

I have recently learned that my husband's great-grandfather,

Leo Oppenheimer
Born 24 August 1848
Died 11 September 1914

| Give dates for the person in case there is more than one person by that name in the cemetery. |

| State full name of person or people buried in the plot. |

is buried in your cemetery. Would it be possible for me to get **copies of your records for him and all the people buried in the plot with him?** I would be happy to pay for this service if you will let me know the cost.

| Request records for all people buried in the plot. |

| Request cost for the service. |

In case you can release this information only to a direct descendant, my husband has signed this letter.

| When researching a person who is not your blood relative, indicate permission from a blood relative of that person. |

Thank you for your help. I enclose a self-addressed, stamped envelope for your convenience in replying.

Sincerely,

[your name]

[your husband's name]

Figure 10-3 Request for information on burials in a cemetery plot

came from the tombstone itself or from the reader (a good transcription will make this distinction by using brackets or different type faces). A reader may cut corners by listing only the years of birth and death when the tombstone gives exact dates or a death date and the age at death.

Many gravestones have deteriorated, making them hard to read. A reader may make errors due to this. Numbers can be especially tricky: A worn *4* may look like a *1*; a worn *8*, like a *3*.

Some other errors aren't the reader's fault. In some cases, stones weren't put on the grave until long after the time of death. At that point, the person who placed the stone might have put dates on the tombstone based on assumptions or even on misreadings of family records (*Jan.* misread as *Jun.*, for instance).

Many family associations have erected memorial stones to an immigrant ancestor and his family, often in a cemetery where many members of the family are buried. Such stones often list the names of the immigrant ancestor or couple, their children, and perhaps their children's children. This may cause a reader to assume that all the people listed on it are buried in that cemetery although some are buried elsewhere.

Another problem with some cemetery readings is transcribers who do researchers the "favor" of alphabetizing the names to make it easy to locate a name. Unfortunately, this means that you lose the possibility of reconstructing family groups by seeing who's buried next to whom. The best transcribers list stones in physical order (and specify which stones are in the same plot) to help you identify family groups.

As with any item documenting your ancestor, it's best to see the original or an exact copy; however, it isn't possible to photocopy a gravestone! If you have questions about a published reading of an ancestor's stone and aren't able to visit the cemetery yourself, consider hiring someone to go to the cemetery and photograph the stone for you. This may reveal interesting information, such as gravestone ornaments that the reading didn't mention. Some carvings on the stone are strictly for decoration, such as a lamb for innocence (usually found on a child's stone) or a skeleton for mortality. Others may show that the deceased was a member of a particular religious or fraternal organization (a clue that could lead to more information on the person if the organization is still in existence) or may have other religious significance.

FUNERAL HOMES

Funeral homes generally keep records of the people whom they have buried. Especially for the time before death certificates were required, these records may contain useful information for the genealogist. Older records are relatively straightforward—giving the name and possibly the age of the deceased, the person who paid for the funeral, and its cost—but occasionally there are notes that will add to your genealogical files.

How Do I Locate Funeral Homes in the Area Where My Ancestors Lived?

There are three ways to locate funeral homes:

- Ask a local funeral home if they have a national directory of funeral homes which you can check for homes in your ancestor's area. If the ancestor lived in a small town, there might not be a funeral home in that town, so have a list of nearby towns.
- Your local library may have a national directory of funeral homes.
- If you can't find a directory of funeral homes, check a telephone book for your ancestral area to see if any funeral homes are listed.

If the funeral home which handled your ancestor's burial has gone out of business, its records might have been taken over by another funeral home in the town or given to a local historical or genealogical society.

How Do I Locate Published Funeral Home Records?

Although funeral home records are published more rarely than other types of information, you may find that a genealogical society has published, usually in its magazine, information from a book of old records from a funeral home. Look in periodical indexes for citations for such articles.

Items to Consider Before Contacting Funeral Homes

Although you may find addresses for funeral homes, you will have to determine whether the funeral home was in business when your ancestors lived in the area. You will also need to determine whether your ancestors used funeral homes. Before the time when state laws regarding such things as embalming were passed, some families simply prepared their dead for burial themselves.

What Do I Say In My Letter to a Funeral Home?

When writing to a funeral home, be concise and ask if they have a record for a specific person's funeral. Give the death date or a potential range for the death date (the shorter the time period, the better), if known. Ask for copies of all

[Your postal address, phone number, and E-mail address]

[date]

Deerlawn Funeral Home
[recipient's address]

Dear Friends:

According to some bills which have been passed through my family, your funeral home handled the burial of my great-grandfather:

Aaron Calvin King — **Give full name of deceased.**
Died 23 October 1924 — **Give date of death.**

Is it possible for me to get **copies of all the records you have relating to this burial?** — **Ask for copies of *all* records.**

I would be happy to pay for this service if you will let me know the cost. — **Offer to pay.**

Thank you for your help. I enclose a self-addressed, stamped envelope for your convenience in replying. — **Always enclose a SASE.**

Sincerely,

[your name]

Figure 10-4 Request to a funeral home for a search of records

papers in the file for the person. (See Figure 10-4 on page 107.) Don't expect a funeral home to search fifty years worth of records in hopes of finding information on an ancestor. They're running a business, not a research service.

CONCLUSION

Religious and cemetery records can be of great help to genealogists by providing information that fills in the vital dates of an ancestor's life. Funeral home records may add more details.

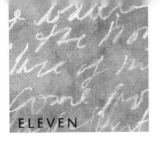

ELEVEN

Newspapers

WHAT MIGHT I FIND IN NEWSPAPERS?

Several types of items in newspapers can aid genealogical research. The most obvious ones are birth, marriage, and death notices and obituaries. You may also find notices for important events like golden wedding anniversaries or family reunions, which often include genealogical information. Less useful for genealogy, but interesting for family history, are articles that mention your ancestor in some other capacity. If your ancestor had a business, you may find advertisements for it.

In older newspapers, don't expect to find the long, detailed articles on vital events that appear in modern newspapers. The further back in time you go, the shorter these notices are. Birth announcements are a relatively modern invention, although the birth of a child might have been treated as a news item: "Jacob Milliron in Wayne Township has been blessed with a daughter" might be the extent of the notice. Often, newspapers only published obituaries, or short death notices, if the family paid for them. If they did appear, they might again be more of a news item, with none of the genealogical details you would hope to find. For example, from 1826: "Death—On Wednesday last, Mr. Alexander Walker, of Allegheny Twp., one of the earliest settlers in Armstrong County."

Once you get to the time period when longer obituaries appear, you may find that they give you more details than you want about the funeral (who preached on what topic, who sang what songs) and less than you want about the deceased and his family. In the late 1800s and the greater part of the 1900s, a woman's first name rarely appeared in the newspaper; her obituary would name her, for example, as "Mrs. John Smith."

If your ancestor lived in one area and migrated to another far away, an obituary might appear in the newspaper of the original area, so look there as well.

If you know from the marriage date and death dates of an ancestral couple that they lived to their fiftieth wedding anniversary, check newspapers around that date. Even now, many couples never reach their fiftieth anniversary; a hundred years ago, this anniversary was a rare occurrence. Often there would be a major celebration with many family members attending, and the newspaper might report it. These articles usually go into great detail about the people who attended and give the numbers of children, grandchildren, and great-grandchildren of the couple.

In the early 1900s, many families held large reunions, and newspapers often reported them. It's hard to predict when you might find such articles, but if you have evidence that the family held a reunion, check the local paper to see if there's an article about it. These articles give details on who attended and some information on the common ancestors. However, treat the information on the ancestors with the same caution with which you would treat an article in a county history.

HOW DO I IDENTIFY NEWSPAPERS FOR MY ANCESTOR'S AREA AND TIME?

There are several ways to determine if newspapers existed in a locality during your ancestors' lifetime. It's possible that a newspaper did exist at the time, but only some copies, or maybe no copies, of the paper now survive. In many areas, there were (and are) only a few newspapers in a county. **The town where your ancestor lived might not have had a newspaper, but the county seat probably did.** This newspaper might have had departments for news from outlying areas, so check the whole paper if possible. Even if you find a paper from the town where your ancestor lived, it's a good idea to look for one from the county seat as well.

Reminder

Check published histories of your ancestor's county; they often have a section describing newspapers published in the county. This may give you an idea of what existed at one time.

In 1937, Winifred Gregory published *American Newspapers 1821–1936: A Union List of Files Available in the United States and Canada*. Although not a complete list of newspapers published during that time period, this book can give you clues as to what newspapers were available. The book includes codes indicating where Gregory found the newspaper, and the paper still may be there.

The articles for each state in *Ancestry's Red Book* discuss some of the major newspapers in the state. Some articles list books with information on newspapers in all or part of the state.

Several annual publications list current newspapers and the initial publishing dates. From them, you can find out if a newspaper that might have been around at the time of the event for which you hope to locate an article still exists. Three of these are

- *Gale Directory of Publications and Broadcast Media*
- *The Standard Periodical Directory*
- *Working Press of the Nation, vol. 1, Newspaper Directory*

The United States Newspaper Program, funded by the National Endowment for the Humanities, has been working to locate and preserve old newspapers. The first phase in each state involved finding collections of old newspapers in locations ranging from university and public libraries and historical societies to old barns. Staff then entered information on these into OCLC, an international library database, making it accessible nationwide. Many college and university libraries, and some public libraries, subscribe to this database. The project's second phase involves microfilming significant newspapers.

Check the United States Newspaper Program Web site at <http://www.neh.gov/preservation/usnp.html> for a listing of the coordinating library and project status for each state. For most states, this also includes a link to a state Newspaper Project Web site, which may include a list of all newspapers located for that state. If you don't have Internet access, contact the coordinating agency for your ancestor's state to ask if they can help you locate newspapers for the area where your ancestor lived. In many cases, the state library is the coordinating agency for the state Newspaper Program; if not, its staff can tell you who is.

If your library has access to OCLC (sometimes available to the public under the name FirstSearch), ask the librarian to help you to search for listings for newspapers from your ancestor's area. You'll need to have the newspaper's title to do this search. Once you've found a listing, you can see what libraries have reported holdings to OCLC.

Bell & Howell Information and Learning (formerly known as UMI) sells microfilm of some newspapers. If you have large numbers of ancestors in an area and want to buy microfilm of newspapers, contact them at (800) 521-0600, extension 3781, to get a copy of their newspaper catalog. Even if you don't want to buy microfilm of newspapers, this catalog will give you an idea of some that are available in libraries and might be accessible via interlibrary loan.

How Do I Locate Copies of Newspapers?

Several of the sources mentioned above for identifying newspapers also give locations.

Often, the local library holds a collection of the town's newspapers. Newspaper offices usually have copies of back issues, often on microfilm, and may also hold copies of newspapers previously published in the town, even those that are not predecessors of the current paper. If they don't have back issues, they can probably tell you who does.

Tip

Also check *Newspapers in Microform, United States,* a cumulated list of microfilm newspaper holdings that libraries have reported to the Library of Congress.

Getting Microfilm and Photocopies of Newspaper Articles Via Interlibrary Loan

If you know the date of a specific event in your ancestor's life (birth, marriage, or death), write to the library and/or genealogical or historical society for the area in which he lived. Ask if they have newspapers available that they can

Library/Archive Source

[Your postal address, phone number, and E-mail address]

[date]

Perry County Historical Society
[address of recipient]

Dear Friends:

I am interested in obtaining a copy of the **obituary** of my ancestor:

William Henderson Crawford ——————— | **Give full name.** |
Died 8 November 1877
Madison Township

| Give date and place of death. |

I understand that you have newspapers for this area and for this time period. Would it be possible for you to search for this obituary for me and make me a copy of it if you find it?

| Anticipate that the library or society might not be able to do the research for you. |

If it is not possible for you to do this search, can you recommend a researcher in your area who could do the search for me?

| Always send a SASE. |

Thank you for your help. I enclose a self-addressed, stamped envelope for your convenience in replying and a donation of $10 for your help. If your charge for this service is more than $10, please let me know.

Sincerely,

| Send a donation, but inquire about the cost in case it is larger than your donation. |

[your name]

Figure 11-1 Letter to a library or historical or genealogical society requesting information from a newspaper

check for a marriage or death notice, and include a donation and a self-addressed, stamped envelope. (See Figure 11-1 above.) See chapters twelve and sixteen for information on locating these repositories. If the first organization to which you write can't help, someone there may refer you to an organization that can help. Be prepared for the possibility of the bad news that no newspapers survive from that time period.

Genealogical societies and libraries sometimes index newspapers for their area or may have a scrapbook or clipping file of articles with genealogical applications. If you don't have a date for the marriage or death of an ancestor, ask if the society or library has an index. (See Figure 11-2 on page 113.) Don't ask them to search a large time span of newspapers unless you're willing to pay them a fee for the search. If you write, "My grandfather died sometime between

```
[Your postal address, phone number, and E-mail address]

[date]

Armstrong County Historical Society
[address of recipient]

Dear Friends:

I am trying to find out the death date of my ancestor:

Valentine S. Reese                    Give full name.
Died between 1910 and 1920
Probably in Kittanning Borough
```
Give range for date of death and (probable) place of death.

Ask if they have an index that might help.

```
Does your society have an index to obituaries for this time period that might
help me? If so, I would appreciate it if you would check it and let me know if
you can locate his obituary and death date.
```

Always send a SASE.

```
Thank you for your help. I enclose a self-addressed, stamped envelope for your
convenience in replying and a donation of $10 for your help. If your charge
for this service is more than $10, please let me know.
```
Send a donation, but inquire about the cost in case it is larger than your donation.

```
Sincerely,

[your name]
```

Figure 11-2 Letter to a library or historical or genealogical society requesting a search of an index

1870 and 1880 in your county. Can you tell me if you have an obituary for him?" the response will probably be a polite refusal or a price quote for research unless the library has an index of obituaries.

Suppose you don't know the date of an event, but can identify a potential time frame for it. Once you've located a newspaper whose dates cover that time period, you may be able to request it on interlibrary loan. Libraries won't lend actual newspapers, but they sometimes lend papers on microfilm. The state library and state archives are more likely to do so than other libraries. Ask your local librarian to find out if the library that owns the paper lends microfilm, and if so, to put in an interlibrary loan request for you.

Even if you do locate a newspaper on microfilm that might include your ancestor's event, some libraries will not lend microfilm, so be prepared for them to decline to send it. You may also find that, even if the library does lend you the microfilm, only some issues of the newspaper have survived, and the ones you'd like to see aren't among them.

A library may decline to send out the microfilm on interlibrary loan or may report that it searched for an event that occurred on a certain date and didn't find a notice of it. If so, you may want to consider hiring someone who lives in the area to do the research for you or to double-check the library's results.

How Do I Locate Articles About My Ancestor in Newspapers?

If you're able to get microfilm of newspapers for the date range in which you hope to find a notice of an ancestor's death or other event, you'll have to search page by page for the article. Soon, you'll get a feel for the newspaper's layout and where items like obituaries are found on a regular basis. Take time to read the other articles in the paper, and you may stumble over other notices that will help your research.

News didn't travel as fast in our ancestors' day as it does now. A death notice might not appear until three or four weeks after a death, especially in a weekly newspaper or one published only two or three times a week. Check newspapers for at least a month after the event before you conclude that there was no article about it.

Sources

OTHER SOURCES OF NEWSPAPER INFORMATION

While looking for newspaper articles relating to your ancestors, investigate whether anyone has published a book of abstracts of articles from newspapers from your ancestral area. The library or genealogical or historical society for the area can probably tell you if such books exist. Then either purchase one or try to borrow it on interlibrary loan. These works often extract items about subjects other than vital events, such as people visiting from out of town or leaving on a trip, houses or businesses burning down, court proceedings, etc., which may add to your knowledge of your ancestor's life. Since these books usually have indexes, you can find information on your ancestors.

Some companies, including Heritage Books and Scholarly Resources, have issued abstracts of newspapers on CD-ROM. See their catalogs or Web sites to find out if they have published any that include your ancestral locality.

CONCLUSION

Newspaper articles can help you find dates for life events before vital records were kept. They may also give information on the extended family of the subject of an article or incidental details about your ancestor's life.

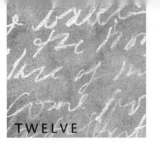

TWELVE

Library Research

Libraries can help the long-distance researcher immensely. Even if you're far from the area where your ancestors lived, libraries in your area may have books that can help you. If they don't, they can probably get books and articles on interlibrary loan for you.

LIBRARIANS ARE YOUR FRIENDS

When you go to a library to do research, introduce yourself to the reference librarian. (But don't go into great detail about your family unless she asks you to. She's busy, three people are in line at the reference desk behind you, and amazing as it may seem, she doesn't want to hear the story about how your great-great-grandfather escaped from a Civil War prison camp.) **Although she's busy, she's there to assist you.** If people didn't ask for help, she wouldn't have a job. Tell her you're doing family history research, and ask if she can recommend any sources to further your research. If you need help with something specific, ask her. If your questions are appropriate, don't worry about "bothering" her.

Reminder

WHAT SHOULD I LOOK FOR IN LOCAL LIBRARIES?

Visit any libraries in your area that are open to you: public, university, genealogical society, historical society, Family History Centers, etc. Since your research and the libraries available to you are a unique mix, it's impossible to predict what useful books you'll find, but each type of library has different items in its collection that might help you. Some are aimed specifically at genealogists; others are more general. Look for books about the state where your ancestors lived; while such a book might not mention your ancestors, it might help you understand their lives better. Use the bibliographies in these books to find other books with useful information. Browse in the history and reference sections for titles that look helpful. Look for collective biographies—books like *Who Was*

Who in America, National Cyclopedia of American Biography, etc. Many of these target specific professions such as composers, authors, physicians, etc. An ancestor who wasn't especially well known might appear in this type of book.

MATERIALS AVAILABLE AT AND THROUGH FAMILY HISTORY CENTERS

See chapter thirteen for information on locating a Family History Center. If there's one near you, be sure to visit it. Call first to ascertain when they're open, as smaller ones have limited hours. If you're aware of your local Family History Center, but haven't visited because you were afraid people there would try to convert you, don't worry. The Church of Jesus Christ of Latter-day Saints (LDS) specifically prohibits recruitment activities at the Family History Centers. When you go, ask the volunteer in charge to explain and demonstrate the various resources available.

Family History Centers have access to many of the vast genealogical resources collected by the LDS. Through a Family History Center, you can rent microfilm of many records from your ancestral area—assuming they have been filmed. But with over 600,000 rolls of microfilm of U.S. resources, chances are good you'll find something to help you. These records include items such as census records, passenger lists, church records, indexes of will books, and many more.

In the Family History Library Catalog (FHLC), along with listings of microfilms of actual records, you'll find listings for hundreds of thousands of books covering the United States and beyond. You'll also find microfilm of many family histories available for rent, including some privately produced ones that don't show up in card catalogs of major libraries. The FHLC is available both at Family History Centers and on the Internet at <http://familysearch.org/Search/searchcatalog.asp>.

Your local Family History Center may also have a collection of books related to genealogical research.

Family History Center Databases on CD-ROM

The LDS has issued several databases on CD-ROM, available at its Family History Centers and at some other major genealogical libraries. The Family History Library has now begun the process of mounting these on the Internet (see the discussion of FamilySearch in chapter nineteen). Beyond the Family History Library Catalog, two major databases—the International Genealogical Index and Ancestral File—will be especially helpful in your search.

International Genealogical Index

The International Genealogical Index has been available for some time on microfiche; it's now published in CD-ROM format as well. This product indexes birth, christening, marriage, and LDS temple ordinance information for a huge number of deceased people (there is no data for living people) all over the world, many of whom are not members of the LDS. Sources for the entries include

Sources

birth, baptismal, and marriage records; census records; and information submitted by individuals. A code in the index tells you the source of the entry.

This database is an index only, not an actual source; follow through by getting the original document from the Family History Library in Salt Lake City and evaluating it. If the original is, for example, a civil marriage record, the entry is probably correct. But if the material was submitted by an individual, try to find out that person's primary source for the information. The LDS doesn't attempt to verify the data included in this index, and some "information" in it is incorrect.

Ancestral File

Ancestral File is a database of linked pedigree information based mostly on information submitted by hobby genealogists. You might find an ancestor in this file with a line that goes back several generations. However, this database includes names and dates only, not sources. Again, the LDS doesn't verify information included in this database, so attempt to verify in primary sources any information that appears to pertain to your line. Either use the information you find as a guide for the direction of your research or contact submitters of the information (names and addresses are available on the CD) to find out what their sources were, and work from there.

HOW CAN I IDENTIFY BOOKS ABOUT MY FAMILY OR LOCALITY OF INTEREST?

Many sources besides the Family History Library Catalog can help you identify books about your family or locality of interest. A major one is *Genealogical & Local History Books in Print*, a listing of county and regional histories and family histories. Even if your library has an older edition of this multivolume work, you can still use it; you need to know if a book about your ancestral county or family exists, not whether it is still in print. However, this reference tool lists only books that were in print when it was published. While it does include currently available reprints, microfilm, and microfiche of older books, it doesn't list older books that aren't available for purchase or ones whose author or publisher didn't pay to have their book included.

Two other books can help you identify county and regional histories. P. William Filby's *A Bibliography of American County Histories* lists all county histories that he could identify; however, because his focus is county histories, he didn't include books whose purpose was primarily biographical. Marion J. Kaminkow's *United States Local Histories in the Library of Congress: A Bibliography* complements Filby's listing: while the two books overlap, each includes sources not listed in the other.

Three other books can help you identify published genealogies. Kaminkow also compiled *Genealogies in the Library of Congress: A Bibliography*, and its supplements for 1972–1976 and 1976–1986. To identify family histories not in the Library of Congress, he surveyed several other major genealogical collections and compiled *A Complement to Genealogies in the Library of Congress:*

For More Info

READ MORE ABOUT IT!

For an in-depth discussion of library materials that may advance your research, read *Printed Sources: A Guide to Published Genealogical Records,* edited by Kory Meyerink.

A Bibliography. Subsequently, in 1991, the Library of Congress published *Genealogies Cataloged by the Library of Congress Since 1986*.

A company called OneLibrary.com produces a CD-ROM product called *Genealogical Library Master Catalog*. This consists of three CD-ROMs, one each for family histories, local histories, and genealogical sources ("original and transcribed records"). The records on the CDs come from the catalogs of eighteen libraries with large genealogical collections, such as the California State Library in Sutro and the New York Public Library. Even if your ancestors didn't live in these states, large genealogical libraries tend to have materials from other states because residents of their state migrated to or migrated from other states in large numbers. Many of these catalogs are available separately on the Internet, but if you prefer to search all eighteen catalogs at once or don't have Internet access, these CD-ROMs are an alternative.

A library with a strong genealogy collection will have most, if not all, of the above books; if your library is small, it may not have them. In this case, ask the librarian to try to get photocopies of the pages relating to your county or family of interest from some or all of these books through interlibrary loan. Your library may also have access to a database, such as WorldCat on First-Search, which allows you to search large collections of titles for a specific word. Search the subject index in this database to locate books on your ancestral county. Or search for your county in the subject indexes in some of the major library catalogs on the Internet listed later in this chapter. Once you identify books that appear relevant to your search, check the catalogs of your local libraries. You'll find some of them there, but if not, don't panic!

INTERLIBRARY LOAN GIVES ACCESS TO THE LIBRARIES OF THE WORLD

Library/Archive Source

Most libraries don't lend books directly to people outside their service area, but **they'll often lend to another library on interlibrary loan**. If you've identified something that you think will help your research and it's not in your local library, ask if your library can request it on interlibrary loan for you. Most libraries provide this service; often, they charge for it. While your library may not charge a fee for interlibrary loan, the library that lends the book or provides the photocopy you need may charge one. When you make the interlibrary loan request, the librarian usually asks whether you're willing to pay and the maximum you're willing to spend. A good librarian tries to locate a library that doesn't charge or, failing that, sends the request to the one that charges the least. Think about how much the information is worth to you. If it's a question of determining whether county histories exist for your ancestral county, you may decide to pursue other means of identifying them. If you've found a citation for an article that appears to take your family line back three generations, that's probably worth something to you. While photocopies made in your library may cost ten cents a page, a library's charges for photocopies via interlibrary loan also cover staff time and postage. Many charge a base fee of two dollars, five dollars or even ten dollars plus an amount per page for photocopying an article.

Tell the librarian the amount you're willing to pay and that you want to know if the material is only available for more than that. If your limit is ten dollars and the only library that can supply the material charges twelve dollars, you want to know. With the possibility of those three extra generations, you might decide that the article is worth it!

Tips to Maximize Results in Obtaining Materials via Interlibrary Loan

To maximize your chance of getting material on interlibrary loan, you need to give your librarian correct information about it. If you say you're looking for a book called *The Kings of Armstrong County* and the title is actually *Genealogy of Jacob King (König) and Mathias King (König) of Northampton County, Pennsylvania*, don't be surprised if he has trouble locating the book. Give as full and correct a citation for the work as possible (author, title, publisher, and publication date of the book). Many genealogies may have the same title (e.g., *History of the Smith Family*). While the librarian may end up getting a reprint of the book, it's important for him to know when it was published to be able to identify it correctly.

Tip

When requesting a magazine article, give the magazine's title; the article's author and title; and the publication date, volume, issue number, and pages of the issue in which the article appears. In some cases, the citation you're working from may not include all this information, so give the librarian as much information as you can.

When requesting material about a county, it would seem logical to request it from the library in that county. However, while libraries often keep historical material relating to their region in a noncirculating special collection, a library halfway across the United States might lend that material. College libraries are more likely to lend a county history than public libraries are.

Many county histories and genealogies are available on microfilm and microfiche. Although library patrons tend to dislike microforms, it's preferable to read your book on microfiche or microfilm than not at all. If the print version of the book isn't available through interlibrary loan, investigate whether you can borrow a microform copy.

If a county history that has information on your ancestor or a family history that follows your line is not circulated through interlibrary loan, your librarian can ask the library that owns it to photocopy specific information from it. It helps if you have the exact pages. If not, make a request like, "Please photocopy all pages from this county history relating to the Schreckengost family" or "Please photocopy all pages from this genealogy showing the lineage of Jacob Milliron who was born 15 March 1818 and died 21 February 1898 and was married first to Leah Schreckengost and second to Margaret Bradenbaugh." The more specific you can make these requests, the better. The library may not fill such a request (especially if the county history has no index), but you don't lose anything by trying.

As a last resort, if you can't get something on interlibrary loan in any form, ask your librarian whether any libraries near you own the material. If you're desperate to see it, you might drive two hundred miles to a library that owns it. Bring along your family group sheets and allow some extra time for your visit—who knows what other interesting items you might find at that library while you're there!

Some Specialized Genealogical Libraries Lend Material Directly on Interlibrary Loan

Besides the Family History Library, a few libraries exist specifically to supply genealogists with material on interlibrary loan. The major one is Heritage Quest (formerly the American Genealogical Lending Library). It has a huge collection of microfilm publications available for a small rental fee. See chapter thirteen for more information. The National Genealogical Society and the New England Historic Genealogical Society have libraries of books for loan to members for a small fee (see appendix A for their addresses).

Look at ads in genealogical magazines to identify other rental libraries. There aren't many of them, and most specialize in a specific locality, so you may not find one for your area.

HOW CAN I IDENTIFY LIBRARIES IN MY ANCESTRAL AREA?

Notes

You may decide to expand your research by writing to libraries in the area where your ancestor lived. **Several types of libraries in your ancestral area may help:**

- the library in the county seat, which often has the best genealogical collection in the county
- the library in the town where your ancestor lived, which might have a local history or genealogy collection
- the county genealogical society
- the county historical society
- the library of a local college or university
- the state library
- the state genealogical society library
- the state historical society library

To identify these libraries, consult the *American Library Directory*, an annual publication that lists all libraries in the United States. The listings in this directory are divided by state, then by town. Look at the listings for the state capital, the county seat, the town where your ancestor lived, and any significant nearby towns. Read the information in the listings for these libraries to see what sorts of holdings they have that might help you. Entries in the *American Library Directory* have an "Automation" section that gives the Internet address for the library's Web page and online catalog if it has them. College and university libraries should be low on your list of resources to contact, unless they have a special collection that seems to have great relevance to your family.

P. William Filby's *Directory of American Libraries With Genealogy or Local*

History Collections is based on the results of surveys he sent to libraries all over the United States and Canada. Of special interest is each library's answer to the question about number of holdings in the genealogy and local history collection. A library with two thousand books in this collection will probably be more useful than one with twenty books; however, one of those twenty books might be just the one you need.

Chapter sixteen lists some resources you can check to locate addresses of genealogical and historical societies. Elizabeth Petty Bentley's *The Genealogist's Address Book* and Juliana Szucs Smith's *The Ancestry Family Historian's Address Book* list libraries in the sections for each state. *America's Best Genealogy Resource Centers*, by William Dollarhide and Ronald A. Bremer lists major genealogical research centers by state, with an analysis of their holdings. None of these lists is comprehensive. If the library in the county seat of your ancestral area isn't listed, it doesn't necessarily mean that it doesn't have a genealogical collection. It just means that it doesn't have a major regional or state collection; for some of these listings, it means only that the library didn't return the survey on which the book was based.

WHAT SHOULD I SAY—AND NOT SAY—WHEN I WRITE?

When writing to libraries, remember that most probably they're understaffed; genealogical and historical society libraries are often staffed by volunteers. Also, public libraries are chartered to serve a specific area and funded by taxes levied on residents of that area. Because librarians are such nice people, they often respond to mail queries even if you don't pay taxes in their area. They're most likely to respond under two circumstances: (1) the queries are short and simple; (2) the requester sends a donation. Some libraries charge a fee for mail research. Don't expect them to perform major feats of research for you. Ask one or, at most, two specific questions at a time. (See Figure 12-1 on page 122.) Do ask if the library has an index to obituaries or marriage notices in local newspapers, and if so, what time period it covers.

Reminder

If the library answers your question, write a thank-you note; depending on how grateful you are and how much time they spent on your request, perhaps even send another donation (did their answer add another generation or more to your pedigree chart? Did they do extensive research and send you baptismal information for all sixteen of your ancestor's children?). Although you may have more questions, hold off for a month or so before sending them another request. You don't want these people to say, "Oh, no, it's another letter from that pest in Wapakoneta who's doing his family history." You want them to say, "Oh, good, it's another letter from that man in Wapakoneta who sent a donation two months ago."

Expect to wait for a response from any of these libraries. If they're understaffed, they may have a large backlog of requests. Writing an angry letter saying, "I wrote to you two months ago; where the *&^% is my information?" won't encourage them to spend much time on your query. Instead, if you're

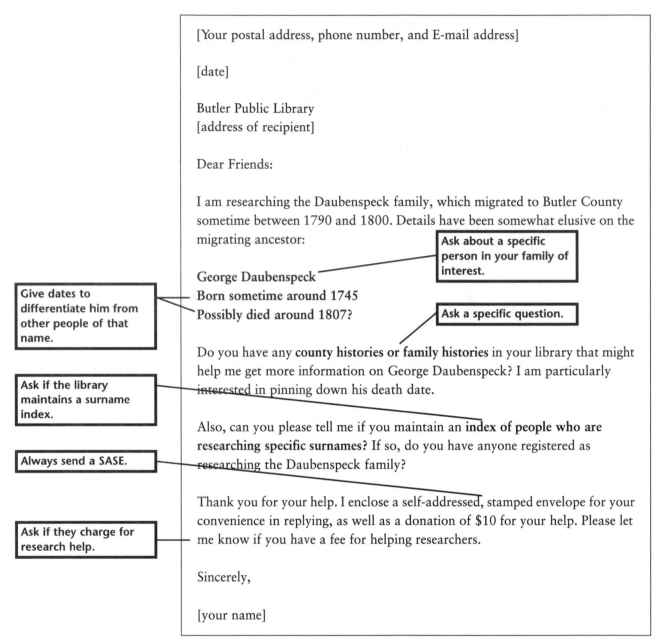

[Your postal address, phone number, and E-mail address]

[date]

Butler Public Library
[address of recipient]

Dear Friends:

I am researching the Daubenspeck family, which migrated to Butler County sometime between 1790 and 1800. Details have been somewhat elusive on the migrating ancestor:

Ask about a specific person in your family of interest.

George Daubenspeck
Born sometime around 1745
Possibly died around 1807?

Give dates to differentiate him from other people of that name.

Ask a specific question.

Do you have any **county histories or family histories** in your library that might help me get more information on George Daubenspeck? I am particularly interested in pinning down his death date.

Ask if the library maintains a surname index.

Also, can you please tell me if you maintain an **index of people who are researching specific surnames?** If so, do you have anyone registered as researching the Daubenspeck family?

Always send a SASE.

Thank you for your help. I enclose a self-addressed, stamped envelope for your convenience in replying, as well as a donation of $10 for your help. Please let me know if you have a fee for helping researchers.

Ask if they charge for research help.

Sincerely,

[your name]

Figure 12-1 Letter requesting research help from a library in the ancestral area

wondering if your letter ever got there, write a gentle inquiry: "I wrote to you last August asking for help with research on the Doverspike family, and I haven't received a reply. I am wondering if my letter got lost in the mail. . . ." You're depending on these people to help you; don't alienate them.

In some cases, you may get a form letter from the library explaining that, while they have genealogical resources, because of staffing problems, they aren't able to do research for mail requests. Such a letter usually includes a list of people who do paid research in the area. At this point, decide whether you want to pay someone to do the research or explore other avenues of getting to the information.

Even if you don't have a specific question about an ancestor to send to these libraries, it's worth writing to ask if they maintain a registry of people doing family history research on a specific name. This is more productive if you're researching an unusual surname. But even with a name like Smith or Williams, by writing to people listed in such an index at the library in the town where your ancestor lived, you may locate people researching your line. And of course, having ascertained that the library does maintain such a registry, send them your list of surnames to add to it.

HOW CAN I FIND LIBRARY RESOURCES ON THE INTERNET?

Web site addresses and mailing addresses for state libraries are in appendix E. Many of these libraries have online catalogs; check these to see if any books are listed relating to your ancestral families and the counties and municipalities you're researching. These Web pages often have links to statewide or regional catalogs—which allow you to search several libraries at one time—or to catalogs for individual libraries in the state.

Some of the largest genealogical collections in the country have mounted their catalogs on the Internet. Even a library outside the area where you're researching may have a significant collection on your area because many people migrated to the library's region from your ancestral area or vice versa. Browse these, and you may identify material that can help you. Even if a library has a catalog online, it may be a work in progress. Catalogs don't appear online magically; someone must enter a record for each book. Since local history collections are often separate from the main collection, a library may delay entering local history books until the main collection is entered. A library may not enter the local history collection at all since it's usually noncirculating. But checking that library's catalog may lead you to books you didn't know existed; perhaps a small, locally produced genealogy of a family in which you're interested isn't in the larger genealogy catalogs, but it is just what you need to expand your family line.

Read any notes about the catalog before you begin to use it to see if there's information about what is or isn't included. Read the instructions for using the catalog; this could save you some frustration in the long run. Major genealogical library collections on the Internet include

- Library of Congress
  http://lcweb.loc.gov/catalog/
- National Genealogical Society
  http://www.ngsgenealogy.org
- Allen County Public Library (Fort Wayne, Indiana)
  http://www.acpl.lib.in.us/genealogy/genealogy.html
- Daughters of the American Revolution
  http://www.dar.org/library/library.html
- New England Historic Genealogical Society
  http://www.nehgs.org/
- Birmingham [Alabama] Public Library/Linn Henley Research Library

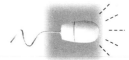

Internet Source

Sources

THE NATIONAL GENEALOGICAL SOCIETY LIBRARY SEARCH SERVICE

If you have trouble getting a book that might help your research, check the National Genealogical Society Library catalog. The NGSearch service will look for one individual, couple, or fact in an indexed book. The five-dollar search fee includes photocopying and postage for up to five pages. If necessary, they will copy more pages at a charge of twenty-five cents per page.

http://www.bham.lib.al.us/
- California State Library, including the Sutro Library
  http://www.lib.state.ca.us/
- Newberry Library (Chicago)
  http://www.newberry.org/nl/newberryhome.html
- Boston Public Library
  http://www.bpl.org/WWW/telref/searchresources.html
- American Antiquarian Society
  http://www.americanantiquarian.org/ (At this writing, catalogs are temporarily unavailable over the Internet. If you're interested, check their site to see if the catalogs have become available.)
- Library of Michigan
  http://www.libofmich.lib.mi.us/
- New York Public Library
  http://catnyp.nypl.org/
- New York State Library
  http://www.nysl.nysed.gov/xcelsior.htm
- Western Reserve Historical Society
  http://www.wrhs.org/sites/library.htm
- Ohio Historical Society
  http://www.ohiohistory.org/resource/archlib/index.html
- Public Library of Cincinnati and Hamilton County
  http://plch.lib.oh.us/
- Library of Virginia
  http://www.lva.lib.va.us/
- State Historical Society of Wisconsin
  http://www.shsw.wisc.edu/library/

The following Web pages have links to large numbers of libraries:
- http://www.CyndisList.com/libes.htm (the library page from Cyndi's List)
- http://sunsite.Berkeley.edu/Libweb/ (lists links to libraries all over the United States and in many foreign countries, sorted by category: academic, public, state, regional consortia, and national libraries)
- http://www.lights.com/hytelnet/ (links to library catalogs all over the world via telnet connections [most computers with Windows 95 or higher have telnet software; if you don't have it, there are sites on the Internet from which you can download it free])
- http://lcweb.loc.gov/z3950/ (from the Library of Congress)
- http://dir.yahoo.com/Reference/Libraries/ (the Yahoo libraries page)

Following the links from the library lists mentioned above could lead you to libraries that are small but helpful. The public library in your ancestral region's county seat may have only a hundred genealogy books, but because those are confined to your ancestral locality, they may include information you need.

Actual Libraries on the Internet

You can also access actual books through the Internet. As of this writing, at least two subscription sites

- http://www.GenealogyLibrary.com
- http://www.heritagebooks.com/library/

offer collections of indexed, scanned family histories, biographies, and other books useful to genealogists. Generally, books on these sites are older books whose copyrights have expired if they were copyrighted; don't expect to find a history of your family published last year. GenealogyLibrary.com also offers scanned census records and other databases.

MY ANCESTOR'S NOT IN THE INDEX!

In the course of researching your family, you'll work with many kinds of indexes: indexes in books, indexes to periodicals and censuses, indexes to CD-ROM products, indexes to deed and will books, and other indexes.

What if you look in an index and don't find your ancestor, who you *know* was in that state for that census or *ought* to have been included in that family history or surely *must* have been written up in some magazine article somewhere? Either your information is wrong, there's a problem with the indexing, or, for census indexes, the census taker missed your ancestor.

Let's assume that you are correct in thinking that your ancestor should be in the index. **You might not find a person in an index for many reasons:**

- The first name isn't listed the way you expect to find it. For example, you think of him as William Thomas Thompson, but he's listed as Thomas William, Thomas, W.T., or T.W. Many genealogists discover that the name by which they know an ancestor is actually a middle name. Perhaps you have the correct first name, but the author of the book or article, only knew the middle name, by which the person was called. Perhaps you know the ancestor by a nickname that doesn't readily convert to the actual given name—Lida for Elizabeth, for example.
- The indexer misread or mistyped the name, and the person is listed somewhere other than where you looked.
- The indexer accidentally skipped the name in the indexing process.
- In indexes to records, the person creating the original record badly misspelled the name, and the indexer used this misspelling.
- In a census index, the census enumerator missed this family, so the person isn't in the census.

If you think that you can't find your ancestor because of an indexing problem, consider how your ancestor's name might have been misread or misheard, and look in the index under potential misspellings.

Notes

For More Info

READ MORE ABOUT IT!

For more thoughts on indexing problems, read Richard Saldaña's *A Practical Guide to the "Misteaks" Made in Census Indexes.* Many of his observations apply to all types of indexes.

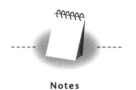

HANSEN'S TEN RULES FOR USING INDEXES

(Reprinted with permission of James Hansen, reference librarian at the State Historical Society of Wisconsin)

1. An index is only an index. It is not a substitute for the record being indexed.

2. The larger the size of the index, the more easily pertinent listings are overlooked.

3. In any given record, any vowel may at any point be substituted for any other vowel.

4. Virtually every pre-WWII record, in whatever form we see it today, originated as an attempt by an individual to put on paper what he or she thought was heard.

5. There is no perfect indexing system.

6. It doesn't matter how you spell your name; it only matters how the indexer spelled it.

7. Just because an index is described as complete or comprehensive doesn't mean it is complete or comprehensive.

8. If you haven't found it in an index, you can only conclude that you haven't found it in an index. You cannot conclude that it's not in the record.

9. The index isn't always in the back of the book.

10. Sometimes it is best to ignore the index altogether.

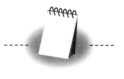

See James Hansen's rules for using indexes (above), but also keep in mind the following:

- Some books only index names the author thought were important. If you think someone ought to be in a book, look up names of related people (e.g., the person's spouse).
- Some books have more than one index. Look carefully to be sure you aren't missing anything.
- Search for women under their maiden and married surnames. Different authors have different approaches to the challenge of indexing married women.
- While automated databases allow you to search for a specific spelling of a name in several huge files of material in one fell swoop, paper indexes can allow you to catch misspelled names by browsing. If you're searching a computer database with no browsing option, you will find the name only if you enter it exactly as it's spelled in the database. If you don't

find the name on your first attempt, try to guess how it might have been misspelled.

- In automated indexes that don't allow browsing, try searching for the person's name with and without the middle name(s) and initial(s).

CONCLUSION

When doing library research, you're almost always dealing with secondary sources. Take anything you find about an ancestor in a book with a grain of salt. (In some cases, a shaker of salt may be necessary!) But library collections hold materials containing information about distant areas that will increase your knowledge of your family and the areas where your ancestors lived. Family History Centers give you access to microfilm of public and church records as well as books. Libraries in your ancestral area may help you with queries relating to your ancestors; make these brief and specific.

Many libraries make their catalog available on the Internet, allowing you to discover books that might be useful. If you can't find these books in your local library, you may be able to get them on interlibrary loan. Some genealogical vendors have made scanned versions of books available on the Internet as a subscription service.

In genealogical research, you may work with many types of indexes. If you don't find your ancestor's name at first, try creative methods for locating the index entry by looking for variant spellings and forms of the name.

THIRTEEN

CD-ROMs, Microfilm, and Microfiche

Reminder

Until recently, genealogists who couldn't get a book on interlibrary loan or a copy of records had to depend on microfilm (usually) or microfiche (occasionally) copies of the material, if they were available. While microfilm is still a major force in genealogy, in recent years CD-ROMs have been making inroads into the territory microfilm once owned. With the advent of census records on CD-ROM, its eventual domination of this area appears even more certain. Microfilm and microfiche require bulky, expensive readers that only the most dedicated genealogists own; others must depend on finding readers at a library. A large percentage of genealogists now have CD-ROM drives in their computers; they can use CD-ROMs in the comfort of their own home at any hour of the day or night. However, don't expect microfilm to go away any time soon! At this point, **many more books and documents that genealogists need are available on microfilm than on CD-ROM.** Also, the useful life of a physical CD-ROM is almost certainly shorter than the lifetime of a roll of microfilm. Data on CDs will eventually degrade (possibly in a time frame as short as ten years); microfilm, properly stored, can last hundreds of years.

These formats make it possible for you to have easy access to items of which there's only one, possibly distant, copy (e.g., deed book indexes) or that are extremely fragile and can no longer be used in their original state (old books). This book discusses many microfilm and CD-ROM products in the chapters about the subjects they cover; this chapter focuses on these products in general. To simplify discussion, assume unless otherwise stated that any mention of microfilm includes microfiche as well.

HOW DO MICROFILMS AND CD-ROMS REPRODUCE MATERIALS?

Most microfilm products are exact copies of original documents, books, etc. Because microfilm is made by a photographic process, there's no reason to change the documents. However, you may also find microfilm of books that give transcriptions of documents.

There are two types of CD-ROM products. One includes actual scanned images of the pages of an item; the other includes transcriptions of material. Microfilm or scanned images of secondary sources are still secondary sources, so CD-ROMs with transcriptions of documents are secondary sources. If you find information relating to an ancestor in a secondary source, no matter what the format, use it only as a guide to getting a copy of the original for verification in case there are errors in the transcription.

Advantages of Microfilm

Microfilm is a format genealogists love to hate—or perhaps the microfilm readers are the source of the problems. Threading film through the machine can be confusing (many readers now have diagrams showing how to load the film), and getting the machine to stop at the page you want to see can sometimes be a challenge. But if you've located material that will help you expand your family tree and your choice is to see it on microfilm or not to see it at all, wouldn't you rather have the microfilm? Microfilm does have some advantages over hard copies:

- Microfilms let you see one-of-a-kind documents, like will book and deed indexes located in distant courthouses.
- Microfilms don't shed dust from red rot (deteriorated leather) and crumbs from disintegrating pages.
- Microfilms are easier to lift than heavy courthouse ledgers.
- Microfilms are easier to copy than heavy courthouse ledgers, which often are larger than the copying area on a copy machine.
- With microfilm, you can use different lenses to enlarge the print for both viewing and copying.

Options for Accessing Microfilm

There are several ways you can get access to microfilm. Three organizations have rental programs for microfilm.

Church of Jesus Christ of Latter-day Saints Family History Library

You can borrow microfilmed materials from the Family History Library in Salt Lake City through its branches, the Family History Centers. The services of Family History Centers are open to all interested individuals; you don't have to be an LDS member. To locate the Family History Center nearest you,

- check the yellow pages for "Churches—Church of Jesus Christ of Latter-day Saints"; call the church and ask
- call (800) 453-3860 and ask for this information
- look at the Family History Centers listing on the FamilySearch Web site at <http://www.familysearch.org/Search/searchfhc2.asp>

The Family History Library sends films to the Family History Center through which you ordered them; you must use them there. The Family History Library has more than two million microfilm publications, covering the genealogical gamut from family history books to deed indexes to census records to passenger arrival lists. They are constantly expanding their collection, but they haven't filmed everything. Check the Family History Library Catalog at your local Family History Center or on the Internet at <http://www.familysearch.com/Search/searchcatalog.asp> to determine what they've filmed for your ancestral area and families.

Heritage Quest and the National Archives

Heritage Quest and the National Archives Census Microfilm Rental Program encourage libraries to become members. If your library is a member and you borrow microfilm through it, you won't have to pay basic membership fees. However, you probably will have to pay the small rental fee that both organizations charge for use of microfilm. If your library isn't interested in joining, you may join Heritage Quest or the National Archives Census Microfilm Rental Program on your own. In this case, microfilm that you borrow will come to whatever address you specify, and you will need a microfilm reader to view it.

Heritage Quest

P.O. Box 329,
Bountiful, UT 84011-0329
http://www.heritagequest.com/genealogy/microfilm/index.html

Heritage Quest has more than 250,000 titles available for rental or purchase, including U.S. census records; military records; ship passenger lists; selected state censuses; county records; vital records; county, local, and family histories; etc. For information on what's available and costs of rental; write to them or check their Web site.

National Archives Census Microfilm Rental Program

P.O. Box 30,
9050 Junction Dr.,
Annapolis Junction, MD 20701-0030
http://www.nara.gov/publications/microfilm/micrent.html

Contact the National Archives Census Microfilm Rental Program to purchase a start-up kit that includes catalogs for the materials they lend on microfilm. These are:

- federal population censuses from 1790 to 1920 (the 1930 census is scheduled for release on 1 April 2002)
- compiled military service records of Revolutionary War soldiers and general indexes to those records
- Revolutionary War pension and bounty land warrant application files

The kit also includes coupons for free rental of your first two rolls of microfilm, guides for using National Archives records for genealogical research, and other catalogs. To learn more about the program, write to them or visit their Web site.

Other Sources for Microfilm Access

- Your librarian may be able to identify another library that will lend microfilm of a book in which you're interested.
- Depending on the microfilm in which you're interested, you might be able to persuade your library to purchase it. It's more likely that you could persuade your library to purchase microfilm of records, like federal census records, for your own state than those for a distant state.
- If you want to get microfilm of original documents kept at the state level and none of the rental sources listed above have it, contact that state's library and archives and ask if they have microfilm of the documents available for loan.

Advantages of CD-ROMs

CD-ROMs have several advantages over books and microfilm:

- Previously you might have had to locate a library that held, for example, a complete run of the *National Genealogical Society Quarterly* or *The New England Historical and Genealogical Register* and then travel to the library to do your research. Even if you got something like census microfilm on loan, unless you owned a reader, you had to take it to the library to use theirs. Now you can purchase CD-ROMs of most of the issues of these and some other magazines and of many books and censuses, then search them in the privacy of your home. You aren't limited to the library's hours; you can work with CDs at two o'clock in the morning if you desire. If you use CDs at your library, you're spared the bother of going back and forth to the shelves to retrieve (sometimes large and awkward) volumes one by one. All you have to do is insert the correct CD into the CD drive.
- Many CDs have comprehensive indexes that allow you to point and click to get to the material in which you're interested.
- Many books are available on CD-ROM at a much lower price than you'd pay for the hardcover equivalent. This means you can own books that you might otherwise have considered too expensive to purchase.

Preview CDs Before You Buy

Brøderbund, which publishes many of the CD-ROMs available today, gives you an opportunity to preview CDs before you buy them. On the Internet, you can search the Internet FamilyFinder at <http://www.familytreemaker.com/iffintro.html> to determine, among other things, whether a name appears in several databases, including Brøderbund CD-ROMs. While you can't see the actual information from the database on the Internet unless you pay for a subscription, you can at least learn whether a family or person with the name you're researching appears on that CD. Brøderbund also has a policy that if you purchase one of their CDs, you can return it for a refund within ninety

For More Info

READ MORE ABOUT IT!

Marthe Arends's *Genealogy on CD-ROM* is an encyclopedic summary (up to its date of publication) of virtually any CD-ROM you might need for your family history research, including both general interest CDs of use to genealogists and CDs created specifically for genealogists. While you can garner the same information from vendors' catalogs, this book categorizes CDs by subject and state, so you can read the section on your state to compare what's available from various publishers. In many cases, Arends's book gives more information about what's on the CD than the publisher's catalog does.

days if you find no ancestors in the material on the disk. However, this means that you must take time as soon as you receive the CD to check for all your ancestral names. This won't take long if you've just begun your research, but if you have many names to check, it could be time consuming.

Warning

When purchasing CDs, be sure you know what you're getting. The title of the CD may be enticing and sound all-encompassing, but then you read the fine print: the CD contains eleven books pertaining to families in six states. If your ancestors lived in only one of these states, perhaps only two or three of the books on the CD have information about your state of interest. What are the chances that one of these books actually mentions your family? Does a CD of vital records for a state include all counties and all years for which these records were kept or only some portion of them?

Unfortunately, many CD vendors' catalogs don't answer these questions, and their customer service departments aren't always helpful in answering questions about content—one of many reasons Marthe Arends's book *Genealogy on CD-ROM* may be helpful, as she gives details about what's on each CD.

Options for Accessing CD-ROMs

There are fewer options for accessing CD-ROMs than there are for microfilms because at this point (probably due to software licensing considerations), very few organizations lend them. Your options are:

- Buy the CD.
- If it's available as an Internet database, subscribe to that database.
- See if your library is interested in purchasing it. As with microfilms, a library will be more likely to purchase a CD-ROM with general information (e.g., P. William Filby's *Passenger and Immigrant Lists Index*) than something with specific information about a distant state. If the library's genealogy collection has many items about another state because many people migrated to your area from there, the library may make an exception to this.

CONCLUSION

For a long time, microfilm has allowed genealogists to see exact copies of documents and books they can't get to personally. CD-ROMs now add another option for this type of access. Both formats have advantages over books, but microfilm requires a reader, which most genealogists don't own; many more genealogists own a computer with a CD-ROM drive.

While several organizations lend genealogical material on microfilm, very few lend CD-ROMs; but much information on CD-ROM is available as (usually subscription) databases on the Internet. CD-ROMs can provide useful information in a cheap and easily searchable format, but know what you're getting before you buy one.

FOURTEEN

Build Your Own Library

As your research progresses, you may find it useful to build your own private library of books and CD-ROMs about genealogy and related subjects. Many books are now available on CD-ROM, and often the CDs cost less than the hard copy. In this chapter, assume that the term *book* also refers to CD-ROM versions of books.

WHAT BOOKS SHOULD I HAVE IN MY GENEALOGY LIBRARY?

The basis of any good genealogical library is a set of how-to books to help you determine what the next step should be in your genealogical research or figure out how to accomplish that next step. See the Preface to this book for a list of good basic books.

If you've identified family histories or genealogical works dealing with your family, you may want to add these to the collection. As you progress in your research, you'll discover related subjects about which you'll want to learn more—such as social history, land records, family health history, or old handwriting—and find books on these subjects to add to your collection.

If many of your ancestors lived in the same area, investigate building a collection of works related to that area. These include county histories, church record transcriptions, cemetery readings, newspaper abstracts, bibliographies, indexes, etc. A telephone book for the area, available at a small charge from the phone company, may give you ideas for research and allow you to determine if anyone with the surname(s) you're researching still lives in the area.

How Do I Find Out What Books Are Available and Where to Get Them?

Start with your local bookstore. Most booksellers have at least a shelf of books on genealogy, so see what you can find there. These will be mostly how-to

Technique

See Also

books or books on specialized subjects like Civil War research, computer and Internet research, finding females, etc. You aren't likely to find books with information on research in a specific geographic area in a bookstore unless the store is in that area. **Also contact the booksellers listed in appendix A and ask for their catalogs.**

Read ads and book reviews in genealogical magazines. Reviews can be especially helpful in steering you away from books that are poorly written or contain erroneous information. You may even find an ad for a book whose title tells you it's exactly what you need to further your research.

Consult a copy of *Genealogical & Local History Books in Print*. This lists county histories, family histories, and other books that can help you in your search, as well as sources for purchasing them.

If possible, go to genealogical conferences. These feature lectures to help you to develop your research skills; most conferences also include at least some book vendors. Visit their tables and look over their wares. Here you'll have an opportunity to examine the books before you purchase them to get an idea of whether they'll help you or not, and you'll find a much larger selection than you found at your local bookstore. Usually, the larger the conference, the more vendors you'll find. If you have a chance to attend one of the two major national conferences (National Genealogical Society or Federation of Genealogical Societies), you may find the exhibit areas so interesting you won't want to leave to attend lectures!

Finally, browse the listings from popular bookstores on Internet sites, such as <http://www.amazon.com> and <http://www.barnesandnoble.com>. Many of these sites sell genealogical books.

Sources

BOOKS IN ALTERNATIVE FORMATS

Bell & Howell Information and Learning, formerly UMI, has issued thousands of family and local history books on microfiche. While some people find this format inconvenient, many of these books are out of print and difficult or impossible to get on interlibrary loan. It's better to have them in an inconvenient format than none at all. Find out if your local library has a microfiche reader you can use, or, like some dedicated genealogists, buy your own microfiche reader. Bell & Howell Information and Learning also sells photocopied reproductions of out-of-print genealogical books bound in hardcover or paperback. They charge a small fee for most of their catalogs.

Many genealogy books (family and county or local histories) are available on microfilm, including some microfilm series that reproduce all of the county histories published in the late 1800s and early 1900s in states such as New York, Pennsylvania, and Ohio. You may find listings for some of these in library catalogs or in *Genealogical & Local History Books in Print*.

Many kinds of genealogy books are available on CD-ROM, which can have several advantages over the actual printed book. CD-ROM vendors often make a new index that enables you to find the listings for an indexed word with a click of your mouse. A CD that includes several books may have one master index, saving you the time you'd have spent checking the individual indexes. A CD is usually cheaper than hard copies of the book or books it contains. And CDs are almost always smaller than books, which helps if you have limited storage space. Major publishers of books on CD-ROM include Ancestry, Brøderbund, and Heritage Books.

The Genealogical Publishing Company has cooperated with Brøderbund in issuing CD versions of books of vital records and collections of historical articles (e.g., *English Origins of New England Families*). These books include either specific extracts of vital records for an area or state or a compilation of articles on families from a specific area. Brøderbund also publishes CDs of books of military records, baptismal records, immigration records, etc.

Ancestry's CD-ROM *Ancestry Reference Library* contains several useful reference books, including *The Source, Ancestry's Red Book, Guide to Genealogical Research in the National Archives,* and more. Brøderbund publishes *The Genealogist's All-in-One Address Book* on CD, which includes *County Courthouse Book, Directory of Family Associations,* and *The Genealogist's Address Book*. In both cases, the cost of the CD is much less than the price of purchasing all these books in hardcover. However, before purchasing these CDs, investigate whether they contain the latest edition of the reference books in question; if not, you're better off buying the actual book.

Many genealogists like to collect audiotapes of genealogical conference lectures on subjects related to their research interests. Repeat Performance, listed in appendix A, has catalogs of several years' worth of tapes of conferences. You can listen to these tapes while driving or doing chores.

CONCLUSION

Collect a library of books, CD-ROMs, audiotapes, and maybe even microfilm and microfiche about genealogical research and the area(s) where your ancestors lived. Then you can research at any time of day or night, without being restricted by the hours of a library.

FIFTEEN

Archival Repositories

\di'fin\ *vb*

Definitions

A rchival repositories are institutions like historical societies, national and state historic sites, historic homes, etc., that preserve collections of original materials of lasting historical value—usually one-of-a-kind documents or photographs.

HOW DO ARCHIVAL REPOSITORIES DIFFER FROM LIBRARIES?

The major difference between libraries and archival repositories is that libraries specialize in collecting published materials and archival repositories specialize in collecting unpublished materials. There may be thousands, even millions, of copies of a published book; usually only one copy of an unpublished item like a diary or letter exists unless it has been transcribed or microfilmed. Therefore, while libraries normally lend most of the materials in their collections, archives have to keep close tabs on their resources. If a library book is lost, it often can be replaced; if the only copy of your great-grandfather's diary is lost, it's gone.

WHAT MIGHT I FIND IN AN ARCHIVE?

Archives hold all sorts of materials in their collections. They may have letters, diaries, ledgers, household account books, records of companies that closed long ago, etc. An archive may hold material about your ancestors or even material your ancestor created. Perhaps a storekeeper with whom your great-grandfather did business kept a ledger showing amounts people owed him for their purchases—or perhaps your ancestor was the storekeeper. Maybe your great-great-grandmother kept a diary that found its way into an archive. Perhaps your grandfather worked for a company that kept record books listing its employees, and when the company closed, the local historical society received its records.

HOW DO I FIND OUT IF MATERIAL BY OR ABOUT MY ANCESTOR MIGHT BE IN AN ARCHIVAL REPOSITORY?

For many reasons, archival materials are harder to track down than books. Unlike libraries, which catalog each individual item in their collection, archival repositories usually catalog collections, giving a general description of their contents, rather than itemizing each individual piece of paper in the collection. On the other hand, while librarians generally use only up to three or four subject headings when cataloging a book, archivists include as many subject headings as are appropriate to help researchers find out what's in the collection.

Another problem in locating archival materials is that they sometimes end up far from where they were created. If your great-grandfather who lived in Pennsylvania wrote a letter to his brother in Michigan, the letter might be in a repository in Michigan. If upon the brother's death his son from Nevada took his papers, the letter might be in a repository in Nevada! You can't rule out any area to search for archival materials. The ledger of a storekeeper who lived in a rural area might be in the state historical society several counties away.

So, maybe archival materials relating to your ancestors exist. They could be anywhere in the country. Finding them seems like looking for a needle in a haystack. How do you start?

One starting point is a publication called the *National Union Catalog of Manuscript Collections,* **or** *NUCMC* (pronounced "Nuck-muck") for short. Many participating archival collections—large and small, all over the United States—have submitted information about their collections to the Library of Congress. NUCMC was published in annual volumes between 1959 and 1993; entries from 1986 to the present are available on the Web at <http://lcweb.loc.gov/coll/nucmc/>. (When you get to this page, click on a search choice under "NUCMC Z39.50 Gateway to the RLIN AMC file" to get to the search screen.) The online version has more access points than the print version. The print version is available in the libraries of major universities and colleges and in some public libraries. Ask your public librarian to help you to find this work in your area.

Library/Archive Source

This data is also available through a computerized library catalog called Research Libraries Information Network (RLIN). Many academic libraries and some large public libraries subscribe to RLIN; if you live in a small town, you may not be able to get access to it there. Ask the staff at the libraries where you research if any of them offer this service. Because it's a subscription service, libraries that have it may allow patrons to use it only under certain circumstances, and the librarian may do the actual search for you.

HOW DO I IDENTIFY ARCHIVAL REPOSITORIES IN THE AREA WHERE MY ANCESTOR LIVED?

Another approach to archival collections is to look for collections in the area where your ancestor lived. The *Directory of Archives and Manuscript Repositories in the United States* can help you locate those in your ancestral area. This directory gives the name, mailing address, access policies, general description of holdings, and other information for archives in the United States and its territories.

Another resource for locating archival repositories and identifying their holdings is *Guide to Archives and Manuscript Collections in the United States: An Annotated Bibliography*. While not all-inclusive (some repositories whose holdings appear in *NUCMC* aren't included in this book), it includes brief information on the collections in various repositories.

Elizabeth Petty Bentley's *The Genealogist's Address Book* and Juliana Szucs Smith's *The Ancestry Family Historian's Address Book* include some listings for archival repositories.

Many archival repositories have made information about their collections available on the Internet. Directories with links to these sites include

- Repositories of Primary Sources
  http://www.uidaho.edu/special-collections/Other.Repositories.html
- Archives and Manuscript Collections Outside Columbia
  http://www.columbia.edu/cu/libraries/subjects/speccol.html
- Archival and Manuscript Repositories in the United States
  http://lcweb.loc.gov/coll/nucmc/other.html
- Archives on the Web
  http://www-personal.umich.edu/~kjostert/archives.html
- Yahoo's links to archives
  http://dir.yahoo.com/Arts/Humanities/History/Archives/

Some repositories have published printed guides to or inventories of their holdings; these may be available in major research libraries.

Reminder

However, **not all repositories have information on their holdings available in NUCMC or on the Internet.** In some cases, you may never find out that a repository has material relating to your family unless you visit it. The finding aids (written descriptions of items in their collections) of some repositories are available only in the repository itself. Some repositories have no finding aids at all; the archivist just knows what's in the collection from long years of working in it. In these repositories, documents the archivist doesn't know about may be lost to history until someone inventories the collection and produces finding aids.

SOME THINGS TO CONSIDER BEFORE CONTACTING AN ARCHIVAL REPOSITORY

Using *NUCMC* or an archival repository's Web site, you might identify specific material which relates to your ancestor. Or you might identify a repository, perhaps a historical society, in the area where your ancestor lived, which you hope *might* have materials relating to your ancestor.

Even if you have located specific materials relating to your ancestor, you may have trouble getting at them. For example, a collection description says that it contains "Two letters from James Black in San Francisco, California, to his son Josiah Braden Black in Butler, Pennsylvania." The description also says that this collection includes three cubic feet of materials. If the collection contains a folder labeled "Letters from James Black," it may be relatively easy for the archivist to locate the letters. On the other hand, the collection could be arranged chronologically, or not at all. If so, it could be difficult for the archivist to find these particular letters. If he does locate them, he may discover that they're written on fragile paper that he doesn't dare try to photocopy.

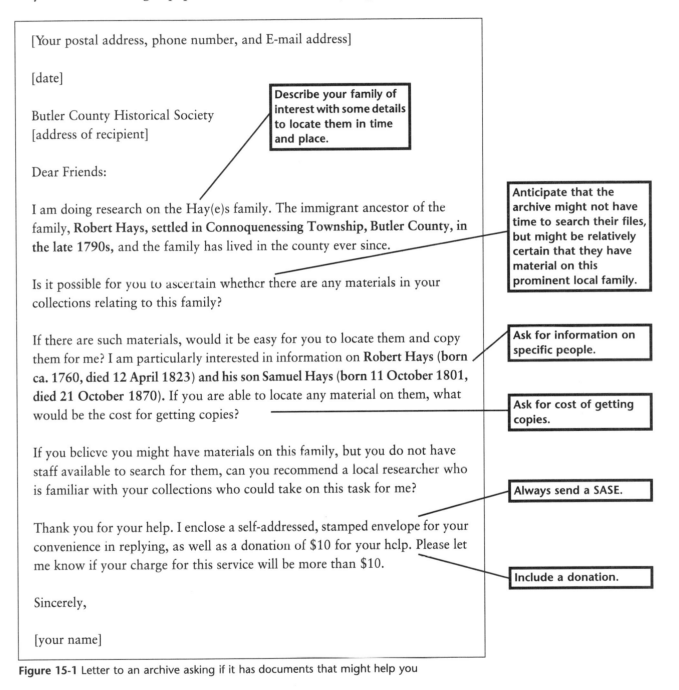

[Your postal address, phone number, and E-mail address]

[date]

Butler County Historical Society
[address of recipient]

Describe your family of interest with some details to locate them in time and place.

Dear Friends:

I am doing research on the Hay(e)s family. The immigrant ancestor of the family, **Robert Hays, settled in Connoquenessing Township, Butler County, in the late 1790s,** and the family has lived in the county ever since.

Anticipate that the archive might not have time to search their files, but might be relatively certain that they have material on this prominent local family.

Is it possible for you to ascertain whether there are any materials in your collections relating to this family?

If there are such materials, would it be easy for you to locate them and copy them for me? I am particularly interested in information on **Robert Hays (born ca. 1760, died 12 April 1823) and his son Samuel Hays (born 11 October 1801, died 21 October 1870).** If you are able to locate any material on them, what would be the cost for getting copies?

Ask for information on specific people.

Ask for cost of getting copies.

If you believe you might have materials on this family, but you do not have staff available to search for them, can you recommend a local researcher who is familiar with your collections who could take on this task for me?

Thank you for your help. I enclose a self-addressed, stamped envelope for your convenience in replying, as well as a donation of $10 for your help. Please let me know if your charge for this service will be more than $10.

Always send a SASE.

Include a donation.

Sincerely,

[your name]

Figure 15-1 Letter to an archive asking if it has documents that might help you

If you don't know for sure that there's anything relating to your ancestor in the archive that collects materials about your ancestral area, you have an even bigger problem. You can hardly ask the archivist to go through every piece of paper in the archives in hopes of finding something relating to your ancestors. However, you can take a chance and write to the archive to ask if they can identify anything in their collections that might relate to your ancestor (see Figure 15-1 on page 139). Don't expect miracles, though.

Many archives are in the same situation as most libraries: they're short of money and staff. Even so, most archivists are eager to use their collections. In either of the above cases, take the chance of writing to the archive in question. If you have found that a collection has information that seems to relate to your ancestors, give them all the information you found about the collection and the names and vital dates of the ancestors in question. Like other professionals, archivists are pressed for time, so don't spend six pages telling the fascinating story of how your multi-great-grandfather was captured by Indians but managed to escape. If the collection description mentioned specific items, like the letters of James Black, explain that you want copies of these and any other relevant items the archivist can identify.

Reminder

Always offer to pay the archivist for research time and copies. Explain that you realize that the condition of the materials may not allow photocoping. Be understanding of the problems involved and grateful for any results you get.

If the archivist responds that she can send you copies of the materials, send a thank-you letter. If there was no charge for the research and/or copies, send a donation to the archive.

In the case where you have identified only that there's an archive (perhaps a historical society) serving the area where your ancestor lived, you must be even more careful in your letter. Basically, you need to ask if the archive might have material relating to your family, but a letter saying "Send me everything you have on the Daubenspeck family" is sure to land in the trash can. A letter saying "I am doing family history research on the Daubenspeck family, members of whom lived in your area between 1760 and 1820, and wonder if you're able to ascertain whether there's anything in your archival collection related to this family" might get a response (see Figure 15-2 on page 141). If you're researching several families in the area, spread out your requests, rather than writing and asking for information on ten or twelve different families at one time. If the archivist can look up the material fairly quickly, you may get a quick answer. If finding answers to the questions in your letter (the one with the list of your twelve ancestral families from the area) will take several hours, the letter may go into a pile for work at some later time—and who knows when the archivist will get back to it?

As usual, offer to pay any expenses involved in getting the materials. Once you receive the materials, pay the bill promptly if there is one, or send a donation to the archive.

CONCLUSION

Archival materials are difficult to identify and access. However, such materials relating to your ancestors will quite possibly contain intimate personal details about their lives and will be well worth the hunt.

[Your postal address, phone number, and E-mail address]

[date]

[Name] University Library
[address of recipient]

Dear Friends:

I am doing research on the Daubenspeck family. Recently, I searched *NUCMC* and discovered a record for papers of Jacob Daubenspeck of Butler County, Pennsylvania, your accession number 1476. The description says that this collection includes "Daubenspeck family records."

> **Give a specific description of the information that led you to write to this archive.**

Would it be possible for you to photocopy these family records for me? I realize that they may be in poor condition or difficult to locate within the collection.

> **Ask if it is possible to get copies.**

If it is possible to photocopy these records, please let me know what the cost would be.

> **Ask for cost of obtaining copies.**

Thank you for your help. I enclose a self-addressed, stamped envelope for your convenience in replying.

> **Always send a SASE.**

Sincerely,

[your name]

Figure 15-2 Letter to an archive when you have identified something specific in their collection that you think might help you

SIXTEEN

Joining Genealogical and Historical Societies

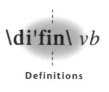

\di'fin\ *vb*

Definitions

WHAT TYPES OF SOCIETIES CAN I JOIN?

Many types of genealogical and historical societies can assist your research. These fall into the broad categories of national, state, locality, lineage, affiliation, and family name societies.

National societies focus on genealogy of a specific country. The two major national societies in the United States are the National Genealogical Society and the Federation of Genealogical Societies. Each holds a conference every year. The National Genealogical Society publishes the *National Genealogical Society Quarterly* (see chapter seventeen for more information) and a newsletter. Among other services, it offers a home study course, *American Genealogy: A Basic Course*. The Federation of Genealogical Societies publishes a quarterly magazine, *Forum*.

State societies focus on research in a state. A few societies, like the New England Historic Genealogical Society, span a multistate region. Only a few states have no state genealogical society, and these generally have county genealogical societies.

Locality societies focus on a specific locality: a group of counties, one county, or even a portion of a county.

Lineage societies accept members based on some characteristic or action of an ancestor. This can range from patriotic service (Daughters of the American Revolution) to occupation (Flagon and Trencher, for descendants of colonial tavern keepers) to place of residence (First Families of Ohio). While people tend to think of lineage societies in terms of those for whom qualifying ancestors date back to colonial times, many lineage societies are based on ancestors who lived much later—for example, Sons of Spanish-American War Veterans. Generally, to join a lineage society, you must submit a documented lineage back to the qualifying ancestor and prove that the ancestor did indeed participate in the activity or live in the area and time period on which society membership is based. If a lineage society allows you to join by paying a fee without providing any kind of proof of your lineage back to a qualifying ancestor, be suspicious of it!

One of the most important reasons for joining a lineage society (aside from asserting your pride in your ancestor's activity) is that the society will place your application form in its archives, thus making your research available to future generations.

Membership in **affiliation societies** is based on a group to which your ancestor belonged, such as a religious or ethnic group. You may or may not have to prove your ancestry to join.

Some **family name societies** are open to descendants of a specific immigrant; some are open to anyone on any line with a specific surname. Some have newsletters or magazines; some maintain a database for people of the name in question; some have informal methods of getting together people who have common ancestors.

Family name societies and their publications vary greatly in quality. It's frustrating to join a family name society only to discover that there are only thirty other members, none of whom share your line. A good strategy with family name societies is to join one or two at a time based on your problem names. Once you have joined, evaluate the materials and services you receive from a society to see if it's worth continuing. Family name societies often don't last long; many are run by one person or a few people who gradually lose the energy with which they started the society, and the decision to leave the society is made for you.

WHAT ARE THE BENEFITS OF JOINING SOCIETIES?

Why bother to join the society for the area where your ancestors lived? It's a few hundred (or thousand) miles away; you can't attend meetings. So how can you benefit from it or other societies, like family name societies or affiliation societies?

Genealogical societies send out listings of publications about the region or topic they cover, including notices of reprints of older books such as county histories, public records, church records, newspaper abstracts, etc., that might help you. Some societies keep surname files (listing people who are searching a specific name), ancestor chart files, etc., that they will search. Of course, you'll send them your surnames to add to the file.

Often, societies offer members the ability to place free or low-cost queries in the society publication. If you're researching a family with a common name, like Smith, and you place a query in a national publication, you could get a lot of letters from people who are researching a different Smith family. But the readership of a county genealogical society publication consists of people interested in that county. Mainly, you'll get responses from people researching Smith in that area, so you'll have a much smaller chance of getting responses from people who aren't researching your line.

Many locality societies offer free or low-cost searches of basic materials

Money Saver

GRADUALLY CUTTING EXPENSES FOR MEMBERSHIPS

Dues can add up if you belong to many societies. However, some offer a lifetime membership for a larger fee—possibly a hundred or a few hundred dollars. For several years, I bought one lifetime membership per year in societies that offered them, thus, after the initial major expenditure, gradually cutting down my overall expense for society membership.

pertaining to their area. Generally, members who write to a society to request help with their research receive faster service than nonmembers. While the society may find nothing about your ancestor, they might find an article in a county history or other source that could greatly expand your knowledge of your family. When you request searches, be patient. Don't assume that a society has a large research staff who will respond immediately. Many societies are staffed by volunteers, and your request may take a while to reach the top of the pile.

Many societies have magazines, newsletters, and other publications that may have information on your ancestral family, information on research peculiarities, abstracts of records, and articles on families in the region—one of which may be yours. Even an article about a family that isn't related to yours may give you clues that will assist your research by mentioning a source of which you weren't aware or giving information about some research facility or source relating to the area.

If you have many ancestors in an area and you can afford it, join any local, regional, and state organizations for that area to assure that you get the best coverage. Someone who writes an article about people in your ancestral area might include information about other counties they lived in, making it too broad for the county society's publication. Or the author might simply prefer to submit the article to the state society's publication because it reaches a larger audience or looks more prestigious on a resume. If you belong only to the local society, you might miss articles that could help you. On the other hand, the state society might not pick up items of purely local interest, which you would miss if you don't join the local society.

HOW DO I IDENTIFY SOCIETIES?

To identify genealogical and historical societies, you can use several sources, including

Sources

- Smith's *The Ancestry Family Historian's Address Book*
- *Ancestry's Red Book: American State, County & Town Sources*
- Bentley's *Directory of Family Associations*
- *Directory of Historical Organizations in the United States and Canada*
- Bentley's *The Genealogist's Address Book*
- *Encyclopedia of Associations*
- *The Handy Book for Genealogists*
- Directories of various kinds of societies in the magazine *Everton's Genealogical Helper*

Check all these sources, as none of them has a complete list.

Many societies have Web sites. Larger societies may even mount their library's catalog on the Internet. Cyndi's List includes a page with links to pages for specific surnames, family associations, and family newsletters at <http://www.CyndisList.com/surnames.htm> and one with links to general societies and groups at <http://www.CyndisList.com/society.htm.>.

The Federation of Genealogical Societies Web page lists genealogical societies at <http://www.familyhistory.com/societyhall/main.asp> (searchable by any combination of society name or keyword—e.g., the name of your county—plus city, state, province, or zip code).

WHY SHOULD I JOIN MY LOCAL SOCIETY IF I HAVE NO ANCESTORS IN THE AREA WHERE I LIVE?

You've investigated societies and joined the ones you think will help you. You've also discovered that there's a local genealogical society in your area—but why bother to join that one?

The local society can help you in many ways, even if you don't have local ancestors. First, you'll have educational opportunities: regular meetings—with speakers—and seminars or conferences. Many speakers cover universal topics: things like deeds, immigration, or useful Internet sites are pretty much the same, no matter where you look at them. Even if the topic seems specific ("What's in the Morgan County Courthouse?"), it may give you ideas for research in your more distant ancestral home. Just getting together and interacting with other genealogists can help you. You'll share research stories, and maybe someone you meet will have a suggestion about how to get around brick walls in your lines. If nothing else, you'll make some new friends.

You live far away from where your ancestors lived; maybe other descendants of your ancestors live in your area, too. Many societies publish lists of ancestral surnames of their members. You may even find a distant cousin in a chance discussion.

Finally, there's the payback factor: as a member of your local society, you can do volunteer work to help other long-distance genealogists who live far from your area, just as people in your ancestral area are helping you.

CONCLUSION

Genealogical and historical societies issue publications that may give you information on your ancestors or may at least assist in refining the strategies you use in searching for them. If possible, join several, including those for the counties and states where you're researching, plus (if they exist) family name societies for your problem names. Just think of all the interesting mail you'll get!

SEVENTEEN

Genealogical Magazines

Printed Source

M any magazines are published for genealogists. If you can afford it, you can have the mail carrier bring you new genealogical information almost every day. Even if you can't afford them all, subscribe to at least one or two and read others at the library.

Genealogical magazines fall into four main categories: general-interest, locality-oriented, surname, and subject-oriented magazines. In this chapter, *magazine* includes all types of periodicals, from one-page historical society newsletters to scholarly journals like the *National Genealogical Society Quarterly*.

GENERAL-INTEREST MAGAZINES AND JOURNALS

General-interest magazines and journals include articles on research techniques and other aspects of searching. Some articles deal with specific families but include lessons you can extrapolate to your own research. Other articles explain the intricacies of working with a certain category of record.

There are seven major magazines for general (i.e., not region-specific) U.S. research. See appendix A for information on contacting the publishers.

Ancestry (bimonthly) is a glossy magazine with lots of color photographs. It includes ads, news from the genealogical world, letters from readers, and book notices. There are articles on research techniques and sources; columns on topics such as ethnic sources, library and archive sources, technology, and the Internet; and "Step-by-Step," for developing research skills. *Ancestry* doesn't publish queries.

Everton's Genealogical Helper (bimonthly) includes how-to articles, articles with background information for researchers, and surveys of research techniques (in a specific area or using certain reference tools), plus ads for books, researchers, software, and other topics related to genealogy. But beyond articles, it includes several departments where readers interact with the editors and each other. One of its major services is paid queries in which genealogists list information about people for whom they are searching in hopes that someone who knows about those people will respond. *Everton's Genealogical Helper's* extensive "Bureau of Missing Ancestors" makes it the major genealogical query magazine in the United States; these queries reach many thousands of readers all over the country. There are other departments to which genealogists can submit humorous or amazing stories from their research ("And would you believe that after I spent ten years searching for my long-lost half sister, I found her living right next door to me!"), get replies to questions about a research problem that has stumped them, place queries searching for lost people who they hope are still alive, or list items they have located that might help some other researcher (e.g., a Bible with family records found in an antique shop). Another department publishes ancestor photographs with information about them. The "Roots Cellar" allows researchers to submit an ancestor's name coupled with the date and place of one event in the ancestor's life. Other columns include news items, calendars of workshops, conferences, family associations meetings; columns on several genealogical software programs; reviews and listings of Web sites; and book notices.

The magazine also includes a rotating series of directories, one per issue:
- Locality Periodicals
- Family Associations
- Family Periodicals
- Genealogical and Historical Societies
- Professional Researchers
- Top Twenty Web Sites [for the year]

Each issue includes a subject index, a locality index, and a complete surname index that picks up surnames from *everything* in the magazine (including commercial ads, book notices, etc.) except the "Roots Cellar," which is alphabetical by surname.

Family Chronicle (bimonthly) is another glossy magazine with color photos. It includes how-to articles, background information for research, software reviews, and articles on items related to research—such as organizing your materials, managing your E-mail, etc. It also contains ads, news items, and letters.

Family Tree Magazine is a new entry in the world of genealogical magazines. It is also a glossy magazine with color photographs and is aimed mainly at new genealogists. It includes articles on ethnic heritage, family reunions, historic travel and using your genealogy in crafts such as scrapbooking. Reviews of Web sites and products—like CD-ROMs, computer software, books, and scrapbook materials and other related craft supplies—appear in this magazine. While it's aimed at beginning genealogists, there's something in it for everyone.

Heritage Quest (bimonthly) includes articles on methodology, articles on computer aspects of genealogy, paid ads for professional genealogists, short news items, book notices, an events calendar, and ads (mostly for Heritage Quest products). There are also question-and-answer columns on Scandinavian, British Isles, and German research, written by independent columnists. Send in a research problem along with a modest fee, and the columnist suggests sources where you might pursue the research. The columns include the most interesting questions the columnist has received, but all inquirers receive a personal answer.

The *National Genealogical Society Quarterly* (*NGSQ*) is a benefit of membership in the National Genealogical Society. It's a scholarly journal without color photos, but don't let this put you off. Articles include methodological case studies, ways a researcher solved a problem, guides to research in a specific state, information on major genealogical resources, etc. This journal uses a peer review system: before an article appears in the magazine, the editor submits it to experts on the subject and asks for their comments. These comments determine whether or not *NGSQ* publishes the article and can result in the article's being significantly rewritten before it actually appears in the magazine. This system guarantees the superior quality of articles for which *NGSQ* is noted.

The book reviews in *NGSQ* differ greatly from those in the glossy magazines in that they are scholarly, detailed, critical, and analytical. It's interesting to read book reviews where the reviewer disliked the book and tells you exactly why. If you're considering writing a book, read these to find out what not to do! The magazine also includes thoughtful and thought-provoking editorials, information on the National Genealogical Society and its benefits, and a few ads. Volumes one through eighty-five of *NGSQ* are available on CD-ROM from Brøderbund.

The American Genealogist or *TAG* (quarterly), is similar to *NGSQ* in that it is a scholarly, peer-reviewed, nonglossy journal, but there are a few differences. *TAG* prints extended genealogical studies of a family, while *NGSQ* generally doesn't. *TAG* articles may deal with studies of a family's European origins, identity problems, etc. The editor delights in short, humorous, and even risqué fillers extracted from ancient documents. There are no ads.

LOCALITY-ORIENTED MAGAZINES

Many genealogy magazines focus on a specific locality, such as a state, a region in a state (or overlapping state lines), a county, or a metropolitan area. These magazines typically publish articles on doing research in the area, resources for research (for example, types of records), repositories, and sometimes the genealogy of families in the area. They often include cemetery readings and abstracts and/or transcriptions of records from the area. They may offer the opportunity to place queries. Some of these magazines are published by a genealogical society that focuses on the area in question, but others are independent.

SURNAME-ORIENTED MAGAZINES

Some surname-oriented magazines focus on one line of a certain family; others include anything about families of widely varying but similar names, e.g., Rader, Reader, Roder, and Rotter. Surname-oriented magazines typically publish articles or collections of tidbits about people of the surname in question and often have free or low-cost queries.

The quality of these magazines varies greatly, from poorly done, photocopied, stapled pages to well-organized printed and bound magazines. Often one person or a few people put together a surname-oriented magazine as a labor of love, devoting much time and effort (and, in some cases, money) to it, making no profit except the friendship and gratitude of many people who may or may not be related. If you subscribe to a surname-oriented magazine, be prepared to share the information you have collected about your ancestors of that name and their families. Editors of these magazines are often desperate for material.

SUBJECT-ORIENTED MAGAZINES

Finally, there are subject-oriented magazines. These may cover a certain time period (the Civil War) or a specific group of people (e.g., an ethnic or religious group). Articles discuss researching ancestors who belonged to the group or lived in the time period in question. Some include queries and columns answering readers' questions about researching the topic.

HOW DO I IDENTIFY GENEALOGICAL MAGAZINES?

Several directories can help you identify magazines you can use. See chapter sixteen for sources that list magazines societies publish. Other sources include

Sources

- *Everton's Genealogical Helper* (lists genealogically oriented magazines in its annual directories, including "Family Periodicals" and "Locality Periodicals"; also publishes notices and ads for new magazines)
- Elizabeth Petty Bentley's *The Genealogist's Address Book* (has for each state an "Independent Publications and Miscellany" section that includes listings for magazines)
- *The Standard Periodical Directory* (look under the subject headings "Genealogy," "History," and "Regional Interest"; in the "Regional Interest" section, read through all listings for your ancestral state)
- *Ulrich's International Periodicals Directory* (the section "Genealogy and Heraldry" includes family periodicals and periodicals of genealogical societies)

WHICH MAGAZINES SHOULD I SUBSCRIBE TO?

With so many genealogical magazines available, how do you decide which ones to subscribe to? The amount of money you have available for subscriptions will affect this decision. **If possible, among the general-interest magazines, subscribe to at least one scholarly journal and one popular magazine.**

Tip

The scholarly journals will expose you to a high standard of research, which you should emulate. Readers have complained that in the numerous case studies and genealogies they have never seen anything about *their* family, so why should they continue to subscribe? This isn't the point! Sometime one of these magazines may include an article that's actually about your family. But even if you never see anything about your own family, case studies can give you insight into ways to approach a problem using resources you might not have thought of using or might not have known existed. This can be especially helpful if the family in the article lives in an area where your ancestors lived; but even if the family is in a different area, the sources used for an article may have information about your ancestors, too.

Everton's Genealogical Helper is the only national query magazine; queries are a major avenue for making contact with other people researching your lines. If you're looking for queries (both the chance to insert them and the chance to read them) you should definitely subscribe to it. The *Helper* also has many more book notices and ads than the other popular magazines.

Once you've chosen which general magazines you'll get, think about subscribing to some locality periodicals. This decision may be made for you if you join one or more societies that focus on the area(s) where your ancestors lived. If no societies cover the area but an independent locality genealogical magazine does, consider subscribing to it. If there isn't even a genealogical magazine for the area, is there a historical magazine or at least a general-interest magazine? This could help you get to know the area and may describe some historic sites your ancestor might have known. A general-interest magazine might publish an article or column on doing genealogical research in the area.

It you have a large number of ancestors in an area, try to obtain back issues of genealogical periodicals about the area. Often publishers and societies have individual back issues available for sale and send out lists of all articles from all issues of the magazine so far. You may find a back issue that includes an article on your family, or at least one discussing some research tool of interest.

Several major genealogical magazines such as *NGSQ*, *The New England Historical and Genealogical Register*, and *The Pennsylvania Genealogical Magazine* have published complete runs (up to the date the CD was published) of their magazines on CD-ROM with one combined every-name index. If you have many ancestors in the area these magazines cover, consider purchasing these CDs. See the Brøderbund catalog or Web site for more information on what's available. The CD prices are a bargain compared with the cost of purchasing the back issues in paper format.

It's probably fiscally impractical for you to subscribe to magazines for all the surnames you're researching. Surname-oriented magazines for your problem lines should lead your list. Once you subscribe, evaluate the magazine's quality and the number of subscribers. If there are only seventeen subscribers and you've had no responses to your queries after a year, seriously consider discontinuing your subscription.

What Do I Do With These Magazines?

The storage question is up to you. If you subscribe to many, they'll pile up. Do save back issues for future reference. You may find two years from now that a family that doesn't mean anything to you today is related to your family. If you find a new ancestral surname, you'll want to check the indexes in old magazines to look for articles or queries dealing with the name.

In the meantime, when you first get the magazines, read them thoroughly.

You may find articles describing research techniques, approaches, or tools to help you. A book review may describe a book about your ancestral area or even a family in which you're interested. Analytical reviews warn you of things to watch out for in a book or let you know the book is superb. So read every word of these magazines, and consider how you can apply what you're reading to your own research.

INDEXES TO GENEALOGICAL PERIODICALS

There are several major indexes to genealogical periodicals. Each has a different approach and covers different lists of periodicals. If you don't subscribe to any magazines related to your ancestral family or area, check periodical indexes to see if they list articles that might help you. If you have access to more than one index, check all of them for the subject in which you're interested to be sure of locating as many relevant articles as possible.

To save space, many indexes to periodicals use abbreviations or even codes to indicate the periodical where an article appears. When using indexes, be certain to verify the translations of these codes before you leave the library. You'd be frustrated if you left a research session with a photocopy of an index page that lists an article that obviously contains lots of information about your ancestor only to discover that you can't tell what magazine the article is in.

Periodical Source Index (PERSI)

The *Periodical Source Index*, known as *PERSI*, is published by the Allen County Public Library in Fort Wayne, Indiana. The first volume of this index appeared in 1988 and indexes serials published in 1986; the library has issued yearly volumes ever since. In the meantime, the library also developed a retrospective index for serials from 1847 through 1985 in sixteen volumes.

The library indexes only magazines that are in its collection, so they might not include the magazine for the area you're researching. But since the Allen County Public Library is one of the largest genealogical libraries in the country, it's worthwhile to check out this index. The index covers more than four thousand periodicals, but a given yearly index doesn't cover this many titles—not all of the titles were published throughout the time span of the index, and the library doesn't have a full run of some magazines. Generally, *PERSI* doesn't include periodicals devoted to a specific surname. *PERSI* is divided into five sections: U.S. Places, Canadian Places, Other Foreign Places, Research Methodology, and Families.

To make things even easier, in 1997, Ancestry began issuing a cumulated version of *PERSI* on CD-ROM. Now, instead of having to look up your topic in multiple volumes, you can look it up once on the CD-ROM and find all references to it in all the volumes at one time. If your library doesn't own the *PERSI* CD-ROM and you have a computer with a CD-ROM drive, this index is a worthwhile purchase. Ancestry updates the CD on a yearly basis.

PERSI is also available as part of a subscription to Ancestry.com on the Internet at its Web site, <http://www.ancestry.com/>.

You need to know a few things about the article citations in both the print and CD-ROM versions *of PERSI*:

- Citations don't include the names of the articles' authors. Sometimes this information is useful, as you might recognize the name of a reputable (or not so reputable) researcher or want to search for an article that a specific person wrote.

- Citations don't give the page number(s) for the article. In some cases, an "article" is actually only a short query. It's laudable that the people in Fort Wayne went to the trouble of indexing queries. However, if, based on your *PERSI* research, your library sends an interlibrary loan request for something that you think is an article but is actually a query, the library that receives the interlibrary loan request may look in the table of contents, find nothing listed for the name in question, and send the request back unfilled.

- In some cases, the iisting for the article includes a descriptive phrase (e.g., "Altman Fam., Pennsylvania") rather than the article's exact title (in this case, "Raising Heretical Questions About Accepted Facts: Altmans of Colonial Pennsylvania"). If you request an article on interlibrary loan based on *PERSI*, suggest to the librarian that she put the "title" as taken from *PERSI* in brackets or otherwise indicate that this may be a description rather than an actual title.

- In some cases, if a magazine has changed its name during the course of its publication, an article may be indexed under a title that's not on that issue of the magazine. If your library shelves magazines in alphabetical order by title, you might look on the shelf for volume twelve of a magazine, find that the issues in your library start with volume twenty, and, not realizing that volumes one through nineteen are shelved elsewhere because they have a different title, think that your library doesn't own that issue.

Despite these minor drawbacks, *PERSI* is still a valuable source for genealogical information.

Genealogical Periodical Annual Index

The *Genealogical Periodical Annual Index* began in 1962 and has been issued annually except for the years 1970 through 1973. Surname, locality, and topical categories are interfiled. The index began by indexing seventy-eight periodicals; it now covers more than 350 English-language genealogical periodicals. Its criteria for inclusion are different from those of *PERSI*, so although its coverage is smaller, it includes some titles that aren't in *PERSI*. It indexes book reviews, so you may find leads to books about your family. This index may be in your local library; it is also available online at <http://www.heritagebooks.com/library/>.

Index to Genealogical Periodical Literature, 1960–1977

This publication by Kip Sperry indexes articles on how to do research rather than on surnames. Use it to locate articles on how someone else solved a problem similar to your current brick wall; you may find some ideas on how to get over it.

Biography and Genealogy Master Index

This is "a consolidated index to more than 3,200,000 biographical sketches in over 350 current and retrospective biographical dictionaries," including works such as *Who's Who in America*, *Dictionary of American Biography*, *American Men & Women of Science*, and *Contemporary Authors*. The listings includes dates for the person where known, which can help if you're looking for a name like James Smith. There are supplements to the original volumes; check them all.

Index to Genealogical Periodicals

This work by Donald Lines Jacobus indexes about fifty magazines plus around fifty-six published books, with a focus on New England and northern Atlantic seaboard research. This index covers large runs of each magazine included. The original volumes were published in 1932, 1948, and 1953. Subsequent reprints include all three volumes, and Carl Boyer's reprint merges the material from the three volumes into one alphabetical sequence each for name, place, and topic to simplify searching.

Other Indexes

Many magazines such as the *National Genealogical Society Quarterly*, *The New England Historical and Genealogical Register*, and the *New York Genealogical and Biographical Register* have published cumulated indexes for large time spans. Some or all issues of these magazines are also included in some of the indexes mentioned above. Check out any indexes for the *National Genealogical Society Quarterly* that you can access; also investigate indexes for any periodicals that cover the area where your ancestors lived.

As was mentioned above, several major genealogical magazines have been issued on CD-ROM, with one cumulated index for all the issues on the CD.

MY LIBRARY DOESN'T HAVE THE MAGAZINE!

Chapter twelve describes the interlibrary loan process. **If you want to get a magazine article on interlibrary loan, have the correct title of the magazine, and have the author, title, publication date, volume and issue numbers, and pages for the article.** In some cases, the citation you found might not include all this information, but the more you can give the librarian, the better.

Important

The Allen County Public Library will supply you directly with copies of all articles indexed in *PERSI* for a moderate fee; see details in *PERSI*. However, you might want to talk to the interlibrary loan librarian at your library before you request materials from the Allen County Public Library; your librarian might identify a library that will supply the article for a smaller fee or free of charge.

CONCLUSION

After a hard day of writing letters, entering data into your computer, or visiting your local library, relax in your comfy chair, read a genealogical magazine, and look for more clues on how to extend your research. Magazines and journals may include information specifically about your ancestors and may also include articles that will give you ideas on how to proceed with your research. Subscribe to at least one general-interest magazine and one scholarly journal, or at least look at these regularly at the library. Also consider subscribing to magazines related to the area(s) where your ancestor(s) lived and special groups (ethnic, religious, etc.) to which they belonged.

Several periodical indexes can help you locate articles relating to your search from older issues of magazines. If your library doesn't have the periodicals you need, you may be able to order articles on interlibrary loan.

EIGHTEEN

Finding Other People Who Are Researching Your Line

Many genealogists spend all their research time working with courthouse and library records, but networking is important, too. Genealogists can't operate in a vacuum. Some pieces of information that you'll never find in a courthouse or library may simply fill in a blank in your pedigree chart, but some may also give you insight into your ancestor's life.

While most resources this book has covered so far are publicly accessible records, it's important to search for distant cousins you don't know who could have information that isn't publicly available. **They may have family Bibles or other papers, and they may know family stories about your common ancestors that have been passed through their line of the family,** but not through yours. You can use several methods to locate these people, including queries (both in magazines and on the Internet), telephone directories, letters to newspapers, and Internet sources.

A person who responds to your query might not have gotten back any further on the line than you have, but each of you might have information about descendants that the other doesn't have. Since research on your ancestors' siblings can help you find information on ancestors, pooling your information may provide clues that will help you extend the line. If not, at least you'll have filled in some blanks on your family group sheets.

Hidden Treasures

QUERIES IN MAGAZINES AND ON THE INTERNET

Queries have always been an important tool in genealogical research, but with the growth of the Internet, they have taken on a new life. In earlier chapters, you learned about subscribing to magazines and joining genealogical societies. One reason was to have access to magazines in which you could place queries. For example, thousands of people all over the country read *Everton's Genealogical Helper*, so a query placed there can reach far-flung descendants of your ancestors. Likewise, potential cousins all over the world can access a query on the Internet. If you have Internet access, it's wise to place queries on the Internet as well as in print vehicles. Researchers often find that people who work with one medium don't bother with the other; working with both will provide the widest possible audience for your queries.

Placing Queries on the Internet

There are many query sites on the Internet. The USGenWeb pages are one good outlet for queries on the Internet (see chapter nineteen for details on USGenWeb). USGenWeb pages exist for every state and for most counties, so people who read your queries are already focused on the area where your ancestor lived. One of the few requirements for USGenWeb pages is that they have a queries section. The main USGenWeb page, with links to the pages for each state, is at <http://www.usgenweb.org/index.html>.

Another site for queries is <http://genforum.familytreemaker.com/>. This site lists family names for which forums exist and gives instructions for starting a forum for a new name. The first page of a forum lists the subject lines of queries that people have posted there. You may be able to tell just from the subject line whether a query can help you; if not, look at it to be sure. Once you're there, post your own query for that family line.

If you have E-mail, you may want to use an E-mail list for your surname(s) of interest. Check the listing at <http://www.rootsweb.com/~maillist/surnames/index.html> to see if your surname is listed and how to join. If no list exists for your surname, consider starting one. You might not see much traffic on the list for a while, but eventually others interested in the surname might find the list and join in.

RootsWeb also sponsors bulletin boards for surnames at <http://genconnect.rootsweb.com/>. Each site has a list of subject lines from queries others have posted about the surname, showing the chain of correspondence following the original query. This allows you to see a query and track the discussion that springs from it. Clicking on any title will take you to that post.

How to Write a Good Query

Whether you're sending the query to a magazine or putting it on the Internet, the rules for writing a good query are the same. **First, some nitty-gritty procedural details:**

Step By Step

- When creating a query for a magazine, type the query using a word processor or a typewriter, if at all possible. If you must put the query on a form the magazine supplies and you have a computer, not a typewriter, print out the query and tape it to the form. Handwriting a query is counterproductive if it appears in print with a name misspelled because someone at the magazine couldn't read your writing.
- Type all surnames in the query in capital letters to set them off from given names. This is especially important when an ancestor's surname can also be used as a given name.
- Often queries are limited to a certain number of words, either by the policy of the publication or because you're paying by the word. You may be tempted

to skimp on words to save money or to fit as many people as possible into the fifty words the society allows you. Don't. It's better to write a longer query or one including fewer people. If you abbreviate it so much that readers aren't sure what you mean, a distant cousin who has information that could help you may not understand it and fail to reply.

- Send queries only to magazines that relate to the topic of the query. Don't send a query for people who live in California to the *Ohio Genealogical Society Newsletter* on the theory that "maybe someone who's researching in Ohio is also researching in California." The people in the query should have some obvious Ohio connection.

- Observe the magazine's rules when writing a query. If they say, "No more than fifty words," don't send a two hundred-word query. If they say, "Only two queries per member per year," don't send five queries at once.

To ensure the best results, include specific dates and places to identify the people you list in the query. Having these cuts down on the number of false drops in replies.

Some people, especially beginning genealogists, write queries like, "Searching for WILLIAMS, SMITH, BOWSER, WILSON, BROWN, THOMPSON, JONES, and SCHRECKENGOST," sometimes with a lengthy list of surnames. You may think advertising only a list of surnames without details will save money, but it's false economy. This type of query has many problems. A person who's researching only one name in the list who has found several queries in a magazine that connect with her lines might not want to waste her time responding to a query for a common surname which gives absolutely no hint that the family is the same as hers.

On the other hand, while your Smiths lived in Nevada, you may get letters from hopeful descendants of Smiths who lived all over the United States and have no connection with your line. Since you placed the ad, to follow the rules of genealogical courtesy—especially if they send you a SASE—you'll have to spend time sending responses saying, "Sorry, we're not researching the same line." If you had posted this query on the Internet, your online mailbox might be swamped with responses from people who are hopeful that your Smiths are their Smiths.

This sort of query can be effective if it includes relatively uncommon names. A person researching Schreckengost, a much less common name, would probably respond to this query. A person researching Thompson, who knew that Great-Great-Grandmother Thompson's sister married a Schreckengost, might write to the person who had placed this query. A query listing several uncommon names, such as "Researching DAUBENSPECK, MILLIRON, and SCHRE-CKENGOST," makes more sense than the example above.

If you decide to place a query listing only surnames rather than specific people, at least give the context of place(s) and time period(s) in which you know that these people lived. A person who has Carrs in Morgan County, Illinois, might not bother to respond to a query on "CARR, anywhere, any time" but would be

Tip

much more likely to respond to your query for "CARR in Morgan County, Illinois, ca. 1850."

As a courtesy, list the names in alphabetical order. The longer your list, the more important this is. Many people check genealogical queries against an alphabetical list of their ancestral surnames, and you make it easier for them if your list and their list are in the same order.

Thus, the first sample query in this chapter would be much more effective if it read "Searching for BOWSER, BROWN, JONES, SCHRECKENGOST, SMITH, THOMPSON, WILLIAMS, and WILSON in Armstrong County, PA, 1840s to 1900."

However, it's better to make your query even more specific, focusing on your problem ancestors in one line. Naming specific people in your query will help to eliminate the number of unrelated people who respond. Indicating a relationship between two or more people helps even more (although if the two people are a father and son with common names, such as James Smith and John Smith, you may still hear from a large number of unrelated people). It's best to focus on one specific person or couple. The query "Information on ancestors of Nancy BOWSER (BAUER?) (born 1804, died 1886), married ca. 1821 Samuel SCHRECKENGOST (born 9 July 1796, died after 1853), in Armstrong County, PA," includes more words than the original query, but you'll get fewer responses to it from people who aren't related to your line. Use parentheses and position to indicate to whom the dates belong. A query written as "Information on ancestors of William SCHRECKENGOST, married 14 August 1890 Susanna Catherine SMITH, born ca. 1866, died 1952" leaves the reader wondering whether William or Susanna Catherine was "born ca. 1866, died 1952."

HOW TO ANSWER QUERIES (AND WHEN NOT TO ANSWER THEM)

Write to someone in response to a query for the following reasons:
- You can tell from the query that you and the inquirer have the same line.
- Based on the information in the query, you and the inquirer possibly have the same line.
- You don't think that you and the inquirer have the same line, but you have some information that may help.

When sending a letter in response to a query, don't overload the person with information. Do you want to spend the time and money to photocopy and mail fifty pages of information only to have the person respond that it was nice of you to send it, but he already had copies of forty-nine of those pages in his files? In your first letter, outline the information you have to share, and ask how much (if any) of this the other person needs (see Figure 18-1 on page 160). The person may be inquiring about a collateral relative, and while you're interested in both the Schreckengost and Bowser lines, he may be interested only in the Bowser line and not care that you can trace the Schreckengosts back six generations.

QUERY SUMMARY: GOOD VS. BAD	
This:	Not This:
Seek information on John CHARLES, David JAMES, and Shadrack JONES.	Seek information on John Charles, David James, and Shadrack Jones.
Why: *Capitalizing entire surnames allows the reader to see that they're surnames, if the surnames aren't in all capitals, the reader might think that the three men share the surname Jones.*	
Searching for BOWSER, BROWN, JONES, SCHRECKENGOST, SMITH, THOMPSON, WILLIAMS, and WILSON, living in Armstrong County, PA, between 1800 and 1940.	Searching for WILLIAMS, BOWSER, SMITH, WILSON, BROWN, THOMPSON, JONES, and SCHRECKENGOST.
Why: *Giving context for the names, especially common names, gives the reader a clue that you share common ancestors before they spend time and money writing to you. Putting the names in alphabetical order helps someone who's checking names against her alphabetical list of names.*	
Information on ancestors of Nancy BOWSER (BAUER?) (born 1804, died 1886), married ca. 1821 Samuel SCHRECKENGOST (born 9 July 1796, died after 1853), in Armstrong County, PA.	Searching for WILLIAMS, BOWSER, SMITH, WILSON, BROWN, THOMPSON, JONES, and SCHRECKENGOST.
Why: *This query gives specifics, leaving no room for confusion. Readers can tell whether they're researching the same person. Use parentheses to clarify to whom dates refer.*	
CARR, KERR, Morgan County, IL, 1840s–1900s	CARR, KERR, anywhere, any time
Why: *Again, give a context for the name(s) you're researching.*	

Tip

As a rule, **your first letter should include your family group sheet for the family in question** (if the query mentions a married couple) **and/or a pedigree chart** (or charts) **showing your ancestry on the line.** You may only have one or two generations on a line and write to someone in hopes that he can help you extend the line. If so, print out a pedigree chart that includes your earliest known ancestor on the line and three more recent generations to give the person a good context for your family. Place your name, address, telephone number, and E-mail address on all family group sheets and pedigree charts you send to make it easier for someone to locate you if, five years from now, he finds something that might help you and wants to get in touch with you. Even if you've moved, your phone number and/or E-mail address might be the same.

[Your postal address, phone number, and E-mail address]

[date]

[name and address of recipient]

Dear Sean,

I saw your query in the latest issue of *Everton's Genealogical Helper* asking for information on Jacob Milliron (Muhleisen) who died in Westmoreland County, Pennsylvania, in August 1786. I am also a descendant of Jacob Milliron. I enclose a family group sheet for Jacob to show you the information I have collected on him and a pedigree chart showing my line of descent from him.

I would be interested to know what your line of descent from Jacob is. Also, I would appreciate knowing if you can add anything to the family group sheet or suggest any documented corrections.

I have collected quite a lot of information on the Milliron family and would be happy to share once I know what you need.

Thank you for any help you can give me on this line. I enclose a self-addressed, stamped envelope for your convenience in replying.

Sincerely,

[your name]

> **Specify the query and family name to which you are responding.**

> **Rather than go into a long description of your family, enclose pedigree charts and family group sheets that show graphically your connection and the information you already have. Your footnotes on the family group sheets will show some of the documents you have.**

> **Ask for *documented* corrections.**

> **Offer to share what you know.**

> **Enclose a SASE.**

Figure 18-1 Letter in response to a query: you know you have the same line

Someone who has advertised one name in your ancestral area may have other lines in common with you as well—you'll never know until you ask. Put together a one-page list of names you're researching to enclose with letters (see Figure 18-2 on page 161 and Figure 18-3 on page 162).

If it's obvious that the inquirer is researching the same line, ask her to let you know, based on the pedigree chart you've enclosed, what other information you might have that she needs. You may descend from two different children of the married couple listed in her query, or you may share four or five generations in common. Also ask if she'll share the information she has on the family. A few genealogists consider the information they have collected their own private property; they are happy to have you send them information but never quite get around to sending you anything. But most genealogists are generous and happy to share whatever they have.

If you only think it's possible that you and the inquirer share the same line,

---

(Your postal address, E-mail address, and phone number)

NEW ENGLAND SURNAMES IN THE LINE OF JAMES W. OPPENHEIMER

(Immigrants indicated in parentheses when known)

Buck
Burnham (Thomas)

Cheney (John and William)
Clement(s) (Robert)
Crosby (Jane, daughter of Robert)

Day
Hildreth (Richard)
Hinchman?
Lawrence (Marie, daughter of Thomas and Joan Antrobus)

Low (Thomas)
Pearson (John)
Pengry (Moses)
Pickard (John)

Plummer (Francis)
Safford (John, Thomas)
Thurston (John)

Todd (Margaret, m. Thomas Low)
Warren (Arthur)
Wheeler (John)
Wise (Humphrey)

Yeoman (Agnes, m. John Wheeler)

Figure 18-2 List of surnames of people you're researching: throughout an area

send the person a pedigree chart showing your connection with the line. For example, in response to the original sample query above including Schreckengost, send a pedigree chart that includes your Schreckengost-Bowser marriage. This puts the family in context and allows the inquirer to see easily if they're the same line he's researching. (See Figure 18-4 on page 163.)

In the third case, you have a "problem ancestor" and have been collecting everything you can on the name in the locality in hopes of finding his ancestors. While Muskingum County, Ohio, is swarming with Crawfords, William Henderson Crawford, who married Elizabeth Wilson there on 4 August 1853, seems to have appeared out of thin air, with no apparent relationship to any of the other Crawfords. In your futile search for his family, you have collected reams of data on those other Crawfords, in hopes that someday you'll be able to fit William in with them. You see a query from someone who's researching a specific Crawford family in Muskingum County. Do you say, "That's not my line;

(Your postal address, E-mail address, and phone number)

NAMES I'M RESEARCHING IN PENNSYLVANIA

Names on my mother's line in Armstrong and surrounding counties (including Clarion, Indiana, Jefferson, and Westmoreland; also Daubenspeck in Butler), from about 1760 on:

Ackerman	Doverspike	King (König)	Reese
Aukerman	Eisenmann	Lytle	Schreckengost
Allen	Fiscus	McMaster(s)	Shellhammer
Altman	Heilman	Milliron/Muhleisen	Walker
Daubenspeck	Hindman	Rader	

In western or northwestern Pennsylvania (family appears in Illinois, but came from Pennsylvania, exact location not established):

John K **Reid/Reed/Read** (1798–1851), married Elizabeth **West** (1794–1890)

On my husband's line, mostly in Butler County, but also some in Westmoreland County:

Black	Hayes/Hays	Plummer	Russell
Burke	Henderson	Roney	Stewart
Frazier	Murray		

and Col. James **Smith** (1737—1812) of Franklin and Westmoreland counties, leader of the "Black Boys" and a Revolutionary soldier (died in Kentucky), and wife Anna **Wilson**. In eastern Pennsylvania, before 1800, ancestors of the various western Pennsylvania lines, plus:

Abraham	Dickson	Harter	Ream/Riehm
Ashbaugh	Eschbach	Hartzell	Scholl
Beck	George	Kiehl	Wynne
Carl/Charles	Geiger	Knau	Zartman
Criswell	Greninger	Linville	

Figure 18-3 List of surnames of people you're researching: several areas

I won't bother with this person," or do you say, "I'll write to this person. I can't prove that this is my line, but I have some information that might help him. Maybe he has some information that will help me!"

The answer is obvious. You take the chance that the inquirer has the long-lost family Bible showing that your William Henderson Crawford is the brother of his Oliver Crawford. Send a family group sheet for your William, explaining that you're having trouble extending his line. Tell the person what you have in your files that might help him, and ask whether he's interested in it (see Figure 18-5 on page 164). Even if he can't help you now, he might put the family group sheet in his files; five years from now, when he finds something that can help you and remembers that you once helped him, he might contact you.

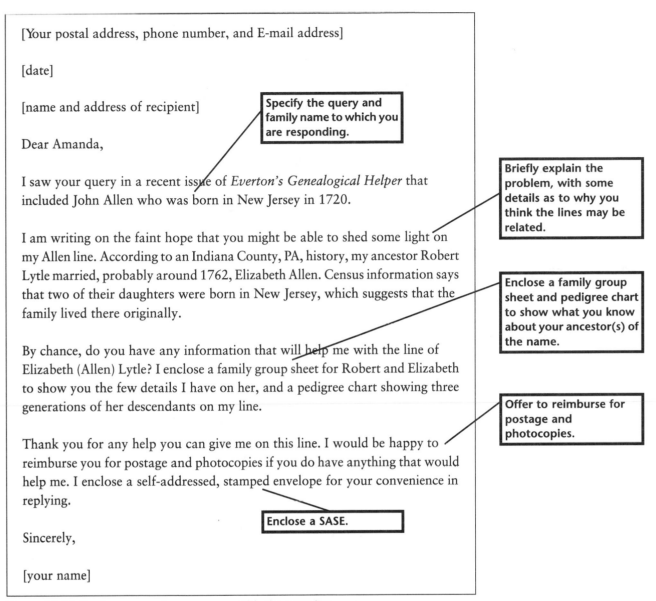

[Your postal address, phone number, and E-mail address]

[date]

[name and address of recipient]

Dear Amanda,

> **Specify the query and family name to which you are responding.**

I saw your query in a recent issue of *Everton's Genealogical Helper* that included John Allen who was born in New Jersey in 1720.

> **Briefly explain the problem, with some details as to why you think the lines may be related.**

I am writing on the faint hope that you might be able to shed some light on my Allen line. According to an Indiana County, PA, history, my ancestor Robert Lytle married, probably around 1762, Elizabeth Allen. Census information says that two of their daughters were born in New Jersey, which suggests that the family lived there originally.

> **Enclose a family group sheet and pedigree chart to show what you know about your ancestor(s) of the name.**

By chance, do you have any information that will help me with the line of Elizabeth (Allen) Lytle? I enclose a family group sheet for Robert and Elizabeth to show you the few details I have on her, and a pedigree chart showing three generations of her descendants on my line.

> **Offer to reimburse for postage and photocopies.**

Thank you for any help you can give me on this line. I would be happy to reimburse you for postage and photocopies if you do have anything that would help me. I enclose a self-addressed, stamped envelope for your convenience in replying.

> **Enclose a SASE.**

Sincerely,

[your name]

Figure 18-4 Letter in response to a query: possibly the same line

At times, you might be tempted to reply to a query when you really shouldn't—the query includes a name you're researching, but the date and/or locality listed in the query differ from those you're researching. For example, you see an ad for "James SMITH (b. ca. 1737 Conococheague Settlement, PA, died ca. 1812, Washington Co., KY), married 1763 Anna Wilson (born ca. 1745, died ca. 1778)." No matter how desperate you are to extend your Smith line, if you've only gotten back to 1900 in New York, don't write to this person just because "she lives in New York, so maybe her Smiths went there later." Nothing in this ad suggests that she's researching Smith in New York, and by writing to her, you'll probably waste both your time and hers.

This caveat doesn't hold quite so true for unusual names. If one of the names in the ad above had been Schreckengost rather than Smith, you might have

Disclaimer about lack of relationship, and then explanation of why you have information on the family.

Give name and address of person who might be able to help.

Offer to supply copies of the information if that person is no longer reachable.

Give information on your problem line in case the other person can help.

[Your postal address, phone number, and E-mail address]

[date]

[name and address of recipient]

Dear Heather,

I saw your query in the latest issue of *Everton's Genealogical Helper* asking for information on John Crawford who married Sarah Johnston on 18 August 1814 in Muskingum County, Ohio.

As far as I know, I have no connection with this John Crawford. However, in trying to identify the parents of my ancestor, William Henderson Crawford, who first surfaces with his marriage to Elizabeth Wilson in Muskingum County in 1853, I have collected quite a bit of information on Crawfords in this area. I have some information on your John Crawford that I received from Lydia Smith who is also researching that line. Her address is 110 Main Street, Anytown, Anystate.

If you write to her and don't get an answer, please let me know and I'll be happy to send you photocopies of what I have from her.

I enclose a family group sheet for my William Henderson Crawford to show you the information I have collected on him in case you might have anything that would help me with his line.

Thank you for any help you can give me on this line. I would be happy to reimburse you for postage and photocopies if you do have anything on it. I enclose a self-addressed, stamped envelope for your convenience in replying.

Sincerely,

[your name]

Enclose a SASE.

Figure 18-5 Letter in response to a query: not the same line, but you can help the person

been justified in writing to the person to see if she had any information that would help you.

CD Source

CD-ROM SOURCES FOR NETWORKING

Several CD-ROM sources can help with networking. Some are collections of family group sheets or family trees submitted by genealogists—usually hobby genealogists. Take the information on these CDs with a grain of salt. Often, submitters to the disks give no sources for the events or relationships, so you don't know whether the submitter had reliable information or whether it was just a guess. Use the information on these CDs as a guide for further research. You can usually find out the submitter's name and address from the CD-ROM itself or through the company that published it. Write to the submitter to offer to share information and to get details about sources. These CDs include

- *Ancestral File* (a lineage-linked database from submitters' family group sheets, available at Family History Centers and selected other libraries; also available on the Internet [see chapters twelve and nineteen for more information])
- *Everton's Computerized Family File* (includes actual family group sheets that have been scanned and indexed; these usually include the submitter's name and address)
- *Everton's Computerized "Roots" Cellar, 1640–1990* (listings include an ancestor's name with one event: birth, death, marriage, or residence; a date and place for the event; and submitter information)
- *International Genealogical Index* (index of many sources, both public records and information from individuals, available at Family History Centers and selected other libraries. Part of it is available on the Internet [see chapters twelve and nineteen for more information])
- *World Family Tree* (a series of CD-ROMs from Brøderbund. These include family group sheets and pedigree charts that Brøderbund collected from hobby genealogists. Request information on a contributor's identity at <http://www.familytreemaker.com/cgi-bin/subinfo.cgi>.)

Remember two things when working with CD-ROM products:
- Some data on these products is quite old, and a person who submitted information may no longer be at the same address or may be dead.
- People can submit anything they want to; vendors include it in the CDs without verifying it. Don't take it as gospel truth.

INTERNET SOURCES FOR LOCATING DISTANT COUSINS

Many Internet sources allow you to locate people researching a specific surname. Some of these sources are

- http://www.CyndisList.com/surnames.htm
  A page from Cyndi's List with links to pages for specific surnames, family associations, and family newsletters.
- http://www.ancestry.com/
  Searches for a name in the Ancestry World Tree files. You get basic data for people it finds by that name, the submitter's E-mail address, and the ability to download file(s) containing information on that name at no charge.
- http://www.familytreemaker.com/iffintro.html
  Internet FamilyFinder: Links to both Web pages and databases, including

Internet Source

Brøderbund CD-ROMs; these include the World Family Tree data. Links to Web pages are free; getting the information from most of the databases requires a subscription.
- http://www.gendex.com/gendex/
  GENDEX WWW Genealogical Index to World Wide Web databases: Search for a name, and get links to Web pages containing genealogical data.
- http://www.one-name.org/
  Guild of One-Name Studies: Check their site to find out if someone is doing a one-name study on a surname in which you're interested. People involved in one-name studies are theoretically researching all occurrences of a specific surname, anywhere in the world.
- http://rsl.rootsweb.com/cgi-bin/rslsql.cgi/
  The RootsWeb Surname List allows you to search a list of more than 600,000 surnames submitted by more than 75,000 genealogists.

PHONE DIRECTORIES

Telephone directories are another source of networking information. In the old days, genealogists recommended that you get someone in your ancestral locality to send you copies of phone book pages for your surnames of interest or that you purchase the local phone book from the telephone company. Then you could write to people of that surname to see if any of them had information on your lines.

Although the principle remains the same, it's now much easier to get addresses for people who share your ancestor's surname. You can still request phone books through the telephone company, but now there are CD-ROM telephone directories that cover the whole United States. If you don't have a CD-ROM drive, you may find such a directory at your local library. If you're researching an unusual surname, search these databases to create a list of people with that name; write to them to find out if they have any information on their family heritage and whether their line connects with yours. Some Internet sites with similar phone books include
- Switchboard
  http://www.switchboard.com/
- Phone Number Search
  http://www.familytreemaker.com/wwphone.html

Warning

Be aware that CD-ROM and Internet phone books aren't always inclusive or accurate.
Once you have gone through phone books to identify people with the surname you're researching, stop and think before you contact them. Should you really contact all these people? Choose people to whom you will write using an equation based on how close they live to your ancestral area and how (un)common the surname is. For a relatively common surname, write only to people who live close to the ancestral area (those in the same county, or at most, those in surrounding counties). If the surname is a common one like Wilson, and your ancestors were

in Illinois, it isn't a good idea to write to the Wilsons in California (not to mention that writing to all the Wilsons in the United States would strain your bank account!). If the name is less common, consider writing at least to those within the state where your ancestor lived and maybe to those in surrounding states. If the surname is so uncommon that you find only ten or twelve listings in the national phone book, by all means, write to all of these people.

Even though you used a telephone book to locate these people, see chapter two for a discussion of why you should contact them by letter rather than by phone. Explain that you're doing family history research, that one of your ancestors

See Also

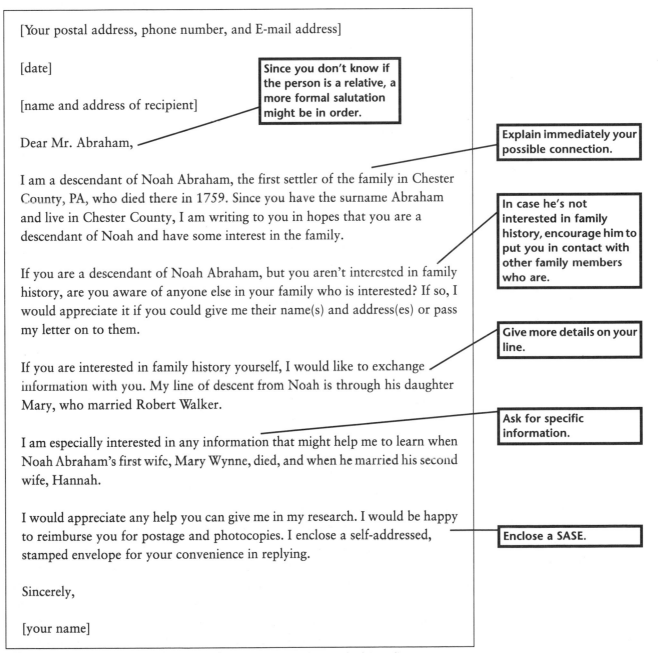

[Your postal address, phone number, and E-mail address]

[date]

[name and address of recipient]

> Since you don't know if the person is a relative, a more formal salutation might be in order.

Dear Mr. Abraham,

I am a descendant of Noah Abraham, the first settler of the family in Chester County, PA, who died there in 1759. Since you have the surname Abraham and live in Chester County, I am writing to you in hopes that you are a descendant of Noah and have some interest in the family.

> Explain immediately your possible connection.

If you are a descendant of Noah Abraham, but you aren't interested in family history, are you aware of anyone else in your family who is interested? If so, I would appreciate it if you could give me their name(s) and address(es) or pass my letter on to them.

> In case he's not interested in family history, encourage him to put you in contact with other family members who are.

If you are interested in family history yourself, I would like to exchange information with you. My line of descent from Noah is through his daughter Mary, who married Robert Walker.

> Give more details on your line.

I am especially interested in any information that might help me to learn when Noah Abraham's first wife, Mary Wynne, died, and when he married his second wife, Hannah.

> Ask for specific information.

I would appreciate any help you can give me in my research. I would be happy to reimburse you for postage and photocopies. I enclose a self-addressed, stamped envelope for your convenience in replying.

> Enclose a SASE.

Sincerely,

[your name]

Figure 18-6 Letter to someone whose name you have found in a telephone directory

had this person's surname, and you're writing in hopes that he might have some information on the family history or know someone who's researching the family (see Figure 18-6 on page 167). Include a pedigree chart showing your line back to your earliest known ancestor of the surname in question.

The person to whom you write might be interested in family history and have some material to share with you. Maybe he isn't interested in family history, but he will send you copies of pages from an old family Bible listing births, marriages, and deaths, which include information that will help you. Or he isn't working on family history himself, but he knows someone who has been working on the family and will give you that person's name and address.

Other people have an interesting response to this sort of letter. While they haven't previously had an interest in the family history, your letter piques their curiosity, and they go out and do some research. Perhaps they go to a graveyard where family members are buried and copy the inscriptions on the stones for you. This could develop into something, because the genealogy virus is hard to shake. By writing this kind of letter, you may plant the genealogy bug in a new family historian, one who's in the right place to dig up some useful information about your family.

There are three other possible reactions to your letter. The person may respond that, yes, this is her family, but she has no information. Or she may reply that she has no connection with the family. And finally, some people won't bother to respond. Possibly they don't answer because they don't know anything and it's too much trouble to write back to you (even though you did include a self-addressed, stamped envelope). You may write to these people again ("I wrote to you three months ago and haven't heard anything . . ."). If you do, be careful how you phrase the letter. The person doesn't owe you anything, and on the chance that she does have some information or connections that might help, you don't want to antagonize her. Any follow-up letters you write should be extremely polite, not demanding or threatening.

LETTERS TO NEWSPAPERS IN THE AREA WHERE YOUR ANCESTOR LIVED

Tip

Chapter eleven tells you how to learn what newspapers were and are published in the area where you ancestors lived. **If you think descendants of your ancestor may still live in the area, consider writing a letter to the local newspaper asking for help.** Make this letter short and to the point (see Figure 18-7 on page 169). Most newspapers like to keep letters short, say, 250 words. If you write a fifteen-page novelette about your ancestors, one of two things might happen. The editor might not print it at all—so your effort will be wasted. Alternatively, the editor might edit the letter. Unfortunately, since the editor isn't familiar with the family, and perhaps your letter rambled a little, the rewritten letter may feature your great-great-great grandmother—married to her grandson. Oops! Descendants who are still in the area and read such a letter won't be impressed. Of course, they may write to you to correct "your error," but they will have a bad impression of you.

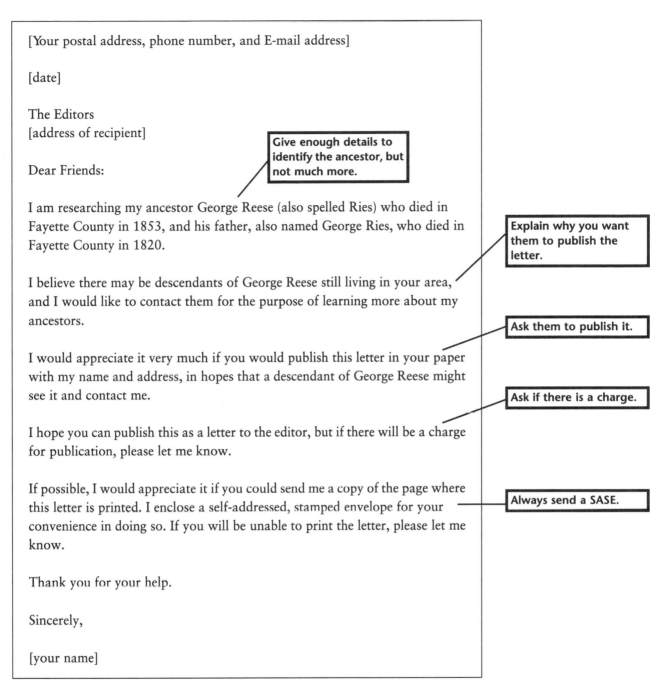

[Your postal address, phone number, and E-mail address]

[date]

The Editors
[address of recipient]

Give enough details to identify the ancestor, but not much more.

Dear Friends:

I am researching my ancestor George Reese (also spelled Ries) who died in Fayette County in 1853, and his father, also named George Ries, who died in Fayette County in 1820.

I believe there may be descendants of George Reese still living in your area, and I would like to contact them for the purpose of learning more about my ancestors.

Explain why you want them to publish the letter.

I would appreciate it very much if you would publish this letter in your paper with my name and address, in hopes that a descendant of George Reese might see it and contact me.

Ask them to publish it.

I hope you can publish this as a letter to the editor, but if there will be a charge for publication, please let me know.

Ask if there is a charge.

If possible, I would appreciate it if you could send me a copy of the page where this letter is printed. I enclose a self-addressed, stamped envelope for your convenience in doing so. If you will be unable to print the letter, please let me know.

Always send a SASE.

Thank you for your help.

Sincerely,

[your name]

Figure 18-7 Letter to a newspaper in the area where your ancestor lived

Make your letter something like the queries discussed earlier in this chapter. Ask only about one or two couples, and give a few identifying details. If someone recognizes these as common ancestors and writes to you, then you can share all those fascinating family stories.

SHARE MAJOR DISCOVERIES

If at some point in your research you make a major breakthrough on a line (e.g., you locate the elusive marriage record for the ancestors who were married in 1756), write to all the people with whom you've corresponded on that line, and let them know. You can do this easily with a photocopied "Dear Cousins" letter. If you haven't been in touch for a while, they might have made a major discovery about which they didn't think to tell you, and your letter will reopen lines of communication.

CONCLUSION

Queries in magazines and on the Internet can help you locate other people who are researching your lines. Take advantage of both by placing your own queries and responding to queries of people who may be related to you. Searches of CD-ROM compilations of family groups, many of which are also available on the Internet, and phone books can also help you identify and contact distant relatives. Some pieces of family information never make it into public records; by contacting distant cousins, you may find priceless information on your line.

NINETEEN

It's All on the Internet, Isn't It?

T o be quite blunt, no. You can find some genealogical information on the Internet, but by no means is all of what you need out there. Things don't just magically appear on the Internet; it takes work to put material up. It also takes money: server space, phone lines, and other items needed for Internet access aren't free. Beyond these considerations, some information you would like to access can't be mounted on the Internet for legal reasons.

On the other hand, some information is available on the Internet, and it can be helpful for long-distance research. The Internet has greatly improved the lot of the long-distance genealogist, and more material is available every day.

LIMITATIONS OF THE INTERNET

Before you learn what's good about the Internet, you need to know a few of its limitations. First, many people are mounting their genealogical research on the Internet. If you find that someone has made information available relating to your family, great! But has he included his sources for the material? If so, go back to the sources and verify. If not, contact the person and ask him what his sources are, especially if you find that he has put up information that conflicts with what you've found (especially if his information conflicts with information that you've verified in primary sources). Are his sources primary or secondary? Are they trustworthy? Anyone can mount anything on the Internet; there are no Internet Police doing fact checking. Many people construct their genealogy from published materials that contain as much fiction as fact and never verify in primary sources. Other people desperately want to be related to a famous person or to have a line that allows them to join a hereditary society. People have been known to bend the truth a little or make a connection between a "father" and "son" with no actual proof of a relationship (after all, they *did* have the same last name, didn't they?) to add this wished-for relationship to their pedigree charts.

Warning

Even if you find the material on a commercial site, be careful. Several companies collect genealogical information from people, put it into CD-ROM and/or Internet format, and sell it. They don't check the material first. They are merely facilitating contacts between genealogists.

As with any transcription, when you find a transcription of primary source materials on the Internet, use it only as a guide. This is no time for thrift. Write for a copy of the original for two reasons. First, the transcription you found on the Internet might include errors. Second, the original might include more information than the transcription, and that additional information might be just what you need to extend your line.

Some Internet sites save you the trouble of writing that letter by actually scanning the original documents and making them available to you online, but for financial reasons (it takes time to scan and index the documents, and scanned documents take up a lot of server space), these sites are few and far between.

Another limitation of the Internet for genealogical research is that many commercial sites make information available on the Internet—for a fee. That's why they're called "commercial." The fees aren't huge, but subscribing to several sites could be expensive. In most cases, these sites help you make the decision about subscribing by letting you do searches up to a certain point. Input a name to get a response telling you how many hits the search got. In some cases, you'll get a response telling you, for example, the state from which the information came (e.g., three hits for George Schreckengost in Pennsylvania and four hits for George Schreckengost in Ohio), so you have some idea whether the hits might pertain to your family. If your George Schreckengost lived all his life in Nevada, you might not want to pay to pursue this search. Given the number of databases the various commercial sites offer, it's tempting to pay the money to access them and take a week or two of vacation to take advantage of those memberships and seek out all the information you can get about your ancestors! Most of the commercial sites continue to add databases on a regular basis.

One more limitation relates to material written about the Internet, not to the Internet itself. The Internet is constantly changing; anything written about it may be obsolete before it hits the paper and certainly has a chance of being obsolete before it's published. Internet addresses change, sites are redesigned, sites stop offering some services and add others. Although this chapter lists some good sites to check, one of the best ways to find out about the Internet is simply to surf it. Also, pay close attention to Internet-related articles in the magazines to which you subscribe. Most genealogical magazines now include short articles or columns describing good sites.

HOW CAN THE INTERNET HELP ME WITH LONG-DISTANCE RESEARCH?

Simply put, the Internet can help you with long-distance research by bringing the whole world to your den or bedroom or whatever room houses your computer. You can find

- transcriptions of records

- genealogical databases
- library catalogs
- scanned images of books
- genealogical information people have mounted

You can send E-mail to people who will respond in a few hours, satisfying your need for instant gratification. If you're curious about the area where your ancestors lived, you might find Web pages with information about the county or town, and possibly pictures. If you go to that area to visit and do research, you can use the Internet to get detailed driving directions with a map and locate a hotel.

MAJOR INTERNET RESOURCES FOR THE GENEALOGIST

You've read in other chapters of this book about some major Internet resources that deal with specific subjects. There are many this book hasn't covered—so many that it's nearly impossible to list them all. However, you should definitely know about some of them.

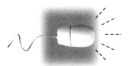

Internet Source

Most people agree that there is one site every genealogist should visit: Cyndi's List, at <http://www.CyndisList.com/>. Cyndi Howells takes all Internet pages related to genealogy that she can identify (thousands of them—maybe hundreds of thousands by the time you read this!) and catalogs them according to subject matter. Start your research here.

The long-distance researcher should definitely look at the USGenWeb sites, starting from their main page at <http://www.usgenweb.org/>. This ambitious project's goal, now close to being reached, is to have a home page for every county in the United States. The main page links to state pages, which in turn link to county pages. Once you've found the home page for your ancestral county, bookmark it and come back to it often. Information that's mounted varies according to what's available to the coordinator for the county, but each county page is required to set up a section where people can exchange queries relating to families who lived in that county. Other information may include items such as cemetery readings, transcriptions of census records, information on county genealogical and historical societies, maps, obituaries, and in general, whatever is available in the county that someone can mount on the Internet. Many counties have E-mail lists for people researching the county. While some of the people on these lists live far from the county in question, some of them live right in the county and might have ready access to information that could help you.

If you have a problem ancestor who appeared out of nowhere, but you have a definite clue about what state he came from (for example, his Texas death certificate says that he was born in Ohio), investigate the state-level pages of the USGenWeb. Actually, look at them even if you know the county your ancestor came from. At the state level, you can post a query for the ancestor for whom you have no specific place of residence in the state. You'll also find background information on the state's history. As with the county pages, material on a state page varies according to what's available.

For More Info

READ MORE ABOUT IT!

Some books about genealogy on the Internet (with dates to suggest how current the Web addresses are) include

- Bentley, *The Genealogist's Address Book* (1998). Not strictly an Internet guide, but includes some Web addresses in its listings.

- Helm and Helm, *Genealogy Online for Dummies* (1999). Not only do you get a book that answers questions about doing genealogical research on the Internet and gives lists of helpful Web sites, you get a CD-ROM loaded with useful programs for Internet genealogy research. Some are demonstrations (test programs to decide whether to purchase them), some are freeware (use them with no strings attached), and some are shareware (try them, and if you continue to use them, pay a registration fee). These include genealogy programs; Internet tools, such as E-mail readers and Web browsers; multimedia tools; and utilities.

- Howells, *Cyndi's List: A Comprehensive List of 40,000 Genealogy Sites on the Internet* (1999). It's fun to surf Cyndi's List on the Internet, but sometimes it's overwhelming. This book can be especially valuable if you have to pay for your Internet time by the minute. Curl up it in your easy chair with it, and plan your next Internet session.

- Howells, *Netting Your Ancestors: Genealogical Research on the Internet* (1997). Gives detailed instructions for getting onto the Internet, using E-mail, working with mailing lists and newsgroups, and using the World Wide Web efficiently. Of course, a book from the creator of Cyndi's List would be incomplete without a list of good Internet sources.

- Kemp, *Virtual Roots: A Guide to Genealogy and Local History on the World Wide Web* (1997). Kemp has put together a directory of Web pages on general subjects (e.g., African Americans, church records, heraldry, Palatines, etc.), the United States (broken down by state and, where available, listing Web addresses for such things as the state home page, archives, genealogical society, historical society, and other state sites), international sites (broken down by country; for most countries, only one or a few Web pages, such as the page for the national library, are listed), and family associations. This book includes only Web addresses, not Internet instruction.

- Renick and Wilson, *The Internet for Genealogists: A Beginner's Guide* (1998). A detailed guide to getting onto and using the Internet, with a list of worthwhile Web pages.

- Schaefer, *Instant Information on the Internet! A Genealogist's No-Frills Guide to the 50 States & the District of Columbia* (1999). "No-frills" means this book includes only Web site addresses, not information on using the Internet. It's divided by state and includes many listings, such as the state archives, library, genealogical society and historical society, and selected other libraries and historical societies. Other headings for each state are "Information Sites," "Selected Indexes and Documents Online," and "Lists and Links."

- Smith, *The Ancestry Family Historian's Address Book* (1997). Not strictly an Internet guide, but includes Web addresses in many of its listings.

Chapter thirteen mentions several CD-ROMs that are available at Family History Centers. Much of the material from these is now available online as well at <http://www.familysearch.org/>. The main page at this site allows you to choose between "Ancestor Search," "Keyword Search," and "Custom Search."

- **Ancestor Search** searches the Ancestral File (more than 35,000,000 names), International Genealogical Index (IGI; more than 600,000,000 names), and an index of thousands of Web sites. You can search simply the first and last name of a person or add the names of the spouse and/or parents. A check box allows you to indicate whether to use exact spelling of surnames or Soundex for searching indexes. In a Soundex search, hunting for someone with the surname Reid can turn up people with names like Read, Reade, and Reed. With Soundex, the search engine also ignores middle initials, so if you search for "John K. Reid," the results will include John M. Read, John Wesley Reed, etc. With an exact spelling search, you'll retrieve only matches for John K. Reid. Searches of Web sites look only for the surnames you've entered.

    Once you've gotten results, you can filter them by choosing to look at results only from Ancestral File, Web sites, or a geographical division of the IGI.
- **Keyword Search** allows you to search for any keyword in the Web sites and SourceGuide.
- **Custom Search** allows you to choose to search only the Ancestral File, the IGI, the Family History Library Catalog, the SourceGuide, the Web sites ("[t]housands of Web sites categorized by our volunteers"), or collaboration lists ("[c]ollaboration mailing lists created by registered users of FamilySearch Internet"). Also use Custom Search to locate a Family History Center near you.

The SourceGuide has three divisions:
- **How-To Guides** includes guides to using various types of resources, such as the IGI, *Periodical Source Index* (*PERSI*), etc.; other resources, such as Latin Genealogical Word List; blank forms, such as Research Log and Family Group Sheets; and research outlines that describe major sources for researching people who lived in the United States, Canadian provinces, European countries, and Latin America.
- **Word Meanings** gives definitions of words from the How-To Guides.

- **Catalog Helper** asks questions about your search and lists subject headings to look under in the Family History Library Catalog and How-To Guides that might help you locate information on your research goal.

Other links from the FamilySearch main page allow you to submit family information to the site, add a site, order family history resources (such as CD-ROMs of Ancestral File or the 1851 British census), learn more about the Church of Jesus Christ of Latter-day Saints, give feedback, and ask for help.

RootsWeb at <http://www.rootsweb.com/> provides all kinds of Internet services for genealogists, including many home pages, and has set up E-mail lists for thousands of family names (see chapter eighteen for more details).

The National Archives realizes that, while genealogical research is not its intended function, many of its records are of great interest to genealogists, and, it has mounted The Genealogy Page at <http://www.nara.gov/genealogy/genindex.html>. This includes links to the text of several NARA publications of use to genealogists, plus other sites of interest.

Look at the home page of the state archives in your ancestral state, and maybe those of other states, too. Many of these archives also have realized that genealogists comprise a large percentage of their customers, so the archives have developed pages to help with genealogical research. See appendix E for their Web site addresses.

Reminder

Internet sites from several genealogical companies make information available for researchers—free of charge, by subscription, or both. Part of the *raison d'être* of these sites is to sell the company's products. However, they do provide useful genealogical information. Many of the commercial sites include online genealogical columns, pages of advice on doing research, etc. Most have databases available for searching, some free and some for a subscription fee. Often both free and fee are available on the same site; free databases may be teasers that eventually tell you there's information about an ancestor on a database or CD-ROM available from the company for a charge. While subscriptions may seem expensive, compared to the price of a trip to a distant courthouse or library, they could be remarkably reasonable. Some major commercial sites include

- Ancestry
  http://www.ancestry.com/
  Check Ancestry's site regularly because it includes a list of new databases, which you can search free for the first ten days after they are available.
- Everton Publishers
  http://www.everton.com/
- Family Tree Magazine
  http://www.familytreemagazine.com
- Family Tree Maker
  http://www.familytreemaker.com/
- Heritage Quest
  http://www.heritagequest.com/

The Web site for the ten-part *Ancestors* series from public television is at <http://www2.kbyu.byu.edu/ancestors/>. These pages include such things as guides to the series (both teacher's guide and viewer's guide), blank forms, and a page of tips and tricks submitted by readers.

If you haven't bought genealogical software or you're thinking about upgrading, Genealogy Software Springboard at <http://www.gensoftsb.com/> provides information on the pros and cons of various software programs, submitted by users of those programs.

Finally, no discussion of genealogical sites on the Internet should neglect the International Black Sheep Society of Genealogists home page at <http://homepages.rootsweb.com/~blksheep/index.html>. This society exists to allow genealogists to glorify the misdeeds and misfortunes of their ancestors. The society itself "includes all those who have a dastardly, infamous individual of public knowledge and ill repute in their family . . . within one degree of consanguinity of their direct lines." Links from the main page include sites such as Historical Links (to Pirate Site, Salem Witch Trials Chronology, etc.). The Member Stories site (a sort of "Black Sheep Anonymous" page, since members are identified only by their first names) includes stories like this one, chosen at random: "Darrell's Grandfather was never married to his Grandmother, but fathered all of her children as well as the children of her 2 sisters."

USING SEARCH ENGINES TO FIND GENEALOGICAL MATERIAL
Genealogy-Specific Search Engines

Internet Source

Several search engines on the Internet are aimed specifically at genealogists. Try searching all of these sites. Because they use different methods of identifying relevant data, a search on one site may yield no hits for a name, while a search on another site may yield several hits for the same name. Some of the pages these sites find require a subscription fee to view the information.

The site Family History SuperSearch, at <http://www.familytreemagazine.com/search/>, allows you to choose which of several genealogical databases (including most of the ones listed in this book) to search simultaneously. You also have the option to search the "Best 3," the "Fastest 3," or "All" of the databases provided).

Internet FamilyFinder, at <http://www.genealogy.com/genealogy/ifftop.html>, allows you to search for a person by name. However, when you get to the resulting pages, you may find that the first and last name you specified appear in a page but belong to different people. The Internet Family Finder doesn't use proximity.

GENDEX WWW Genealogical Index, <http://www.gendex.com/gendex/>, allows you to search the Web by surname and find names linked in family groups.

RootsWeb has a surname search engine at <http://surhelp.rootsweb.com/srchall.html> that allows you to search by name, Soundex code, names that start with certain letters (you must use at least three letters), names with wild card characters, and names with identified alternate spellings. These searches can be helpful if the spelling of your family's name has changed over the years. You can search the USGenWeb and WorldGenWeb, personal genealogy pages, surname-oriented pages, "other," or all of these combined. These options give you much flexibility in doing searches.

GeneaNet, <http://www.geneanet.org/>, allows you to do a simple surname search or a more advanced search where you specify surname, location, type of record desired, etc.

I Found It!, <http://www.gensource.com/ifoundit/>, is a directory of genealogical sources on the Internet.

YourFamily.com at <http://www.yourfamily.com/>, is specifically designed to find family home pages on the Internet.

GenealogyPortal.com at <http://www.genealogyportal.com/>, allows you to search for sites using these categories: names and personal sites, archives and libraries, guides to research, historical sites (to give you background information on events in your ancestor's life), location-specific sites (including historical and genealogical societies), primary records, research supplies, and software and utilities.

General Search Engines

If your surname is unusual, try searching it with a general search engine (note: don't try this if you're researching the name Smith!). If the surname is relatively common, but the person's given name is uncommon (Eliphalet, for example), search the given name and surname as a phrase. There are many general search engines on the Internet. Perhaps you already have a favorite; search with it, and then try searching with another one. The results can be quite varied, as each search engine works differently.

SOME E-MAIL RESOURCES FOR THE LONG-DISTANCE GENEALOGIST

In addition to Web sites, **the Internet also enhances your research through the capabilities of E-mail.** Beyond personal E-mail, several types of E-mail resources are available to the genealogist.

E-mail newsletters provide a wealth of information from experts. These include

Internet Source

- *Eastman's Online Genealogy Newsletter* (sign up at <http://www.ancestry.com/columns/eastman/eastnew.htm>)
- *RootsWeb Review* and *Missing Links* (sign up at <http://www.rootsweb.com/>)
- *DearMYRTLE's Daily Genealogy Column*, written by Pat Richley (sign up at <http://www.dearmyrtle.com/>)
- *Ancestry Daily News* (sign up at <http://www.ancestry.com/dailynews/dailynews.htm>)
- George Morgan's "Along Those Lines" (at <http://members.aol.com/alon

glines/>; mounted each Friday at the Genealogy Forum on America Online, at the Ancestry.com Web site, and in the *Ancestry Daily News*)
- Heritage Quest's *Genealogy Bulletin* (see it or subscribe to it at <http://
www.genealogybulletin.com/>)
- Family Tree Magazine's E-mail newsletter (subscribe to it at <http://www
.familytreemagazine.com/newsletter.asp>)

The Web sites for most of these include archives of back issues, so you can go
back and browse them for useful information.

Other E-mail resources include
- E-mail lists devoted to people researching a specific name (discussed in
chapter eighteen)
- E-mail lists aimed at people researching in a specific area, such as the ones
from the USGenWeb project

ONLINE COLUMNS AND MAGAZINES

Some online columns and magazines not available through E-mail include
- Myra Vanderpool Gormley's "Shaking Your Family Tree," at <http://www
.ancestry.com/columns/myra/shaking_family_treenew.htm>
- *Everton's Genealogical Helper*, at <http://www.everton.com/genealogy/
helper/>
- *Journal of Online Genealogy*, at <http://www.onlinegenealogy.com>
- *International Internet Genealogical Society Newsletter*, at <http://www
.iigs.org/newsletter/index.htm.en>

I'M GOING TO PUT UP AN INTERNET
PAGE ABOUT MY ANCESTORS!

**Let the world (literally) know what you've found out. But please, use only verified
information, and give sources for it.** Don't add to the huge amount of misinforma-
tion currently on the Internet. It's also unwise to mount information about
living people. This is an invasion of their privacy. Unscrupulous people might
misuse the information, possibly with grave consequences.

In your Web page, identify yourself. Give your mailing address as well as
your E-mail address so that a person who finds your page while surfing in the
library has a way to get in touch with you.

Idea Generator

BUT I DON'T HAVE A COMPUTER! HOW CAN
I ACCESS THIS WEALTH OF INFORMATION?

You've read this far and are dazzled to learn what the Internet can do for you.
But you don't have a computer! How can you access all these wonderful sites? You
have several options. First, check your local library. Many libraries have computers with Internet access for public use. Some offer classes on how to use the
Internet; if not, a friendly librarian may show you some basics of Internet use.

Idea Generator

Or perhaps a friend will come to the library to help you get started.

If your library isn't the solution, do you have a friend with a computer and Internet access who will let you use it? If so, remember that this friend is probably paying monthly fees for Internet access. Offer to reimburse her for some of this since you're benefiting from it. Don't make a pest of yourself. Your friend may regret her kindness if you drop by every evening to spend four hours on the Internet! If you get that hooked on the Internet, go to the next option.

Your ultimate option, if you've tried the Internet and decided you like what's available, is to buy a computer. Prices of computers have dropped drastically in the past few years. If you're nervous about this, enlist a friend who is knowledgeable about computers to help you choose and install your computer. Perhaps someone at the local genealogical society can assist you. Most computer users had help from someone else when they bought their first computer and are happy to pass on the favor.

CONCLUSION

The Internet offers a wealth of data to genealogists; take advantage of the information you can collect there. Remember to verify in primary sources anything you find on the Internet. Beyond the possibility of expanding your family information, you'll find E-mail newsletters and magazines, as well as instructional material available from many Internet genealogy sites. If you don't have a computer, you may be able to access the Internet on a friend's or at your local public library.

TWENTY

Why Not Go There Yourself?

Are you curious about the area where your ancestors lived? If you've gotten books about the area and seen pictures of it, have they whetted your appetite to see the real thing? Even if you don't live there, perhaps you could go there on a vacation. Probably, the more research you do, the more interested you'll be in making the trip. You could finally follow the directions in those first genealogy books you picked up: "Go to the courthouse and. . . ."

You may raise objections and find reasons why you can't make the trip. But unless the reason you're doing long-distance research is that you're confined to your home, work on overcoming the obstacles rather than making excuses. Small children at home? Perhaps a friend or relative would look after them for a week or so. Lack of money? **Look for economical places to stay (perhaps you'll even get an invitation to stay with a newfound distant cousin in the area) and start saving for the trip.** No time off work? You probably get at least a day or two. Organize it so that you can make the trip. If you have to take a business trip in the general direction of where your ancestors lived, perhaps you can use a few vacation days to take a side trip to your ancestral area.

Money Saver

WHY SHOULD I GO?

You'll be glad if you make the trip. Having immersed yourself in your ancestors' lives, it's rewarding to go somewhere and say, "Peter Heilman once walked here; he stood here and saw the same things I'm seeing." Most genealogists also find it fulfilling to visit the graves of ancestors. You can't meet the person, but the gravestone makes him real—not just a name on a chart. In the case of a close relative, like a grandfather, who died before you were born, seeing the grave may allow you to reach closure with your sense of emptiness—while other children around you had grandfathers, you had none. Some aspects of the visit may cause sadness. Even if you already knew about it, actually seeing the row of tiny gravestones for the five children who died of diphtheria within eight days of each other makes this sad situation more real than any written word can.

Likewise, it's thrilling to go to the courthouse and touch and see the papers in your ancestor's estate file, including his actual signature on his will—which he himself once held—and his children's signatures (including your next ancestor) on receipts for the money they received. While you might have hired a genealogist to do research for you, there's always a nagging doubt: maybe that person missed something important. You may want to retrace some of that researcher's steps just to be sure. You might have thought of new ways to approach a problem in the line. You might not have been able to hire a researcher who lived in the area, or you hired one who might have worked with microfilm records at a central state repository and didn't have access to some records for your ancestor.

WHERE SHOULD I GO?

If all your ancestors in the United States lived in one place, your choice of where to visit will be obvious. But many people have ancestors scattered across several states. How do you choose where to start?

Is there one ancestor or ancestral line that particularly fascinates you? You'd really like to see where these people lived and try to unearth some of the facts that they seem to have tried so hard to hide from future generations. If so, you'll find it satisfying to begin your research here.

Idea Generator

If your choice isn't so obvious or motivated, remember the first rule of research: Start with yourself and work backward. **Go to the area where the ancestors closest in time to you lived and see what you can find out about them.** In their records, you may find clues that will further your research on the ancestors who migrated to that area and save you hours you might otherwise have spent doing research on them by mail.

When you go to the area, if you have time, consider scheduling a visit to the state capital to look at resources in the state library and the state archives. If the state historical and/or genealogical societies aren't in the capital, consider going to their towns as well, to tap their resources. While the holdings of all these repositories probably overlap, each has something that the other doesn't have, and you may find something useful at each.

PREPARE FIRST

Timesaver

Now that you've decided you will go to your ancestral area and have worked out solutions for potential obstacles, take time to think things through. Do as much planning and research as possible from home before you leave. If any libraries you plan to visit have a catalog available on the Internet, search it; make a list of books you want to look at and their call numbers so that you won't waste valuable on-site research time doing this. **Learn which repositories in the area hold what records for what time periods.** You don't want to spend half an hour trying to locate a deed at the courthouse only to learn that it's in the county hall

[Your postal address, phone number, and E-mail address]

[date]

[address of recipient]

Dear Friends:

I am planning a trip to Monroe County from September 15 through September 20 of this year to do research on my ancestors. I plan to spend some time using your resources. Your answers to the questions below will help me plan my time. If you prefer, you can write responses directly on this letter and return it to me.

> Give the exact dates you plan to be there.

If you have a brochure or research guide describing your collection, especially if it answers any of these questions, please send me a copy.

> Ask for a research guide.

- What days and hours are you open? Are there any days you will be closed between September 15 and 20?
- Do I need to be a member of your society to use your collection?
- Do you charge a fee for use of your collection?
- Do I need to make an appointment in advance to use your collection?
- Is there a hotel or motel near your facility that you would recommend? I'm nervous about choosing a hotel I know nothing about and would appreciate a recommendation.

> Ask specific questions to help you plan your time in the area and to find out restrictions on use of the collection.

Thank you for your help. I enclose a self-addressed, stamped envelope for your convenience in replying.

> Always send a SASE.

Sincerely,

[your name]

Figure 20-1 Letter to a courthouse, library, historical society, etc., requesting information prior to a visit

of records two blocks down the street (see appendix B for a list of books that tell you what repositories hold what records). Write to the research facilities you'll visit or check their Web sites to learn their hours. (See Figure 20-1 above.) Then make a schedule to take maximum advantage of each repository's schedule. If the library is open on Tuesdays until 9:00 P.M., and all other repositories close at 5:00 P.M. on Tuesday, plan to head for the library on Tuesday evening.

Compile a prioritized list of research goals, including the steps you need to take to fulfill those goals. Allow too much time for each goal, not too little. Things always take longer than you think they will. On the other hand, have

RESEARCH TRIP GOALS

Prioritize your list of goals for a research trip and include steps you think you need to take to fulfill those goals. Following is a sample goal with research steps.

GOAL:

Try to pin down, or at least narrow down, the death date for Mary (Wynne) Abraham (she was alive in 1738 when she sold land in Philadelphia; deceased in 1758 when her husband Noah Abraham wrote a will naming wife "Hannah").

RESEARCH STEPS:

1. Look to see if Mary had an estate file.
2. Check for grantor deed records for Noah where his wife was interviewed regarding surrendering her dower right in the land.
3. Check Chester County Historical Society and Library to see if they have any files on the Abraham family that might shed light on the problem.
4. Check cemetery readings for a possible transcription of her gravestone.
5. Check church records for a burial record for Mary or marriage record for Noah and Hannah (note: need to figure out what churches were in Chester Co. at this time period).

more work planned than you expect to accomplish. If it's simply not possible to do some of the research you hoped to do, it's best to have enough research to keep you busy.

If you schedule your trip in the summer, after repositories close for the day, **use the time before sunset to visit cemeteries.** Write to the local historical or genealogical society and ask if they have maps or directions to help you find the cemeteries you need to visit. Then plan your route in a logical manner so you won't zigzag all over the county. And when scheduling the places you'll visit, put cemeteries early in the trip. If you save the cemeteries for the last day, it's guaranteed to pour rain, even if the area is having its worst drought in fifty years.

Do, however, be prepared to be flexible if an opportunity comes up. If someone offers to drive you out to see the original 1830 family homestead on Tuesday afternoon, don't reply, "Gosh, I'm sorry, I have the DAR Library scheduled for then."

If possible, identify a hotel within walking distance of the major repositories you want to visit, and make a reservation well in advance of your trip. This will save you from having to worry about parking problems. If (in the absence of a genuine physical disability) you're thinking, "But I can't carry all my stuff!" reconsider what you need to carry. Even if you drive to the repository, you'll have to carry your stuff around with you all day. You don't want to be overburdened while researching.

SPEAKING OF WEATHER . . .

Keep weather in mind when choosing the time for your trip. Most genealogists enjoy cemeteries, but slogging through a foot of snow to get to your ancestor's tombstone takes some of the fun out of the experience. Likewise, if you're looking through a large cemetery for an elusive tombstone when it's ninety-five degrees with 95 percent humidity and the blackflies think you're God's gift to insects, you may decide your timing is off. Some courthouses and libraries don't have air conditioning, so they're not ideal August vacation spots. On the other hand, if you do go in summer, take a sweater. Some courthouses use air conditioning with a vengeance!

Are There Historical Sites in the Area?

Read any tourist literature you can find about the area. Are there historic sites dating from your ancestors' time? Take a break from your research to visit some of them. If your ancestor didn't attend that old log church that the historical society has preserved, maybe he attended a similar one. Numerous genealogists tell strange-but-true stories of visiting a museum in their ancestral area and finding items on display that had belonged to relatives.

What Should I Take With Me?

Some books on researching at distant repositories give long lists of what to bring with you. This list won't be so long. You *don't* want to bring your six file drawers of materials on your family from the area. Travel light. You can only carry so much from your motel to the places where you'll do research, and some repositories may limit what you can bring in. A good approach is to print out and put in a binder family group sheets for all the families you even remotely think you might research. Then when you find a document listing Aunt Sally's birth date, you can check to see if you already had this information and if the

MAKE SURE YOUR FAMILY DOESN'T GET BORED

Are you bringing family with you on your research trip? If they're along because they want to help with the research, that's wonderful! But some family members may not want to spend quite so much time researching as you do—or they may not want to research at all. In this case, when you plan the trip, investigate things they can do while you're having fun in the courthouse. Don't expect courthouse employees to baby-sit your four-year-old while you look at deeds; and don't expect the fifteen-year-old to suddenly have a 180 degree change in attitude, becoming enthralled with research and wanting to spend her whole trip helping you (although if that happens, great!).

For More Info

READ MORE ABOUT IT!

Books on planning and making a research trip include

- Balhuizen, *Searching on Location: Planning a Research Trip*
- Carmack, *Organizing Your Family History Search*
- Parker, *Going to Salt Lake City to Do Family History Research* (although this deals specifically with research trips to Salt Lake City, many of the tips apply to any research trip)
- Warren and Warren, *Getting the Most Mileage From Genealogical Research Trips*

Timesaver

A USEFUL FORM YOU CAN REPRODUCE

For a full-sized blank copy of the Records You Hope to Find form, see page 234. You are free to photocopy this form for personal use.

Tip

date matches what you had. Never bring actual source documents, especially not originals. Too many genealogists tell sad stories about folders they accidentally left behind and never saw again. Put your name and address on everything you bring, from folders to binders to pads, in case you accidentally leave something somewhere. After you've spent three solid days in the courthouse taking notes, you would be sad to lose that binder.

Make charts listing records you hope to find for your ancestors; check off the ones you already have, so you won't waste time searching for them (see Figure 20-2 on page 187). Also have lists of records you need by type (marriage license, death certificate, etc.), listing the people for whom you need them in alphabetical order (see Figure 20-3 on page 188). When you go to the marriage license index, you can breeze through your list. For marriages, list the names of both the bride and the groom, in case one is badly mangled in, or missing from, the index.

Some repositories only admit members of certain societies, and some societies charge more to use their library if you aren't a member. Bring membership cards for any local, state, or national genealogical societies to which you belong. Also bring writing implements and several pads of paper or a loose-leaf binder with lots of paper for taking notes. Some repositories don't allow you to use pens, so be sure to have pencils (mechanical pencils are best since you don't have to sharpen them).

For organizing the notes and photocopies you collect, bring empty file folders, a stapler, and paper clips. Stamped envelopes and self-stick address labels may come in handy.

Save change before you go, or buy rolls of coins so you'll have lots to use in photocopy machines. If you find material relevant to your research, it's faster to photocopy it than to copy it by hand, and a photocopy won't have transcription errors. You'll be especially sorry if you insist on saving a few pennies by copying something by hand and then get home and can't decipher your notes on a crucial point ("is that a 7 or a 9?"). Besides, you've spent good money to get to this place to do research, and it's much more efficient to spend five minutes photocopying a document or pages from a book than to spend ten or twenty or thirty minutes transcribing it. In that time, you could look at two or three other

CHART SHOWING RECORDS YOU HOPE TO FIND FOR YOUR ANCESTORS IN A COUNTY

Records needed from Morgan County, IL (formed from Sangamon County in 1823)
Birth and death records from 1878 on; marriage records from 1828 on

ANCESTOR'S NAME (INCLUDING MAIDEN NAME FOR WOMEN)	BIRTH DATE	BIRTH CERT	BAPT	MARRIAGE: MARRIAGE DATE	CERT	NEWSP	DEEDS: GRANTOR	GRANTEE	DEATH DATE	DEATH: CERT	OBIT	ESTATE	GRAVE LOCATED?
Crawford, John Harley	3 Sept 1858	E	E	24 Apr 1889	E				12 Feb 1930	E			
Crawford, Susan Frances (REED)	11 Nov 1864	N/A		24 Apr 1889	E				2 May 1895				
Dickson, Joseph	15 Feb 1775	E	E	ca. 1798	E				25 Jun 1844	N/A			
Dickson, Susan (-?-)	19 Oct 1774	E	E	ca. 1798	E				5 Dec 1841	E			
Kile, George W.	14 Dec 1838	E	E	ca. 1858	E				2 Mar 1873	N/A			
Kile, Sarah Jane	2 Mar 1838	E	E	ca. 1858	E				8 Apr 1873	N/A			
Reed, Andrew Jackson	1 Jan 1829	E	E	6 Feb 1851	E				14 Feb 1895				
Reed, Elizabeth (WEST)	9 Nov 1794	E	E	1 Feb 1822	E				14 Jun 1870	N/A			
Reed, John K.	7 Jan 1798	E	E	1 Feb 1822	E				23 Feb 1851	N/A			
Reed, Susan Frances (WILLIAMS)	12 Aug 1831	E	E	6 Feb 1851	E				15 Dec 1884				
Thompson, Nannie Jane (KILE)	1 Jul 1864	E	E	25 Sep 1890					27 Jun 1947	E			
Thompson, Sarah Ann. (CARR)	ca 1834	E	E	1 Apr 1856	E				??				
Thompson, William H.	ca 1829	E	E	1 Apr 1856	E				??				
Thompson, William Thomas	22 Dec 1861	N/A		25 Sep 1890					6 Feb 1904	E			
Williams, Elias	8 Oct 1781	E	E	bef 1802	E				5 Mar 1847	N/A			
Williams, Fanny (-?-)	??	E	E	bef 1802	E				22 May 1841	N/A			
Williams, Josiah	29 Mar 1808	E	E	1 Jan 1829	E				14 Oct 1864	E			
Williams, Sarah Amos (DICKSON)	12 Mar 1810	E	E	1 Jan 1829	E				13 Apr 1880	E			
Wilson, Nancy (ROLLINS)	6 Sept 1818	E	E	6 Jan 1871					18 Mar 1900				

For Reference:
- Note date when county was formed and dates when records are available on the county level.
- Include women's maiden names.
- Have birth, marriage, and death dates handy on the chart.
- Enter "N/A" (not available) for records that fall into a time period when records of that type weren't created.
- Enter "E" (elsewhere) for records that would have been created in another county.

Figure 20-2 Sample chart showing records you hope to find for your ancestors in a county

MARRIAGE RECORDS AND/OR NEWSPAPER ANNOUNCEMENT OF MARRIAGE (MORGAN CO., IL)	
Carpenter, Celestia to Andrew Jackson Reed	??
Dickson, Sarah Amos to Josiah Williams	1 Jan 1829
Fyffe, Katie to Andrew Jackson Reed	??
Reed, Andrew Jackson to Celestia Carpenter	??
Reed, Andrew Jackson to Katie Fyffe	??
Reed, Andrew Jackson to Susan Frances Williams	6 Feb 1851
Williams, Josiah to Sarah Amos Dickson	1 Jan 1829
Williams, Susan Frances to Andrew Jackson Reed	6 Feb 1851

Figure 20-3 List of records needed by category

documents that might have some crucial piece of information you need.

Bring the names, addresses, and phone numbers of people in the area you want to contact. You're all hyped up to call fifth cousin Lillie Smith, but you don't have her phone number—and the phone book lists seventy-two Smiths (or no one by the last name in question is in the phone book because your relative's phone number is unlisted). The name may seem unusual to you, so you decide to look it up in the phone book when you get there. But you may discover that the area you're visiting is the epicenter for this unusual name, and the phone book has two columns of people by this name.

Pack comfortable but sensible clothes. You'll find a more detailed discussion of clothes later in this chapter, but for now, know that many courthouses have few or no chairs for researchers. You may be on your feet for quite a while as you look at wills and deeds. You won't be happy wearing spike heels. Wear clothes with pockets; some repositories require that patrons put purses and briefcases in lockers, so pockets will hold valuables you want to keep with you. If you plan to visit any cemeteries, bring walking shoes and something that covers your legs (jeans are good). Some cemeteries are well maintained, and others aren't; you may find yourself trampling through high grass, brush, and poison ivy.

WHAT REPOSITORIES SHOULD I VISIT?

By this time in your research, you probably have a list of repositories in the area, but consider the following:

- courthouse (see appendix B)
- public library (check the *American Library Directory*)
- genealogical and historical societies (see chapter sixteen)

CEMETERIES: TAKE ONLY PICTURES, LEAVE ONLY FOOTPRINTS

In reading books on genealogical research, you may find many suggestions for things to put on tombstones to enhance the engravings in them for easier reading, to preserve them, etc. *Do not do any of these things.* Virtually anything you put on a tombstone has the potential to harm it. Even shaving cream, long a favorite of genealogists, has chemicals in it that damage stones. And gravestone rubbing, once pushed as a nondestructive way to copy a stone, is now known to cause subtle wear and tear to the stone (not to mention defacing of the stone if you slip and rub the crayon on the stone rather than the paper). The only thing you can do safely to enhance reading or photographing a stone is to use a large mirror to reflect light onto it at different angles. You might say, "Well, I'll just use a little shaving cream, and it's only this once." But what if the next fifteen descendants who visit the graveyard say the same thing? Be considerate of future researchers, and respect your ancestors, who rest under those stones.

- Family History Center (They may have a book collection. See Chapter thirteen for ways to find a nearby Family History Center.)
- local DAR library (Contact the DAR to find out if there's a local chapter.)
- cemeteries (see chapter ten for information on locating cemeteries)

You may have identified others; add them to this list.

If you've corresponded with distant relatives who live in the area, write to them to tell them you're coming. At the very least, suggest getting together for lunch so you can put a face with the name. If they're also researching, ask them if they'll show you the ropes at the various research repositories in the area. If you've hired a genealogist in the area, that person might spend a few hours showing you around local repositories (but may charge the regular research rate to do so). Any of these people may know places to research that you haven't heard of or helpful records that you might not know about. Ask for this information before the trip so you won't be frustrated after the trip when someone asks you, "Oh, did you look at the [fill in the blank] records?" **A local person might volunteer to drive you to cemeteries that are small and difficult to locate, thus saving time you might have spent wandering around on country roads trying to decide which of seventeen large barns is the large barn at which you're supposed to turn to get to the old family graveyard.**

If your visit includes a Sunday (or other day on which your ancestors regularly attended religious services), attend services at the church your ancestor attended. Introduce yourself to people after the service. Chances are, someone will say something like, "Oh, you're researching the King family? You must talk to Nellie Hoffman. Her mother was a King."

MAKING AN IMPRESSION

Earlier, you learned that you need to be careful of the impression you make when writing to people, because you want to be careful how they remember you and genealogists in general. The same thing holds true for personally visiting a research site. If you're loud, boisterous, and rude, the repository personnel, who perhaps were already somewhat prejudiced against genealogists, may extrapolate that behavior to all genealogists and be less helpful to the next one who visits them. Please don't spoil it for other genealogists!

Reminder

You create an impression not only in the way you act, but also in the way you look. Don't go to the courthouse dressed for a trip to the beach—wearing a halter top and shorts or a stained T-shirt with cut offs and flip-flops. You'll be mingling with lawyers and title researchers, and in this sort of attire, you will stand out unfavorably. For courthouse and library research, you'll get more respect from staff if you dress conservatively. This doesn't mean you have to wear a suit and tie, but do dress presentably.

Another rather sneaky way to create a good impression is bribery. Have you written to people at this repository and gotten help from them? Remember the principle of "send a donation"? When you're on a research trip, a donation is also nice, but make it in a slightly different format. You can catch more flies with honey than with vinegar, and in this case, honey can be a box of candy. Even though employees try to treat all researchers at their repository equally, they may be just a teensy bit nicer to the sweet person who brought them that chocolate. For the best effect, bring in the chocolate on your first day of research and mention how much you appreciate the help they gave you in response to your letter(s) to them. People like to be told that they've done a good job.

If people help you out by driving you to cemeteries or showing you around the courthouse, offer to pay for gas and/or buy them a meal. It's better to do too much for them than too little.

INTRODUCE YOURSELF AND ASK FOR HELP

Even if you didn't bring candy, introduce yourself to the people at the repository. You don't need to make a long introduction; just tell them your name and that you're researching your family history (many people agree that at repositories where there's prejudice against genealogists the term *family history* seems to go over better). Then ask if they can give you a brief overview of anything in the repository that might help you. Even if you've come with a local researcher who's going to show you the ropes, ask the employees. If your local contact hasn't asked the employees, he might learn something, too.

Reminder

Also ask how their indexes work. For example, **several systems for indexing deeds are a little more complicated than a normal index.** Once you've had an explanation, the indexes will probably seem simple; but without that explanation, they can be very confusing.

Chance Encounters

While researching at a library, courthouse, or other repository you may become friendly with a fellow researcher. Invite her to have lunch with you. If she's a local resident, she will know a good place to eat and can give you advice on researching in the area. If she's a fellow long-distance researcher on a visit, she could be lonely and may welcome a chance to chat and share genealogical success stories. In either case, you may find out you're related!

NO MATTER HOW MUCH YOU PLAN, YOUR TIME WILL BE TOO SHORT

Schedule your time to use it to the best advantage. When you return to your motel at night, go over the materials you've collected during the day, and correlate them with what you already have. In the process, you may see the need for further research or identify another person you need to pursue. Be prepared to revise your research strategy or schedule based on this analysis.

Also, as all genealogists will tell you, on your last day, you'll stumble on some source that looks as if it will be supremely useful to you—and you won't have the time to work with it. That's OK; you've visited your ancestral area and seen some gravestones and the old homestead. It's a beautiful area, so wouldn't you love to come back next year on your vacation? Start planning that trip—and remember to make a note of that last-day find.

Timesaver

I'M HOME!

Once you're home, you have two chores. First, write thank-you notes to people who helped you, like the distant cousin who drove you to the family cemetery. Second, integrate the material you collected with the material you already had. Fill in those pedigree charts and family group sheets, or enter the data into your computer.

When you start working with the material, despite all the lists and charts you brought to remind you of what you wanted to accomplish, you almost certainly will utter exclamations beginning with "Oh, no!" as in "Oh, no! I didn't look up Uncle Vern's obituary!" **Make a list of these items as soon as you think of them. Start a wish list for your next trip,** or return to this book to see if you can access the material from home.

Tip

CONCLUSION

While you can accomplish a lot through long-distance research, nothing can substitute for seeing, in person, the area where your ancestor lived. If you make such a trip, plan in advance so you have all the information you need to do your research and can make the best use of your time.

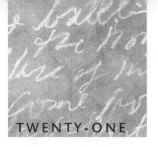

TWENTY-ONE

Hiring a Professional Genealogist

Y ou've talked to every living relative you can identify; you've written scads of letters requesting vital documents and estate files; you've gotten books and magazine articles on interlibrary loan; but still you're stuck on a line. You can't think of anything else you can do from a distance, and while you'd like to make a trip to your ancestral home, it just isn't possible right now. You're sure that there must be *some* record that would help you over this hump, and you want it soon. This is a time to consider hiring a professional genealogist to do some research on your family.

DECIDING TO HIRE A PROFESSIONAL GENEALOGIST

You might decide to hire a professional genealogist when you think you've exhausted all records you can access from a distance but have a strong feeling that your ancestral area holds information that will help with your line.

You might have written to a repository to ask for information, only to be told

- they charge a large fee for the research (For example, some probate courts in New York charge as much as seventy dollars to look up a probate file. This could pay for two or three hours of a professional genealogist's time.)
- they don't do research for genealogists (in this case, they usually send a list of researchers)

One important factor in the decision is whether you're willing to pay someone to do the research for you. While good professional genealogical research isn't cheap (costs may run thirty dollars per hour or more), weigh this against the money you might spend to visit the area. If you go there to do the research yourself, you'll have to pay for lodging, meals, and transportation. Even if you plan eventually to see the area where your ancestors lived, hiring a professional to do some of the research before you get there might actually save you money.

LOCATING THE GENEALOGIST

Several sources list professional genealogical researchers. The Association of Professional Genealogists publishes *Directory of Professional Genealogists* and has a smaller directory available in pamphlet form and on the Internet at <http://www.apgen.org/directory.html>. This directory includes the three-page section "So You're Going to Hire a Professional Genealogist?" which supplements this chapter and is available from the association in pamphlet form or on its Web site.

Sources

The Board for Certification of Genealogists (BCG) offers a rigorous program that ends in one of five certifications:

- CG (Certified Genealogist)
- CLS (Certified Lineage Specialist; this new category, added in the fall of 1999, replaces the former CALS [Certified American Lineage Specialist] and CAILS [Certified American Indian Lineage Specialist])
- CGRS (Certified Genealogical Record Specialist)
- CGI (Certified Genealogical Instructor)
- CGL (Certified Genealogical Lecturer)

A person who has received any of these certifications is highly qualified to do research, but if you're looking for a specific kind of research that corresponds to one of the specialties, you'll probably want to look for someone with the appropriate certification. BCG-certified genealogists must renew their certification every five years.

The BCG Web site at <http://www.gencalogy.org/~bcg/> includes "Roster of BCG Certified Individuals" listing individuals by geographical area of specialty and by the nongeographic specialties African American, Native American, Lineage Societies, and Miscellaneous.

The Family History Library in Salt Lake City has an accreditation program for genealogists that involves testing in a specialized subject area. Those who pass the test may use the designation AG (Accredited Genealogist) after their name. To get information on researchers with this qualification, write a letter describing the geographical area(s) where you're looking for a researcher, and send it with a SASE to

Salt Lake Distribution Center
1999 W. 1700 South
Salt Lake City, UT 84104-4233

They'll send you a list of people accredited for the areas in which you're interested.

Everton's Genealogical Helper includes a directory of genealogists in its September/October issue (remember that genealogists pay to have these listings appear; the magazine doesn't endorse them). Ads placed by genealogical researchers appear in all issues of *Everton's* and in many other genealogical magazines.

If none of these sources turn up genealogists researching in your ancestral area, write to the local genealogical and/or historical society to see if they can supply a list of researchers (see chapter sixteen for ways to identify the society to which to send your request).

HIRING THE GENEALOGIST

In the process of identifying potential researchers, you may find several researchers in your ancestral area. The range of fees among these genealogists can be wide, say, from fifteen to fifty dollars per hour. Now that you're conscious of your roots, you may say, "I'm Scottish!" (or German or some other heritage associated with being careful with money). Your impulse is to choose the cheapest one. Be forewarned: You get what you pay for. If you choose your researcher from the listing of the Board for Certification of Genealogists, you know that the genealogist has gone through a rigorous accreditation process. **If you pick a genealogist at random from an ad in a magazine, you have no idea what, if any, credentials the person might have.** Anyone can place an ad in a magazine offering to do genealogical research for a fee, so be cautious in approaching your potential researcher.

Warning

Write a query letter to the potential researcher(s) you have identified, and outline (briefly) the problem you hope to solve (see Figure 21-1 on page 195). Ask if this is something that they'd be willing to take on. Also ask

- what their fees are
- what their fees include (researchers usually charge separately for photocopies and postage, and they may charge separate fees to cover travel expenses, mileage, parking, etc.)
- what background, education, and research experience they have
- what their professional affiliations are
- if they have published any articles

The responses you get to these letters may help narrow your choice. One person may send a professional looking brochure; another may send a letter handwritten on a scrap of paper torn from a notebook. If the fees of the second person are much lower than those of the first but their standards of research and presentation of results parallel their communication techniques, you'll probably be better off with the more expensive researcher. Likewise, you may see clues in their writing style, grammar (or lack thereof), and spelling that will help you choose one over the other. Having looked at these clues, consider their answers to your questions about background and research experience. Someone who has been researching in the area for twenty years probably has a lot more experience with its records than someone who just moved there. If the person has published articles, read them to see what clues they contain about the person's expertise or lack thereof.

The researcher may give you other information that will help in your decision. Perhaps she only handles certain types of research (missing heirs, for example), and your problem doesn't fall within that area. She may say she has a

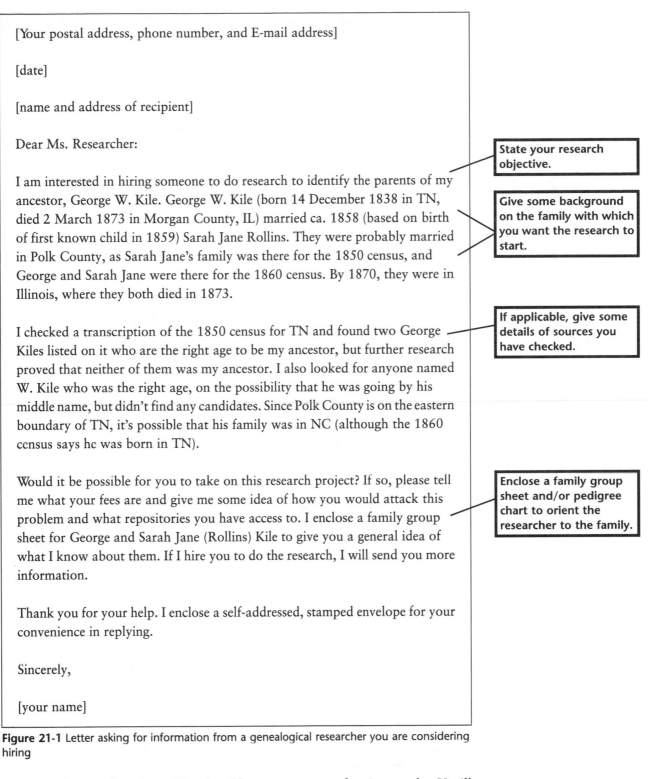

[Your postal address, phone number, and E-mail address]

[date]

[name and address of recipient]

Dear Ms. Researcher:

I am interested in hiring someone to do research to identify the parents of my ancestor, George W. Kile. George W. Kile (born 14 December 1838 in TN, died 2 March 1873 in Morgan County, IL) married ca. 1858 (based on birth of first known child in 1859) Sarah Jane Rollins. They were probably married in Polk County, as Sarah Jane's family was there for the 1850 census, and George and Sarah Jane were there for the 1860 census. By 1870, they were in Illinois, where they both died in 1873.

I checked a transcription of the 1850 census for TN and found two George Kiles listed on it who are the right age to be my ancestor, but further research proved that neither of them was my ancestor. I also looked for anyone named W. Kile who was the right age, on the possibility that he was going by his middle name, but didn't find any candidates. Since Polk County is on the eastern boundary of TN, it's possible that his family was in NC (although the 1860 census says he was born in TN).

Would it be possible for you to take on this research project? If so, please tell me what your fees are and give me some idea of how you would attack this problem and what repositories you have access to. I enclose a family group sheet for George and Sarah Jane (Rollins) Kile to give you a general idea of what I know about them. If I hire you to do the research, I will send you more information.

Thank you for your help. I enclose a self-addressed, stamped envelope for your convenience in replying.

Sincerely,

[your name]

State your research objective.

Give some background on the family with which you want the research to start.

If applicable, give some details of sources you have checked.

Enclose a family group sheet and/or pedigree chart to orient the researcher to the family.

Figure 21-1 Letter asking for information from a genealogical researcher you are considering hiring

backlog of research and wouldn't be able to get to yours for six months. You'll have to decide whether to wait for her or use another researcher. How does her response compare to that of other researchers you've contacted? Consider your time frame for this project. For example, were you hoping to put together something for a Christmas present for your family?

Based on what you've told her about your problem, the researcher may mention some sources she'd consult in seeking an answer. The strategy she suggests may help you decide whether she's the researcher for you.

A Few Words About Fees

Reminder

As was mentioned above, several genealogists in the same area may charge widely varying rates for their research. Decide how important the genealogist's fee structure is toward making your choice. **If the genealogist is certified or accredited, you know you're getting a superior, tested researcher, and it's probably worth it to pay higher fees**—although how much higher is a question you have to answer for yourself. Note that a higher hourly rate does not necessarily mean higher fees. If an experienced researcher charges a higher rate but takes less time to find the information than another researcher with a lower rate does, the total charge at the lower rate might actually be higher. In addition to research fees, researchers often charge for reimbursement of expenses, like mileage (especially if they live in a different county from the one where your ancestors lived) and parking. They'll almost certainly bill you for the costs of any photocopies they make.

Professional genealogists often request a deposit of the cost of several hours of research before they begin work. Many researchers have had unfortunate experiences when disgruntled clients tried to get out of paying bills, perhaps because they were disappointed with the results. Good professional genealogists work hard for their clients, but in some cases, records with the information the clients want simply don't exist. Unfortunately, a search with no results can take longer than a search with positive results. The researcher may find the information in the first record she looks at, but if it isn't there, she will search several other sources to find an answer or at least a clue.

When setting terms with the researcher, don't be chintzy. You know from experience that genealogical research is time consuming. If you authorize the researcher to work for only two hours, you're giving him barely enough time to review the material you sent about the problem and write a report. While you may have to invest a lot of money in this professional researcher, it may seem reasonable compared with the time and money you'd have to invest to travel and do the research yourself.

Writing to the Genealogist You Want to Hire

Once you've settled on a researcher and agreed on fees, you need to tell the researcher what you want done (see Figure 21-2 on page 197). To begin with, you may set a small task to see how she handles it before you turn her loose on your entire ancestry. Her report on this first problem may validate your choice or make you decide to look for another researcher.

Tip

Give the researcher some specific goals. Telling her "I want to trace my ancestors in Morgan County, Illinois, back as far as possible" is vague and leaves a lot of room for interpretation. What if she spends a lot of time on a line that isn't all that important to you, while not spending time on the line in which you were really interested? Telling her "I want to identify the parents of Sarah

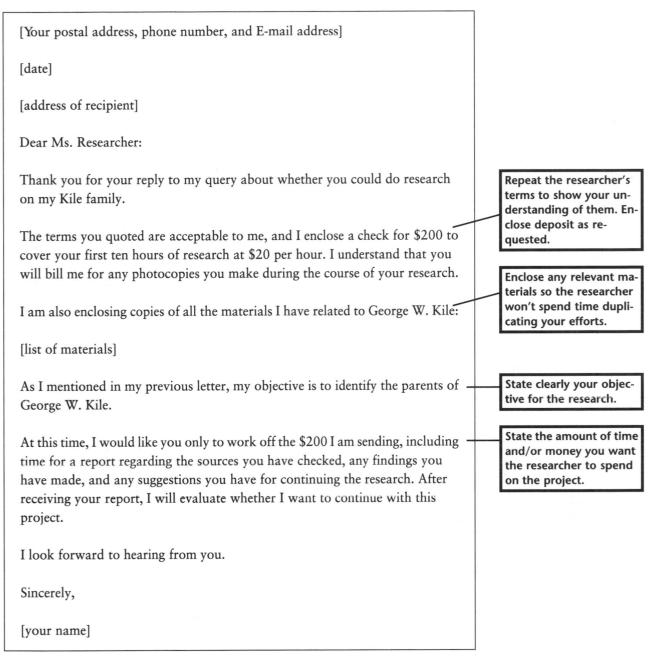

[Your postal address, phone number, and E-mail address]

[date]

[address of recipient]

Dear Ms. Researcher:

Thank you for your reply to my query about whether you could do research on my Kile family.

The terms you quoted are acceptable to me, and I enclose a check for $200 to cover your first ten hours of research at $20 per hour. I understand that you will bill me for any photocopies you make during the course of your research.

Repeat the researcher's terms to show your understanding of them. Enclose deposit as requested.

I am also enclosing copies of all the materials I have related to George W. Kile:

Enclose any relevant materials so the researcher won't spend time duplicating your efforts.

[list of materials]

As I mentioned in my previous letter, my objective is to identify the parents of George W. Kile.

State clearly your objective for the research.

At this time, I would like you only to work off the $200 I am sending, including time for a report regarding the sources you have checked, any findings you have made, and any suggestions you have for continuing the research. After receiving your report, I will evaluate whether I want to continue with this project.

State the amount of time and/or money you want the researcher to spend on the project.

I look forward to hearing from you.

Sincerely,

[your name]

Figure 21-2 Letter of hire to a genealogical researcher

Ann Carr, who married William Thompson in Morgan County, Illinois, on 1 April 1856" gives her a specific goal.

Send the researcher pedigree charts and family group sheets for the family she'll be researching, and enclose copies of relevant documents. Give her a complete list of sources you've consulted and copies of those with relevant information. You don't want to get your first report and find that she's spent a hundred dollars of your money looking at sources you've already searched. Don't expect the researcher to read your mind. Authorize work, including time to write a report (putting together a report can take two to three hours), up to a certain dollar amount.

Reminder

Evaluating the Results

When the genealogist has either fulfilled your objective or spent the full amount of money you've authorized, she should send you a formal report. This should summarize her findings and conclusions, document the sources she checked (possibly with explanations of why she checked a specific source, if she thinks you might question it), and specifty what she found or didn't find. **Negative results don't necessarily mean only that she's a bad genealogist; they may mean only that the information wasn't in the logical sources (and may not be in *any* source).** The report should include photocopies (or transcriptions, if photocopying wasn't possible) of any relevant documents, maps, censuses, information from books, etc. If the researcher couldn't achieve some or all of your objectives, she should tell you what sources she checked, so you can rule those out in the next phase of your search. If you're dissatisfied with the report, you can ask another researcher to check these same sources to be absolutely sure there's nothing in them.

Finally, based on what she has looked at and found, the researcher may make suggestions for further research on this problem. Perhaps, given the amount of money you authorized, she wasn't able to check all the sources she thought might be helpful. Towards the end of the time you authorized, she may have stumbled on a clue that could lead to more information on your line, but she didn't have time to pursue it.

The researcher may suggest that you pursue certain documents she's identified. Perhaps she found that your great-grandfather had a death certificate, but state regulations allow only a descendant to request it. If she's a good researcher, she'll also tell you the address to which to write and the fee for the document.

You may not be totally happy with the results if the researcher didn't achieve your objective, but the contents of the report will show whether she did a good job, given the available sources.

If you have a problem with a researcher's work, write to the researcher and express your concerns. If she doesn't answer them satisfactorily, and she's a member of either the Association of Professional Genealogists or the Board for Certification of Genealogists, those bodies offer an arbitration system. Contact them for details.

If you're satisfied with the researcher's results, or at least with her approach to research, you might decide to ask her to continue working on your line in the area.

CONCLUSION

Hiring a researcher in a distant location may be the next best thing to being there. However, determine the qualifications of a researcher before making your choice as to whom to hire, and then be careful that you communicate specifically what you want this person to accomplish. Also detail what you have already done, to avoid paying for searches of materials you have already researched. Be prepared to pay for quality research.

Useful Addresses for Genealogists

M any book distributors sell CD-ROMs and genealogy software as well. Some vendors have clubs you can join to get materials at reduced prices. Internet addresses were correct at the time of publication but are always subject to change.

AllCensus
591 Whispering Lakes Blvd., Tarpon Springs, FL 34689
(CD-ROMs)
Phone: (727) 937-8331   *E-mail:* comments@allcensus.com
Web site: http://www.allcensus.com/

Ancestry.com
P.O. Box 476, Salt Lake City, UT 84110-0476
(books, CD-ROMs, software, magazines, online databases)
Phone: (800) 262-3787   *Web site:* http://www.ancestry.com/

Appleton's Books & Genealogy
8700 Pineville-Matthews Rd. #610, Charlotte, NC 28226
(books, CD-ROMs, software)
Phone: (800) 777-3601   *Fax:* (704) 341-0072
E-mail: catalog.request@appletons.com
Web site: http://www.appletons.com/

Association of Professional Genealogists
P.O. Box 40393, Denver, CO 80204-0393
E-mail: apg-admin@apg.com   *Web site:* http://www.apgen.org/

Barnette's Family Tree Book Co.
5215 San Jacinto, Houston, TX 77004
(books, CD-ROMs, software)
Phone: (713) 684-4633; (888) 591-8733 for orders
E-mail: general correspondence: mic@barnettesbooks.com; questions about
   books: info@barnettesbooks.com; place an order: order@barnettesbooks
   .com; *Web site:* http://barnettesbooks.com

Bell & Howell Information and Learning
(formerly known as UMI)
300 N. Zeeb Rd., P.O. Box 1346, Ann Arbor, MI 48106-1346
(microfilm of newspapers; microfiche copies of out-of-print genealogical and
  local history books)
Phone: (800) 521-0600   *Fax:* (734) 761-4700   *E-mail:* info@umi.com
Web site: http://www.umi.com/hp/Support/Research/Topics/
  Geneology.html/   (sic)

Betterway Books
1507 Dana Ave., Cincinnati, OH 45207
(books, magazine, Web site with SuperSearch capability)
Phone: (800) 289-0963   *E-mail:* bookorders@familytreemagazine.com
Web site: http://www.familytreemagazine.com/store/

Board for Certification of Genealogists
P.O. Box 14291, Washington, DC 20044
Web site: http://www.genealogy.org/~bcg/

Brøderbund Software
P.O. Box 6125, Novato, CA 94948-6125
(CD-ROMs, software)
Phone: (800) 548-1806   *Fax:* (319) 395-7449
Web site: http://www.familytreemaker.com/

[U.S.] Bureau of Land Management
7450 Boston Blvd., Springfield, VA 22153
E-mail: glomail@es.blm.gov (for eastern states only)
Web site: http://www.glorecords.blm.gov

Census Microfilm Rental Program
(National Archives)
P.O. Box 30, Annapolis Junction, MD 20701-0030
Web site: http://www.nara.gov/publications/microfilm/micrent.html

Census View
P.O. Box 39, Ripley, OK 74062
(CD-ROMs)
Phone: (918) 372-4624   *E-mail:* censusvu@galstar.com
Web site: http://www.galstar.com/~censusvu/

Civil Reference Branch
(for passport applications before 1926)
Textual Reference Division
National Archives and Records Service, Suitland, MD 20409

Clearfield Company
200 E. Eager St., Baltimore, MD 21202
(books)
Phone: (410) 625-9005   *Fax:* (800) 599-9561 or (410) 752-8492
E-mail: sales@genealogical.com
Web site: http://www.GenealogyBookShop.com/

Daughters of the American Revolution, National Society,
1776 D St. NW, Washington, DC 20006-5303

Phone: (202) 628-1776   *Web site:* http://www.dar.org/

Everton Publishers, Inc.

P.O. Box 368, Logan, UT 84321

(books, CD-ROMs, software, magazines, online databases)

Phone: (800) 443-6325   *Fax:* (435) 752-0425

E-mail: magazine@everton.com or order@everton.com

Web site: http://www.everton.com/

Family Chronicle

10 Gateway Blvd., Ste. 490, Toronto, ON, Canada M3C 3T4

(books, magazines)

Phone: (888) 326-2476   *E-mail:* magazine@familychronicle.com

Web site: http://www.familychronicle.com/

Family History Library

35 N.W. Temple St., Salt Lake City, UT 84150

Phone: (801) 240-2331   *Fax:* (801) 240-1584

E-mail: fhl@byu.edu   *Web site:* http://www.familysearch.org/

Family Tree Magazine

1507 Dana Ave., Cincinnati, OH 45207

Phone: (800) 289-0963   *E-mail:* letters@familytreemagazine.com

Web site: http://www.familytreemagazine.com/

Federation of Genealogical Societies

P.O. Box 200940, Austin, TX 78720-0940

Web site: http://www.fgs.org

Frontier Press

P.O. Box 126, Dept. 212, Cooperstown, NY 13326

(books, CD-ROMs, software)

Phone: (607) 547-9415; orders: (800) 772-7559   *Fax:* (607) 547-9415

E-mail: kgfrontier@aol.com   *Web site:* http://www.frontierpress.com

Genealogical Publishing Company

1001 N. Calvert St., Baltimore, MD 21202-3897

(books, CD-ROMs)

Phone: (800)296-6687   *Fax:* (800) 599-9561 or (410) 752-8492

E-mail: sales@genealogical.com

Web site: http://www.GenealogyBookshop.com/

Global Data CD Publishers

1623 W. 3640 S., Saint George, UT 84790

(CD-ROMs)

Phone: (435) 674-7516   *E-mail:* globalcd@infowest.com

Web site: www.gencd.com/txtidx.htm

Hearthstone Bookshop

5735A Telegraph Rd., Alexandria, VA 22303

(books, CD-ROMs)

Phone: orders: (888) 960-3300 other calls: (703) 960-0086

Fax: (703) 960-0087   *E-mail:* info@hearthstonebooks.com

Web site: http://www.hearthstonebooks.com

Heritage Books, Inc.
   1540 E. Pointer Ridge Pl., Bowie, MD 20716
   (books, CD-ROMs)
   Phone: (800) 398-7709 or (301) 390-7709
   Fax: (800) 276-1760 or (301) 390-7153
   E-mail: heritagebooks@pipeline.com
   Web site: http://www.heritagebooks.com

Heritage Quest Genealogical Services
   P.O. Box 329, Bountiful, UT 84011-0329
   (books, CD-ROMs, software, magazines, online databases, microfilm rental
      program)
   Phone: (800) 760-2455 and (800) 658-7755   *Fax:* (801) 298-5468
   E-mail: sales@heritagequest.com
   Web site: http://www.heritagequest.com

Higginson Book Company
   148-GH Washington St., Salem, MA 01970
   Phone: (978) 745-7170   *fax:* (978) 745-8025
   E-mail: higginsn@cove.com
   Web site: http://www.higginsonbooks.com/

Immigration and Naturalization Service
   FOIA/PA, 2nd Floor ULLB, 425 I St. NW, Washington, DC 20536

Jonathan Sheppard Books
   P.O. Box 2020, Plaza Station, Albany, NY 12220
   (reprints of old maps from various time periods, many states and countries)
   Fax: (518) 766-9181

Masthof Press
   RR1, P.O. Box 20, Morgantown, PA 19543
   (books)
   Phone: (610) 286-0258   *Fax:* (610) 286-6860
   E-mail: masthof@ptdprolog.net

Millisecond Publishing Company
   P.O. Box 6168, Kamuela, HI 96743
   (CD-ROMs)
   Phone: (800) 565-0018   *E-mail:* kristine@familyforest.com
   Web site: http://www.familyforest.com/

National Archives and Records Administration
   (for military records)
   General Reference Branch (NNRG-P)
   700 Pennsylvania Ave. NW, Washington, DC 20408
   E-mail: inquire@nara.gov (to request forms)
   Web site: http://www.nara.gov/research/ordering/ordrfrms.html

National Archives and Records Administration
   (to request leaflets)
   Product Development and Distribution Staff (NWCP)
   National Archives and Records Administration, Room G-7
   700 Pennsylvania Ave. NW, Washington, DC 20408

Phone: (202) 501-5235 or (800) 234-8861

E-mail: inquire@nara.gov (to request leaflets)

National Archives and Records Administration

(for immigration records) Attn: NWCTB

700 Pennsylvania Ave. NW, Washington, DC 20408-0001

E-mail: inquire@nara.gov (to request forms)

National Genealogical Society

4527 Seventeenth St. N., Arlington, VA 22207

Phone: (703) 525-0050 or (800) 473-0060

E-mail: ngs@ngsgenealogy.com

Web site: http://www.ngsgenealogy.org/

New England Historic Genealogical Society

101 Newbury St., Boston, MA 02116

Phone: (617) 536-5740; Circulating Library: (888) 906-3447; Membership
& Education: (888) 286-3447; Sales Department: (888) 296-3447

Fax: (617) 536-7307   *E-mail:* nehgs@nehgs.org

Web site: http://www.NewEnglandAncestors.org

OneLibrary.com

131 130th St. S., Glyndon, MN 56547-9551

(CD-ROMs)

Phone: (218) 498-2183 or (218) 498-0235   *Fax:* (218) 498-2901

E-mail: info@onelibrary.com   *Web site:* http://www.onelibrary.com

Palladium

899 Northgate Dr., Fourth Floor, San Rafael, CA 94903

(CD-ROMs, software)

Phone: (415) 446-1700   *Fax:* (415) 446-1730

E-mail: webstar@palladium.net

Web site: http://www.palladium.net/Palladium/products/ultimate/cat_f.htm

Passport Office

(for passport applications after 1926)

Department of State, Washington, DC 20520

Picton Press

P.O. Box 250, Rockport, ME 04856

(books)

Phone: (207) 236-6565   *Fax:* (207) 236-6713

E-mail: sales@pictonpress.com   *Web site:* http://www.pictonpress.com/

Repeat Performance

2911 Crabapple Ln., Hobart, IN 46342

(audiotapes of talks from genealogical conferences)

Phone: (219) 465-1234   *Fax:* (219) 477-5492

Web site: http://www.repeatperformance.com/

The Reunion Network

2450 Hollywood Blvd. #301, Hollywood, FL 33020

(magazine and conferences on how to plan a successful reunion)

Phone: (800) 225-5044 or 954-922-0004   *Fax:* (954) 922-1518

E-mail: reunioninfo@reunionfriendly.com

Web site: http://www.reunionfriendly.com/

Reunions Magazine

P.O. Box 11727, Milwaukee, WI 53211-0727

Phone: (414) 263-4567;   *Fax:* (414) 263-6331

E-mail: reunions@execpc.com   *Web site:* http://www.reunionsmag.com/

RootsWeb Genealogical Data Cooperative

P.O. Box 6798, Frazier Park, CA 93222-6798

(provider of many Internet genealogical services, including Web sites, E-mail
  lists, databases, and server space for mounting data)

E-mail: webspinner@rootsweb.com   *Web site:* http://rootsweb.com

S-K Publications

P.O. Box 8173, Wichita, KS 67808-0173

(censuses published as books and CDs)

Phone: (316) 685-3201   *Fax:* (316) 685-6650

E-mail: genie@skpub.com   *Web site:* http://www.skpub.com/genie/

Scholarly Resources, Inc.

104 Greenhill Ave., Wilmington, DE 19805

(books)

Phone: (888) 772-7817 or (302) 654-7713   *Fax:* (302) 654-3871

E-mail: sales@scholarly.com   *Web site:* http://www.scholarly.com/

Social Security Administration

Office of Central Records Operations, FOIA Workgroup

P.O. Box 33022, 300 N. Greene St., Baltimore, MD 21290

Web site: http://www.ssa.gov/foia/foia_guide.htm

Superintendent of Documents

P.O. Box 371954, Pittsburgh, PA 15250-7954

(government publications, many aimed at consumers, including Bureau of
  Land Management CD-ROMs)

Tuttle Antiquarian Books, Inc.

28 S. Main St., Rutland, VT 05701

(books)

Phone: (802) 773-8229   *Fax:* (802) 773-1493

E-mail: tuttbook@together.net   *Web site:* http://www.tuttlebooks.com/

UMI

(see Bell & Howell Information and Learning)

Willow Bend Books

65 E. Main St., Westminster, MD 21157

(books, CD-ROMs)

Phone: (800) 876-6103   *E-mail:* willowbend@willowbend.net

Web site: http://www.willowbend.net

Where to Find Vital Records, Estate Records, and Land Records

T hree main reference works provide information on obtaining vital records, estate records, and land records, including information on which materials are kept at the state and local level in each state, addresses of repositories, and what materials are in a given repository. Each book has its own focus and gives somewhat different information. You may find it worthwhile to buy two or even all three of these titles.

When working with these books, don't just jump to the listing for your county of interest. Read the main introduction to find out how the book is organized, and read the introduction for your ancestral state so that you understand what's involved in researching there.

ANCESTRY'S RED BOOK

For each state, this book has a short article (where applicable) on
- vital records
- census records
- background sources
- land records
- probate records
- court records
- tax records
- cemetery records
- church records
- military records
- periodicals, newspapers, and manuscript collections
- archives, libraries, and societies
- special focus categories
- county resources

For reasons of space, many of these topics are covered only at the state level (e.g., "Archives, Libraries, and Societies" generally mentions only the state archives, the state library, and the state historical and genealogical societies). Following these articles is a section listing the counties (towns of Connecticut, Maine, Massachusetts, New Hampshire, Rhode Island, and Vermont) giving:

- courthouse address
- date formed
- parent county or counties
- some data regarding dates of records for births, marriages, deaths, and/or deeds available at that level (not all of these topics are listed for each state)

There's also a map showing the counties and their county seat. The editor chose an expert on the state to write each article, which means that the coverage is slightly different from article to article. In some cases, the writer depends on a general statement under "Vital Records" to tell you when counties in the state began to keep specific records, when actually, for various reasons, counties may or may not have records back to that date.

THE HANDY BOOK FOR GENEALOGISTS

This book gives in a compact format information on what's available in each county. However, it doesn't list contact information for the towns in the six states that keep records at the town level. If you're researching in the other states, you might want to consult the *Handy Book* first.

For each state, the book gives a brief history, including information on the dates at which various records began to be kept at the state level and the address(es) from which they are available. There are also listings of

- archives, libraries and societies
- available census records and census substitutes (types of records and years available only; no citations)
- atlases, maps, and gazetteers
- bibliographies
- genealogical research guides
- genealogical sources
- histories

County data follows this, including

- name
- map index (coordinates for the county on the state map at the end of the section on that state; these maps show county boundaries only, no cities)
- date created
- parent county or other entity
- address and phone number of courthouse
- information on what offices hold what records and the years available

In many cases, this listing gives much more specific information about dates of availability of records than *Ancestry's Red Book* does. At the end of the book are maps of each state showing the counties, a set of maps showing major migration trails in the United States, and a few other maps of interest. The *Handy Book* also includes brief information on records for selected foreign countries. A single index to all counties in the United States may be helpful if you have a reference to an ancestor in "Burke County," but you don't know the state. This index allows you, in this case, to narrow your search to three states.

COUNTY COURTHOUSE BOOK

For each state, *County Courthouse Book* gives
- the capital
- when it became a state
- a brief description of the court system in the state
- a listing of courthouses, including information on contacting towns in the six states that keep records at the town level.

Entries for a few New York counties include listings of city and town clerks and the records they hold. This is the only book of the three that acknowledges that New York keeps some records on the town level.

For each courthouse, the book gives
- address
- phone number
- parent counties
- a short note on obtaining land records, naturalization records, vital records, and probate records from the courthouse (may include such items as the name and title of person to contact for different types of records, cost of the records, dates for which the courthouse holds records, etc; content varies from county to county)
- a short set of notes taken from the survey

County Courthouse Book also includes brief listings for American Samoa, Guam, Puerto Rico, and the Virgin Islands.

While the level of detail in some of these listings could be helpful, specifics like fees and individuals' names may have changed since the information was gathered.

This book has one major flaw: Ms. Bentley compiled it based on responses to surveys that she sent to the counties and towns, so content varies from listing to listing. Some counties and towns didn't answer all the questions on the survey. Some didn't return the survey at all; for those, the book lists only the address and phone number of the courthouse, the date of organization, and the parent county. If someone in your ancestral county or town took time to return the survey, you're in good shape. If they didn't, *County Courthouse Book* won't be of much use to you. Sample listings for Armstrong County, Pennsylvania, from the three books follow for comparison.

A COMPARISON OF INFORMATION IN THE THREE BOOKS

Ancestry's Red Book

Map	County Recorder of Deeds	Date Formed Parent County/ies	Deeds	Register of Wills
G6	Armstrong Market Street Kittanning 16201	1800 Allegheny/ Lycoming/ Westmoreland	1805	1805

Armstrong was attached to Westmoreland County until 1804.

The Handy Book for Genealogists

Name	Map Index	Date Created	Parent County or Territory From Which Organized
Armstrong	C4	12 Mar 1800	Allegheny, Lycoming, Westmoreland

Armstrong County, Market Street, Kittanning, PA 16201   (724) 543-2500 (Co Reg & Rcdr has b, d, & bur rec 1893–1905, m rec from 1895, pro & land rec from 1805)

County Courthouse Book

Armstrong County Courthouse
Market Street, Kittanning, PA 16201
Phone (412) 543-2500
County organized 1800 from Allegheny, Lycoming, and Westmoreland Counties.
Land records: Contact Beverly A. Casella, Acting Recorder of Deeds
Naturalization records: Contact Nancy Heilman, Prothonotary
Vital records: Contact Beverly A. Casella, Acting Clerk of Orphans Court
Probate records: Contact Beverly A. Casella, Acting Register of Wills
No probate search service; copies $1.00 per page by mail, plus SASE, no minimum; "Very helpful to have names spelled correctly and approximate dates."

[Note: The author doesn't define what the notations "No probate search service" or "Probate search service," included in some listings, mean. These notations may be misleading because, for example, personnel at the Armstrong County, Pennsylvania, Courthouse will indeed check their probate indexes to see if they have an estate for a given name and will photocopy materials from estates upon request. The area code is different from that given in the *Handy Book* because the area code changed between the time of publication of *County Courthouse Book* and the later *Handy Book*—an example of why it's best to use the latest reference possible.]

Where to Write for Vital Records at the State Level

The most recent birth, death, marriage, and divorce records in a state are usually recorded at the state level. The dates given in this appendix reflect what is kept at the state level only. There may be earlier records at the county or town level. See appendix B for some references that will help you identify what records are kept at those levels.

Fees for vital records run from four to twenty-five dollars and even higher, depending on the circumstances. There may be extra fees for paying by credit card, ordering by phone, etc. If you don't know the exact date of the event, there may be additional fees for searching indexes. Check the Web site or contact the office to verify the current charges before ordering records. If you telephone to request the charges, you may be able to get them from a recorded announcement. If so, listen carefully to the full announcement in order to be certain what information the repository wants from you. Some repositories ask for information like your driver's license number. Send the fee in the form of a check or money order; do not send cash.

In many cases, Web sites for these offices give specific instructions for ordering records, including order forms you can print out. If you write to the office without an order form, give as much information about the person or people involved in the record as you can to ensure getting the right record. Enclose a self-addressed, stamped envelope with your request.

Specifically request a photocopy of the record; otherwise, you may receive a transcription or computer-generated record that doesn't include all the details from the original. Even if you do request a photocopy, a transcription may be all that is available.

Internet addresses in this appendix were correct at the time of publication; however, Internet addresses often change. Use search engines to find sites whose addresses have changed.

An Internet site called VitalChek at <http://www.vitalchek.com/states.asp>

has links to Web pages for many state repositories of vital records, including large cities like New York and Philadelphia.

Alabama
Center for Health Statistics
State Department of Health

    P.O. Box 5625, Montgomery, AL 36103-5625   (334) 206-5418
    http://www.alapubhealth.org/vital/vitalrcd.htm
    Birth and Death Records: since January 1908
    Marriage Records: since August 1936
    Divorce Records: since January 1950

Alaska
Department of Health and Social Services
Bureau of Vital Statistics

    P.O. Box 110675, Juneau, AK 99811-0675   (907) 465-3392
    http://health.hss.state.ak.us/dph/bvs/bvs_home.htm
    Birth and Death Records: since January 1913
    Marriage Records: since 1913
    Divorce Records: since 1950

Arizona
Vital Records Section
Arizona Department of Health Services

    P.O. Box 3887, Phoenix, AZ 85030   (602) 255-3260
    http://www.hs.state.az.us/vitalred/vitalred.htm
    Birth and Death Records: since July 1909
    Marriage and Divorce Records: contact clerk of superior court where license
      or divorce was issued

Arkansas
Division of Vital Records
Arkansas Department of Health

    4815 W. Markham St., Little Rock, AR 72205-3867   (501) 661-2134
    http://health.state.ar.us/htm/vr_faq.htm
    Birth and Death Records: since February 1914, and some Little Rock and
      Fort Smith records from 1881
    Marriage Records: coupons since 1917 (for full certified copy, contact the
      county clerk in county where license was issued)
    Divorce Records: coupons since 1923 (for full certified copy contact the
      circuit or chancery clerk in county where divorce was granted)

California
State Department of Health Services
Office of Vital Records

304 S St., Sacramento, CA 95814

(phone number not available; no phone requests)

http://www.dhs.ca.gov/hisp/chs/OVR/Ordercert.htm

Birth and Death Records: since July 1905

Marriage and Divorce Records: since 1905; divorce record fee is for identification of county where certified copy can be obtained; certificates are available from the state only for actions between 1962 and June 1984

Colorado
Vital Records Section
Colorado Department of Public Health and Environment

4300 Cherry Creek Dr. S, Denver, CO 80246-1530   (303) 692-2224

http://www.state.co.us/gov_dir/cdphe_dir/hs/cshom.html

Birth Records: since 1910

Death Records: since 1900

Marriage and Divorce Records: certified copies are not available from state office; fee for verification, date, and place of event; copies available from county clerk in county where event occurred

Connecticut
Vital Records
Department of Health Services

150 Washington St., Hartford, CT 06106   (860) 509-7897

http://www.state.ct.us/dph/OPPE/vr-birth.html

Birth and Death Records: since July 1897

Marriage Records: since July 1897

Divorce Records: state office does not have divorce decrees and cannot issue certified copies; contact clerk of superior court where divorce was granted

Delaware
Public Archives
Hall of Records

121 Duke of York St., Dover, DE 19901   (302) 739-5318

http://www.archives.lib.de.us/research/vital.htm

Birth Records: since 1920

Death Records: since 1930

Marriage Records: since 1930

Divorce Records: certified copies are not available from state office; fee for search and verification of essential facts of divorce

District of Columbia
Vital Records Branch

825 North Capitol St. NE, First Floor, Washington, DC 20002

(202) 442-9009

http://www.ci.washington.dc.us/services_faq.html#15
Birth Records: since 1874
Death Records: since 1855 (no death records were filed during the Civil War)
Marriage and Divorce Records: since 16 September 1956 (for records before this date, contact Clerk, U.S. District Court for the District of Columbia, Washington, DC 20001)

Florida
Department of Health and Rehabilitative Services
Office of Vital Statistics
P.O. Box 210, 1217 Pearl St., Jacksonville, FL 32231-0042
(904) 359-6900
http://www.doh.state.fl.us/ (within this Web site, use the "Choose Subject" box to choose "Vital Records and Statistics"; on the next page, click on "Certificates" to get to a page where you can click on listings for various types of certificates)
Birth Records: some birth records dating back to April 1865, but the majority of records date from January 1917
Death Records: some death records dating back to August 1877, but most records date from January 1917
Marriage and Divorce Records: since 6 June 1927

Georgia
Georgia Department of Human Resources
Vital Records Unit
Room 217-H, 47 Trinity Ave. SW, Atlanta, GA 30334   (404) 656-4750
http://www.ph.dhr.state.ga.us/epi/vitalrecords/index.shtml
Birth and Death Records: since January 1919
Marriage and Divorce Records: since 9 June 1952

Hawaii
Office of Health Status Monitoring
State Department of Health
P.O. Box 3378, Honolulu, HI 96801   (808) 586-4533
http://www.hawaii.gov/health/records/vr_howto.html
Birth and Death Records: since 1853
Marriage and Divorce Records: since July 1951

Idaho
Vital Statistics Unit
Idaho Department of Health and Welfare
450 W. State St., Boise, ID 83720-9990   (208) 334-5988
(no official Web site from the state of Idaho giving information on vital statistics has been located)

Birth and Death Records: since July 1911 (heirloom birth certificate available; suitable for framing)

Marriage and Divorce Records: since May 1947

Illinois
Division of Vital Records
Illinois Department of Public Health
535 W. Jefferson St., Springfield, IL 62761   (217) 782-6553
http://www.idph.state.il.us/vital/vitalhome.htm
Birth and Death Records: since January 1916
Marriage and Divorce Records: Indexes since January 1962; selected items may be verified for fee; certified copies are not available from the state office

Indiana
Vital Records Department
Indiana State Department of Health
2 N. Meridian St., Indianapolis, IN 46204   (317) 233-2700
http://www.state.in.us/isdh/bdcertifs/bdcert.html
Birth Records: since October 1907
Death Records: records since 1900
Marriage Records: marriage index since 1958; certified copies available from the county where marriage was registered
Divorce Records: contact the county clerk in county where divorce was granted

Iowa
Iowa Department of Public Health
Bureau of Vital Records
Lucas State Office Building, First Floor, Des Moines, IA 50319-0075 (515) 281-4944
http://idph.state.ia.us/pa/vr.htm
Birth and Death Records: records since July 1880
Marriage Records: since July 1880
Divorce Records: brief statistical records only since 1906

Kansas
Office of Vital Statistics
Kansas State Department of Health and Environment
900 Jackson St., Topeka, KS 66612-1290   (785) 296-1400
http://www.kdhe.state.ks.us/vital/
Birth and Death Records: since July 1911
Marriage Records: since May 1913
Divorce Records: since July 1951

Kentucky
Office of Vital Statistics
Department for Health Services
    275 E. Main St., Frankfort, KY 40601   (502) 564-4212
    http://www.kdla.state.ky.us/arch/vitastat.htm
    Birth and Death Records: since January 1911; some earlier records from
        1852 forward survive
    Marriage and Divorce Records: since June 1958

Louisiana
Vital Records Registry
    P.O. Box 60630, New Orleans, LA 70160   (504) 568-5152
    http://www.dhh.state.la.us/OPH/vrinfo.htm
    Birth Records: since July 1914; birth records for city of New Orleans are
        available from 1892
    Death Records: since 1942
    Marriage and Divorce Records: contact clerk of court where event took place

    (For birth records over one hundred years old and death and marriage
records over fifty years old, contact the Louisiana State Archives.)

Maine
Office of Vital Records
    221 State St., Station 11, Augusta, ME 04333   (207) 287-3184
    http://www.state.me.us/dhs/main/faq.htm
    Birth and Death Records: since 1892; records for 1892–1922 are available
        at the Maine State Archives
    Marriage and Divorce Records: since 1892; records for 1892–1922 are
        available at the Maine State Archives

Maryland
Division of Vital Records
Department of Health and Mental Hygiene
    Metro Executive Building, 4201 Patterson Ave., P.O. Box 68760,
        Baltimore, MD 21215-0020   (410) 764-3069
    http://www.dhmh.state.md.us/html/vitalrec.htm
    Birth and Death Records: since August 1898; records for the city of Baltimore
        are available from January 1875
    Marriage Records: since June 1951
    Divorce Records: since January 1961; certified copies are not available from
        state office; only verification is available

Massachusetts
    470 Atlantic Ave. Second Floor, Boston MA 02201   (617) 753-8600

http://www.magnet.state.ma.us/dph/vitrecs.htm

Birth and Death Records: since 1901; for records from 1841–1905, contact the Massachusetts Archives

Marriage Records: since 1901; for records from 1841–1905, contact the Massachusetts Archives

Divorce Records: index only since 1952; obtain from probate court in county where divorce was issued

Michigan
Vital Records Requests
P.O. Box 30195, Lansing, MI 48909   (517) 335-8655

http://www.mdch.state.mi.us/PHA/OSR/vitframe.htm

Birth and Death Records: since 1867

Marriage Records: since April 1867

Divorce Records: since 1897

Minnesota
Minnesota Department of Health
Vital Records
717 Delaware St. SE, P.O. Box 9441, Minneapolis, MN 55440
   (651) 215-5800

http://www.health.state.mn.us/divs/chs/data/bd_1.htm

Birth and Death Records: since January 1908

Marriage Records: statewide index since January 1958; certified copies are not available from the state office

Divorce Records: index since January 1970; certified copies are not available from state office

Mississippi
State Department of Health
Mississippi Vital Records
P.O. Box 1700, Jackson, MS 39215-1700   (601) 576-7960

http://www.msdh.state.ms.us/phs/index.htm

Birth and Death Records: since 1912

Marriage Records: statistical records only from January 1926 to 1 July 1938 and since January 1942; records from 1 July 1938 to 1941 kept by circuit court in county of issue

Divorce Records: since January 1926; certified copies are not available

Missouri
Missouri Department of Health
Bureau of Vital Records
930 Wildwood, P.O. Box 570, Jefferson City, MO 65102-0570
   (314) 751-6400

http://www.health.state.mo.us/BirthAndDeathRecords/
BirthAndDeathRecords.html
Birth and Death Records: since January 1910
Marriage and Divorce Records: indexes since July 1948

Montana
Bureau of Records and Statistics
State Department of Health and Environmental Science,
Helena, MT 59620 (406) 444-2614
(no official Web site from the state of Montana giving information on vital
records has been located)
Birth and Death Records: since late 1907
Marriage and Divorce Records: since July 1943, some items may be verified;
certified copies are not available from state office; apply to the county
where the event occurred

Nebraska
Nebraska Department of Health and Human Services Finance and Support
Vital Records
P.O. Box 95065, Lincoln, NE 68509-5065 (402) 471-2871
http://www.hhs.state.ne.us/ced/cedindex.htm
Birth and Death Records: since late 1904
Marriage and Divorce Records: since January 1909

Nevada
Division of Health-Vital Statistics
Capitol Complex
505 E. King St., Room 102, Carson City, NV 89710 (775) 684-4242
http://www.state.nv.us/health/hdprgms.htm
Birth and Death Records: since July 1911
Marriage and Divorce Records: indexes since January 1968; certified copies
are not available from the state health department

New Hampshire
Bureau of Vital Records
Health and Welfare Building
6 Hazen Dr., Concord, NH 03301 (603) 271-4651
(no official Web site from the state of New Hampshire giving information
on vital records has been located)
Birth and Death Records: since 1640
Marriage Records: since 1640
Divorce Records: since 1808

New Jersey
New Jersey Department of Health and Senior Services
Vital Statistics Registration
P.O. Box 370, Trenton, NJ 08625-0370   (609) 292-4087
http://www.state.nj.us/health/vital/vital.htm
Birth and Death Records: since June 1878; records from May 1848 to May
1878 available at Archives and History Bureau, State Library Division,
State Department of Education, Trenton, NJ 08625
Marriage Records: since June 1878
Divorce Records: available at Public Information Center, CN 967,
Trenton, NJ 08625

New Mexico
Vital Statistics
New Mexico Health Services Division
P.O. Box 26110, Santa Fe, NM 87502   (505) 827-2338
(No official Web site from the state of New Mexico giving information on
vital records has been located)
Birth and Death Records: since 1920, plus delayed records since 1880
Marriage Records: contact county clerk in county where license was issued
Divorce Records: contact clerk of superior court where divorce was granted

New York (except New York City)
Vital Records Section
State Department of Health
Empire State Plaza, Albany, NY 12237-0023   (518) 474-3077
http://www.health.state.ny.us/nysdoh/consumer/vr.htm#genealogy
Birth and Death Records: since 1880
Marriage Records: since 1880
Divorce Records: since January 1963

For all records in the five boroughs of New York City, records before 1914
in Albany, Buffalo, and Yonkers, or before 1880 in any other city, write to
registrar of vital statistics in the city where the event occurred. Local
registrars maintain records for their own jurisdictions. Frequently, the local
registrar is the town or city clerk. Requests for copies of marriage certificates
obtained in New York City must be made through the office of the city clerk
in the borough in which the certificate was obtained, which may not be the
borough in which the marriage took place. If you need assistance in
identifying a local registrar, call the New York State Department of Health
at (518) 474-3077.

North Carolina
Department of Environment, Health, and Natural Resources
Division of Epidemiology

Vital Records Branch

1903 Mail Service Center, Raleigh, NC 27699-1903   (919) 733-3526

http://www.schs.state.nc.us/SCHS/certificates/

Birth Records: since October 1913

Death Records: since 1 January 1946; death records from 1913 through 1945 are available from the North Carolina Division of Archives and History

Marriage Records: since January 1962

Divorce Records: since January 1958

North Dakota

Division of Vital Records

State Capitol

600 E. Boulevard Ave., Bismarck, ND 58505   (701) 328-2360

http://www.health.state.nd.us/ndhd/admin/vital/

Birth and Death Records: some records since July 1893; records from 1894 to 1920 are incomplete

Marriage Records: since July 1925

Divorce Records: Index of records since July 1949; some items may be verified; contact the district court clerk in county where divorce was granted for certified copies

Ohio

Bureau of Vital Statistics

Ohio Department of Health

P.O. Box 15098, Columbus, OH 43215-0098   (614) 466-2531

http://www.odh.state.oh.us/records/records-f.htm

Birth Records: since 20 December 1908

Death Records: since 1 January 1937; records for deaths which occurred 20 December 1908–31 December 1944 can be obtained from the Ohio Historical Society, Archives Library Division, 1985 Velma Ave., Columbus, OH 43211-2497

Marriage and Divorce Records: since September 1949; items may be verified; will not provide certified copies

Oklahoma

Vital Records Service

Oklahoma State Department of Health

1000 N.E. Tenth, Oklahoma City, OK 73117   (405) 271-4040

or

Vital Records Service, Tulsa Office

108 N. Greenwood St., Tulsa, OK 74120   (918) 582-4973

http://www.health.state.ok.us/program/vital/brec.html

Birth and Death Records: since October 1908

Marriage and Divorce Records: contact clerk of court in county where event occurred

Oregon
Oregon Health Division
Vital Statistics Section
P.O. Box 14050, Portland, OR 97293-0050   (503) 731-4095
http://www.ohd.hr.state.or.us/cdpe/chs/certif/certfaqs.htm
Birth and Death Records: since January 1903; some earlier records for the city of Portland since about 1880 are available from the Oregon State Archives; heirloom birth record available
Marriage Records: since 1906
Divorce Records: since 1925

Pennsylvania
Division of Vital Records
State Department of Health Central Building
101 S. Mercer St., P.O. Box 1528,
   New Castle, PA 16103   (724) 656-3100
http://www.health.state.pa.us/HPA/apply_bd.htm
Birth and Death Records: since January 1906; wallet card-style birth certificate available
Marriage and Divorce Records: Make application to the county clerk (for marriage record) or prothonotary (for divorce record) in the county where the event occurred

Rhode Island
Division of Vital Records
Rhode Island Department of Health
Room 101, Cannon Building, 3 Capitol Hill, Providence,
   RI 02908-5097   (401) 222-2812
(no official Web site from the state of Rhode Island giving information on vital records has been located)
Birth and Death Records: since 1853
Marriage Records: since January 1853
Divorce Records: write to Clerk of Family Court, 1 Dorrance Plaza, Providence, RI 02903

South Carolina
Office of Vital Records and Public Health Statistics
South Carolina Department of Health and Environmental Control
2600 Bull St., Columbia, SC 29201   (803) 734-4830
http://www.state.sc.us/scdah/vit.htm
Birth and Death Records: since January 1915

Marriage Records: since July 1950, records since 1911 are recorded with the probate judge in the county where the license was issued
Divorce Records: since July 1962

South Dakota
Vital Records
South Dakota Department of Health
600 E. Capitol, Pierre, SD 57501-2536   (605) 773-4961
http://www.state.sd.us/doh/VitalRec/index.htm
Birth and Death Records: since July 1905, and some earlier records
Marriage and Divorce Records: since July 1905

Tennessee
Tennessee Vital Records
Central Services Building
421 Fifth Ave. N., First Floor, Nashville, TN 37247-0460
(615) 741-1763
http://www.state.tn.us/health/vr/
Birth Records: for entire state since January 1914; records of some births that occurred in the major cities from 1881 to 1913 are also available
Death Records: Vital Records Office keeps death records for fifty years; older records are kept at the Tennessee Library and Archives; records for entire state available since January 1914; for Nashville, since July 1874; for Knoxville, since July 1887; for Chattanooga, since 6 March 1872
Marriage and Divorce Records: since July 1945

Texas
Bureau of Vital Statistics
P.O. Box 12040, Austin, TX 78711-2040   (512) 458-7111
http://www.tdh.state.tx.us/bvs/default.htm
Birth and Death Records: since 1903
Marriage Records: search and verification of essential facts in records since January 1966; certified copies are not available from the state office
Divorce Records: search and verification of essential facts in records since January 1968; certified copies of marriage licenses or divorce decrees are only available from the county or district clerk in the county in which the event occurred

Utah
Bureau of Vital Records
Utah Department of Health
288 North 1460 West, P.O. Box 141012, Salt Lake City, UT 84114-1012   (801) 538-6105
http://www.health.state.ut.us/bvr/

Birth and Death Records: since 1905; if event occurred from 1890 to 1904 in Salt Lake City or Ogden, write to the city board of health

Marriage and Divorce Records: since 1978; only short form certified copies are available

Vermont
Vermont Department of Health

108 Cherry St., Burlington, VT 05402-0070   (802) 863-7275 or (800) 439-5008

http://www.state.vt.us/health/bcert.htm for birth certificates (no official Web site from the state of Vermont giving information on marriage or death records has been located)

Birth and Death Records: for records since 1981, contact the Vermont Department of Health; for records before 1981, contact Division of Public Records

Marriage Records: for records since 1981, contact Vermont Department of Health; for records before 1981, contact Division of Public Records

Divorce Records: since 1981

Virginia
Office of Vital Records

P.O. Box 1000, Richmond, VA 23208-1000   (804) 225-5000

http://www.vdh.state.va.us/misc/f_08.htm

Birth and Death Records: from January 1853 to December 1896, and since 14 June 1912; only the cities of Hampton, Newport News, Norfolk, and Richmond have records between 1896 and 14 June 1912

Marriage Records: since 1853

Divorce Records: since January 1918

With the exception of the years 1896 to 1912, the Office of Vital Records has records of births, deaths, and marriages since 1853. There are no records prior to 1853, and there was no law for the registration of births and deaths between 1896 and 14 June 1912.

Washington
Department of Health
Center for Health Statistics

P.O. Box 9709, Olympia, WA 98507-9709   (360) 236-4300

http://www.doh.wa.gov/EHSPHL/CHS/cert.htm

Birth and Death Records: since July 1907

Marriage and Divorce Records: since January 1968

West Virginia
Vital Registration

Building 3, Room 516, State Capitol Complex, Charleston, WV 25305   (304) 558-2931 http://www.wvdhhr.org/bph/oehp/hsc/vr/birtcert.htm

Birth and Death Records: since January 1917

Marriage Records: since 1921; certified copies available from 1964

Divorce Records: index since 1968; certified copies are not available from state office

Wisconsin

Vital Records

P.O. Box 309, Madison WI 53701-0309   (608) 266-1371

http://www.dhfs.state.wi.us/VitalRecords/index.htm

Birth and Death Records: since 1 October 1907; some records between 1857 and 1907; scattered records earlier than 1857

Marriage Records: since April 1836; records before 1 October 1907 are incomplete

Divorce Records: Records since October 1907

Wyoming

Vital Records Services

Hathaway Building, Cheyenne, WY 82002   (307) 777-7591

http://wdhfs.state.wy.us/vital_records/

Birth and Death Records: since July 1909

Marriage and Divorce Records: since May 1941

The National Archives and Its Regional Records Service Facilities

These facilities have selected genealogical microfilm holdings including complete census population schedules, Revolutionary War pensions, and other basic records, plus records specific to the region they cover. Call before visiting to verify that the facility has the microfilm publications in which you are interested. For contact information and addresses for the facilities, check NARA's Web site at <http://www.nara.gov/regional/nrmenu.html> or write to NARA at National Archives and Records Administration, Washington, DC 20408.

NARA has Regional Records Service Facilities in the following cities:

- Anchorage, Alaska
- Laguna Niguel, California
- San Francisco (San Bruno), California
- Denver, Colorado
- Atlanta (East Point), Georgia
- Chicago, Illinois
- College Park, Maryland
- Suitland, Maryland
- Boston (Waltham), Massachusetts
- Pittsfield, Massachusetts
- Kansas City, Missouri
- Lee's Summit, Missouri
- St. Louis, Missouri
- New York, New York
- Dayton, Ohio
- Philadelphia, Pennsylvania
- Fort Worth, Texas
- Seattle, Washington

Addresses of State Libraries and Archives

Alabama

Alabama Public Library Service
   6030 Monticello Dr., Montgomery, AL 36130
   http://www.apls.state.al.us/

Alabama Department of Archives & History
   624 Washington Ave., Montgomery, AL 36130-0100
   http://www.archives.state.al.us/

Alaska

Alaska State Library
   P.O. Box 110571, Juneau, AK 99811-0571
   http://www.educ.state.ak.us/lam/library/pub/quickinfo.html

Reference Services
Alaska State Archives
   141 Willoughby Ave., Juneau, AK 99801-1720
   http://www.educ.state.ak.us/lam/archives/

Arizona

Arizona Department of Library, Archives, and Public Records
   State Capitol, Ste. 200, 1700 W. Washington St., Phoenix, AZ 85007
   http://www.lib.az.us/index.html

Arkansas

Arkansas State Library
   One Capitol Mall, Little Rock, AR 72201
   http://www.asl.lib.ar.us/

Arkansas History Commission
   One Capitol Mall, Little Rock, AR 72201
   http://www.state.ar.us/ahc/

California

California State Library
Library and Courts Building
914 Capitol Mall, Sacramento, CA 95814
http://www.library.ca.gov/

California State Archives
1020 "O" St., Sacramento, CA 95814
http://www.ss.ca.gov/archives/archives.htm

Colorado

Colorado State Library
201 E. Colfax Ave., No. 309, Denver, CO 80203-1799
http://www.cde.state.co.us/index_library.htm

Colorado State Archives
1313 Sherman St., Room 1B-20, Denver, CO 80203
http://www.state.co.us/gov_dir/gss/archives/

Connecticut

Connecticut State Library
231 Capitol Ave., Hartford, CT 06106
http://www.cslnet.ctstateu.edu/

State Archives
Connecticut State Library
231 Capitol Ave., Hartford, CT 06106
http://www.cslnet.ctstateu.edu/archives.htm

Delaware

The State Library of Delaware
43 S. DuPont Highway, Dover, DE 19901
http://www.lib.de.us/

Delaware Public Archives
Hall of Records
121 Duke of York St., Dover, DE 19901
http://www.archives.lib.de.us

Florida

State Library of Florida
Division of Library and Information Services
Department of State
R. A. Gray Building
500 S. Bronough St., Tallahassee, FL 32399-0250
http://dlis.dos.state.fl.us/index_flash.html

Florida State Archives
R.A. Gray Building
500 S. Bronough St., Tallahassee, FL 32399-0250
http://dlis.dos.state.fl.us/barm/

Georgia

Office of Public Library Services
1800 Century Pl., Ste. 150, Atlanta, GA 30345
http://www.public.lib.ga.us/

Georgia Department of Archives and History
Ben W. Fortson Jr. Archives and Records Building
330 Capitol Ave. SE, Atlanta, GA 30334
http://www.sos.state.ga.us/archives/

Hawaii

Hawaii State Library
478 S. King St., Honolulu, HI 96813-2901
http://www.hcc.hawaii.edu/hspls/hsl/hslov.html

Hawaii State Archives
Department of Accounting and General Services
Kekauluohi Building
Iolani Palace Grounds, Honolulu, HI 96813
http://www.hawaii.gov/dags/archives/

Idaho

Idaho State Library
325 W. State St., Boise, ID 83702
http://www.state.id.us/isl/hp.htm

Idaho State Historical Society
1109 Main St., #250, Boise, ID 83702-5642
http://www2.state.id.us/ishs/

Illinois

Illinois State Library
300 S. Second St., Springfield, IL 62701-1796
http://www.library.sos.state.il.us/

Illinois State Archives
Margaret Cross Norton Building
Capitol Complex, Springfield, IL 62756
http://www.sos.state.il.us/depts/archives/arc_home.html

Indiana

Indiana State Library
140 N. Senate Ave., Indianapolis, IN 46204
http://www.statelib.lib.in.us/

Indiana State Archives
117 State Library Building, 140 N. Senate Ave., Indianapolis, IN 46204
http://www.ai.org/icpr/webfile/archives/homepage.html

Iowa

State Library of Iowa

    1112 E. Grand Ave., Des Moines, IA 50319

    http://www.silo.lib.ia.us/

State Historical Society of Iowa

    600 E. Locust, Des Moines, IA 50319-0290

    or

    402 Iowa Ave., Iowa City, IA 52240-1806

    http://www.culturalaffairs.org/shsi/index.html

Kansas

Kansas State Library

    300 S.W. Tenth Ave., Room 343-N, Topeka, KS 66612-1593

    http://skyways.lib.ks.us/KSL/

Kansas State Historical Society

    Kansas History Center

    6425 S.W. Sixth Ave., Topeka, KS 66615

    http://www.kshs.org/

Kentucky

Kentucky Department for Libraries and Archives

    300 Coffee Tree Rd., P.O. Box 537, Frankfort, KY 40602-0537

    http://www.kdla.state.ky.us/

Louisiana

State Library of Louisiana

    P.O. Box 131, Baton Rouge, LA 70821

    http://smt.state.lib.la.us/

Louisiana State Archives

    3851 Essen Ln., Baton Rouge, LA 70809-2137

    http://www.sec.state.la.us/arch-1.htm

Maine

Maine State Library

    LMA Building

    64 State House Station, Augusta, ME 04333

    http://www.state.me.us/msl/mslhome.htm

Maine State Archives

    84 State House Station, Augusta, ME 04333-0084

    http://www.state.me.us/sos/arc/

Maryland

Maryland State Law Library

    Robert C. Murphy Courts of Appeal Building

    361 Rowe Blvd., Annapolis, MD 21401-1697

    http://www.lawlib.state.md.us/

Maryland State Archives
350 Rowe Blvd., Annapolis, MD 21401
http://www.mdarchives.state.md.us/

Massachusetts
State Library of Massachusetts
George Fingold Library
State House
24 Beacon St., Boston, MA 02133
http://www.state.ma.us/lib/
Massachusetts Archives
220 Morrissey Blvd., Boston, MA 02125
http://www.magnet.state.ma.us/sec/arc/arcidx.htm

Michigan
Library of Michigan
717 W. Allegan St., P.O. Box 30007, Lansing, MI 48909-7507
http://www.libofmich.lib.mi.us/
State Archives of Michigan
717 W. Allegan St., Lansing, MI 48918-1800
http://www.sos.state.mi.us/history/archive/archive.html

Minnesota
Minnesota State Library Agency
Library Development and Services Library
1500 Highway 36 W, Roseville, MN 55113
http://cfl.state.mn.us/library/Libdev.htm
Minnesota Historical Society
345 Kellogg Blvd. W, St. Paul, MN 55102-1906
http://www.mnhs.org/

Mississippi
Mississippi Library Commission
1221 Ellis Ave., Jackson, MS 39289-0700
http://www.mlc.lib.ms.us/
Mississippi Department of Archives and History
P.O. Box 571, Jackson, MS 39205-0571
http://www.mdah.state.ms.us/

Missouri
Missouri State Library
P.O. Box 387, Jefferson City, MO 65102-0387
http://mosl.sos.state.mo.us/lib-ser/libser.html
Missouri State Archives
State Information Center
P.O. Box 1767, Jefferson City, MO 65102
http://mosl.sos.state.mo.us/rec-man/arch.html

Montana

Montana State Library
P.O. Box 201800, 1515 E. Sixth Ave., Helena, MT 59620-1800
http://msl.state.mt.us/

Montana Historical Society
225 N. Roberts, Helena, MT 59620
http://www.his.mt.gov/

Nebraska

Nebraska Library Commission
The Atrium
1200 North St., Ste. 120, Lincoln, NE 68508-2023
http://www.nlc.state.ne.us/index.html

Nebraska State Historical Society
P.O. Box 82554, 1500 R St., Lincoln, NE 68501
http://nebraskahistory.org/

Nevada

Nevada State Library and Archives
100 N. Stewart St., Carson City, NV 89701
http://www.clan.lib.nv.us/

New Hampshire

New Hampshire State Library
20 Park St., Concord, NH 03301
http://webster.state.nh.us/nhsl/index.html

New Hampshire Division of Records Management and Archives
71 S. Fruit St., Concord, NH 03301
http://www.state.nh.us/state/index.html

New Jersey

New Jersey State Library
P.O. Box 520, Trenton, NJ 08625-0520
http://www.njstatelib.org/

New Jersey State Archives
New Jersey State Library Building
185 W. State St., Level 2, P.O. Box 307, Trenton, NJ 08625-0307
http://www.state.nj.us/state/darm/archives.html

New Mexico

New Mexico State Library
1209 Camino Carlos Rey, Santa Fe, NM 87505-9860
http://www.stlib.state.nm.us/

New Mexico State Records Center and Archives
1205 Camino Carlos Rey, Santa Fe, NM 87505
http://www.state.nm.us/cpr/

New York

New York State Library

Cultural Education Center

Empire State Plaza, Albany, NY 12230

http://www.nysl.nysed.gov/

New York State Archives and Records Administration

New York State Education Department

Cultural Education Center, Albany, NY 12230

http://www.sara.nysed.gov/

North Carolina

State Library of North Carolina

Archives and History/State Library Bldg.

109 E. Jones St., Raleigh, NC 27611

http://statelibrary.dcr.state.nc.us/

North Carolina Division of Archives & History

4610 Mail Service Center, Raleigh, NC 27699-4610

http://www.ah.dcr.state.nc.us/

North Dakota

North Dakota State Library

604 E. Boulevard Ave., Dept. 250, Bismarck, ND 58505-0800

http://ndsl.lib.state.nd.us/

State Historical Society of North Dakota

State Archives and Historical Research Library

North Dakota Heritage Center

612 E. Boulevard Ave., Bismarck, ND 58505-0830

http://www.state.nd.us/hist/sal.htm

Ohio

State Library of Ohio Main Library

65 S. Front St., Eleventh Floor, Columbus, OH 43215-4163

http://winslo.state.oh.us/

Ohio Historical Society

Archives/Library

1982 Velma Ave., Columbus, OH 43211-2497

http://www.ohiohistory.org/resource/statearc/index.html

Oklahoma

Oklahoma Department of Libraries

200 N.E. Eighteenth St., Oklahoma City, OK 73105-3298

http://www.odl.state.ok.us/

Archives & Records

Oklahoma Deptartment of Libraries

200 N.E. Eighteenth St., Oklahoma City, OK 73105-3298

http://www.odl.state.ok.us/oar/

Oregon

Oregon State Library
  250 Winter St. NE, Salem, OR 97310
  http://www.osl.state.or.us/oslhome.html
Oregon State Archives
  800 Summer St. NE, Salem, OR 97310
  http://arcweb.sos.state.or.us/

Pennsylvania

State Library of Pennsylvania
  P.O. Box 1601, Harrisburg, PA 17105-1601
  http://www.statelibrary.state.pa.us/Libstate.htm
Pennsylvania State Archives
  P.O. Box 1026, Harrisburg, PA 17108-1026
  http://www.state.pa.us/PA_Exec/Historical_Museum/DAM/psa.htm

Rhode Island

Rhode Island State Library
  82 Smith St., State House Room 208, Providence, RI 02903
  http://www.sec.state.ri.us/library/web.htm
Rhode Island State Archives
  337 Westminster St., Providence, RI 02903
  http://www.state.ri.us/archives

South Carolina

South Carolina State Library
  1500 Senate St., P.O. Box 11469, Columbia, SC 29211
  http://www.state.sc.us/scsl/index.html
South Carolina Archives and History Center
  8301 Parklane Rd., Columbia, SC 29223
  http://www.state.sc.us/scdah/

South Dakota

South Dakota State Library
  Mercedes MacKay Building
  800 Governors Dr., Pierre, SD 57501-2294
  http://www.state.sd.us/deca/ST_LIB/st_lib.htm
South Dakota State Archives
  900 Governors Dr., Pierre, SD 57501-2217
  http://www.state.sd.us/deca/cultural/archives.htm

Tennessee

Tennessee State Library and Archives
  403 Seventh Ave. N, Nashville, TN 37243-0312
  http://www.state.tn.us/sos/statelib/tslahome.htm

Texas

Texas State Library and Archives Commission
1201 Brazos, P.O. Box 12927, Austin, TX 78711-2927
http://www.tsl.state.tx.us/

Utah

Utah State Library Division
250 N. 1950 W, Salt Lake City, UT 84116-7901
http://www.state.lib.ut.us/index.htm
Utah State Archives and Records Service
P.O. Box 141021, Salt Lake City, UT 84114-1021
http://www.archives.state.ut.us/

Vermont

Vermont Department of Libraries
109 State St., Montpelier, VT 05609-0601
http://dol.state.vt.us/
Vermont State Archives
Redstone Building
26 Terrace St., Drawer 09, Montpelier, VT 05609-1101
http://www.sec.state.vt.us/ (click on the Archives Division link)

Virginia

The Library of Virginia (includes the State Archives)
800 E. Broad St., Richmond, VA 23219-8000
http://www.lva.lib.va.us/

Washington

Washington State Library
Joel M. Pritchard Library, Capitol Campus
Sixteenth and Water streets, Olympia, WA 98504-2460
http://www.statelib.wa.gov/
Washington State Archives
1120 Washington St. SE, P.O. Box 40238, Olympia, WA 98504-0238
http://www.secstate.wa.gov/archives/default.htm

West Virginia

West Virginia Library Commission
1900 Kanawha Blvd. E, Charleston, WV 25305
http://wvlc.lib.wv.us/
Archives and History Library
The Cultural Center
1900 Kanawha Blvd. E, Charleston, WV 25305-0300
http://www.wvculture.org/history/wvsamenu.html

Wisconsin

Division for Libraries, Technology, and Community Learning

125 S. Webster St., P.O. Box 7841, Madison, WI 53707-7841

http://www.dpi.state.wi.us/dlcl/

State Historical Society of Wisconsin

816 State St., Madison, WI 53706

http://www.shsw.wisc.edu/archives/index.html

Wyoming

Wyoming State Library

Department of Administration & Information

Supreme Court & State Library Building

2301 Capitol Ave., Cheyenne, WY 82002-0060

http://www-wsl.state.wy.us/

Wyoming State Archives

Barrett Building

2301 Central Ave., Cheyenne, WY 82002

http://commerce.state.wy.us/cr/archives/

http://spacr.state.wy.us/cr/archives/

CHART SHOWING RECORDS YOU HOPE TO FIND FOR YOUR ANCESTORS IN A COUNTY

Records needed from County: _____ State: _____ (formed from _____ County in _____)

ANCESTOR'S NAME (INCLUDING MAIDEN NAME FOR WOMEN)	BIRTH DATE	BIRTH CERT	BAPT	MARRIAGE: MARRIAGE DATE	CERT	NEWSP	DEEDS: GRANTOR	GRANTEE	DEATH DATE	CERT	DEATH: OBIT	ESTATE	GRAVE LOCATED?

You are free to copy this form for personal use. For instructions on filling it in, see page 187.

For Reference:
- Note date when county was formed and dates when records are available on the county level.
- Include women's maiden names.
- Have birth, marriage, and death dates handy on the chart.
- Enter "N/A" (not available) for records that fall into a time period when records of that type weren't created.
- Enter "E" (elsewhere) for records that would have been created in another county.

Bibliography

This list is only a selection of the many books available to help you with your genealogical research.

AIS Microfiche Indexes of U.S. Census and Other Records. Bountiful, Utah: Accelerated Indexing Systems International, 1984. (A microfiche set of census indexes is available at some Family History Centers.)

Allen, Desmond Walls. *First Steps in Genealogy: A Beginner's Guide to Researching Your Family History.* Cincinnati: Betterway Books, 1998.

Allen, Desmond Walls, and Carolyn Earle Billingsley. *Social Security Applications: A Genealogical Resource.* Conway, Ark.: Research Associates, 1995.

American Library Directory. New York: R. R. Bowker, latest edition.

Arends, Marthe. *Genealogy on CD-ROM.* Baltimore: Genealogical Publishing Company, 1999.

———. *Genealogy Software Guide.* Baltimore: Genealogical Publishing Company, 1998.

Association of Professional Genealogists. *Directory of Professional Genealogists.* Denver, Colo.: Association of Professional Genealogists, latest edition.

Balhuizen, Anne Ross. *Searching on Location: Planning a Research Trip.* Salt Lake City: Ancestry, 1992.

Baxter, Angus. *Do's and Don'ts for Ancestor-Hunters.* Baltimore: Genealogical Publishing Company, 1988.

Bentley, Elizabeth Petty. *County Courthouse Book.* 2nd ed. Baltimore: Genealogical Publishing Company, 1995.

———. *Directory of Family Associations.* Baltimore: Genealogical Publishing Company, 1993.

———. *The Genealogist's Address Book.* 4th ed. Baltimore: Genealogical Publishing Company, 1998.

Bentz, Edna M. *If I Can, You Can Decipher Germanic Records.* San Diego, Calif.: Edna M. Bentz, several editions.

Billingsley, Carolyn Earle, and Desmond Walls Allen. *How to Get the Most Out of Death Certificates*. Conway, Ark.: Research Associates, 1991.

Carmack, Sharon DeBartolo. *The Genealogy Sourcebook*. Los Angeles: Lowell House, 1997.

———. *Organizing Your Family History Search: Efficient & Effective Ways to Gather and Protect Your Genealogical Research*. Cincinnati: Betterway Books, 1999.

Cerny, Johni, and Arlene Eakle. *Ancestry's Guide to Research: Case Studies in American Genealogy*. Salt Lake City: Ancestry, 1985.

Colletta, John Philip. *They Came in Ships*. Salt Lake City: Ancestry, 1993.

Croom, Emily Anne. *The Genealogist's Companion and Sourcebook*. Cincinnati: Betterway Books, 1994.

———. *Unpuzzling Your Past: A Basic Guide to Genealogy*. 3rd ed. Cincinnati: Betterway Books, 1995.

———. *The Unpuzzling Your Past Workbook: Essential Forms and Letters for All Genealogists*. Cincinnati: Betterway Books, 1996.

Daughters of the American Revolution. *DAR Patriot Index*. Washington, D.C.: National Society, Daughters of the American Revolution, 1994.

DeWitt, Donald L., comp. *Guide to Archives and Manuscript Collections in the United States: An Annotated Bibliography*. Westport, Conn.: Greenwood Press, 1994.

Directory of Archives and Manuscript Repositories in the United States. 2nd ed. Phoenix: Oryx Press, 1988.

Directory of Historical Organizations in the United States and Canada. Nashville, Tenn.: AASLH Press, 1990–.

Doane, Gilbert H., and James B. Bell. *Searching for Your Ancestors: The How and Why of Genealogy*. 6th ed. Minneapolis: University of Minnesota Press, 1992.

Dollarhide, William, and Ronald A. Bremer. *America's Best Genealogy Resource Centers*. Bountiful, Utah: Heritage Quest, 1998.

Dollarhide, William. *The Census Book*. Bountiful, Utah: Heritage Quest, 1999.

Eichholz, Alice, ed. *Ancestry's Red Book: American State, County & Town Sources*. Salt Lake City: Ancestry, latest edition.

Encyclopedia of Associations. Farmington Hills, Mich.: Gale Research, latest edition. (See specifically the section "Veterans, Hereditary and Patriotic Organizations.")

Filby, P. William, comp. *A Bibliography of American County Histories*. Baltimore: Genealogical Publishing Company, 1985.

———. *Directory of American Libraries With Genealogy or Local History Collections*. Wilmington, Del.: Scholarly Resources, 1988.

Filby, P. William, and Mary K. Meyer, eds. *Passenger and Immigration Lists Index: A Guide to Published Arrival Records of About 500,000 Passengers Who Came to the United States and Canada in the Seventeenth, Eighteenth, and Nineteenth Centuries*. Detroit: Gale Research, 1981. (Beyond the original volumes, there are annual supplements to this title.)

Gale Directory of Publications and Broadcast Media. Farmington Hills, Mich.: Gale Research, latest edition.

Genealogical & Local History Books in Print. Springfield, Va.: Genealogical Books in Print, 1st–4th eds.; Baltimore: Genealogical Publishing Company, 5th ed., 1996–1997. Volumes include: *Family History Volume, General Reference & World Resources Volume, U.S. Sources & Resources Volume, Alabama-New York,* and *U.S. Sources & Resources Volume, North Carolina-Wyoming.* Volumes may be purchased as a set or separately.

Genealogical Periodical Annual Index. Bowie, Md.: Heritage Books, 1962–.

Genealogies Cataloged by the Library of Congress Since 1986. Washington, D.C.: Library of Congress, 1991.

Greenwood, Val D. *The Researcher's Guide to American Genealogy.* Baltimore: Genealogical Publishing Company, latest edition.

Gregory, Winifred, ed. *American Newspapers 1821–1936: A Union List of Files Available in the United States and Canada.* New York: H. W. Wilson Co., 1937.

The Handy Book for Genealogists. Logan, Utah: Everton Publishers, Inc., latest edition.

Hawkins, Kenneth J., comp. *Research in the Land Entry Files of the General Land Office.* Washington, D.C.: National Archives and Records Administration, 1998.

Heads of Families at the First Census of the United States Taken in the Year 1790, [name of state]. Washington, D.C.: Government Printing Office, 1907–1908 (and reprints).

Heisey, John W. *Genealogy Helps, Hints & Hope.* Morgantown, Pa.: Masthof Press, 1995.

Helm, Matthew L., and April Leigh Helm. *Genealogy Online for Dummies.* 2nd ed. Foster City, Calif.: IDG Books Worldwide, 1999.

Hinckley, Kathleen W. *Locating Lost Family Members & Friends.* Cincinnati: Betterway Books, 1999.

Hone, E. Wade. *Land & Property Research in the United States.* Salt Lake City: Ancestry, 1997.

Howells, Cyndi. *Cyndi's List: A Comprehensive List of 40,000 Genealogy Sites on the Internet.* Baltimore: Genealogical Publishing Company, 1999.

———. *Netting Your Ancestors: Genealogical Research on the Internet.* Baltimore: Genealogical Publishing Company, 1997.

Index of Revolutionary War Pension Applications in the National Archives. Arlington, Va.: National Genealogical Society, 1976.

Jacobus, Donald Lines. *Genealogy as Pastime and Profession.* Baltimore: Genealogical Publishing Company, 1968.

———. *Index to Genealogical Periodicals.* Baltimore: Genealogical Publishing Company, 1973 reprint. Reprinted again by Genealogical Publishing Company, 1997, for Clearfield Company. Revised cumulated version issued by Carl Boyer 3rd. Newhall, Calif.: Carl Boyer 3rd, 1983.

Kaminkow, Marion J., comp. *A Complement to Genealogies in the Library of Congress: A Bibliography.* Baltimore: Magna Carta, 1981.

————., ed. *Genealogies in the Library of Congress: A Bibliography*. Baltimore: Magna Carta, 1972. Supplement for 1972–1976, published 1977; supplement for 1976–1986, published 1987.

————. *United States Local Histories in the Library of Congress: A Bibliography*. Baltimore: Magna Carta, 1975.

Kemp, Thomas Jay. *Virtual Roots: A Guide to Genealogy and Local History on the World Wide Web*. Wilmington, Del.: Scholarly Resources, Inc., 1997.

Lackey, Richard S. *Cite Your Sources: A Manual for Documenting Family Histories and Genealogical Records*. Jackson, Miss.: University Press of Mississippi, 1985.

Meyerink, Kory L., ed. *Printed Sources: A Guide to Published Genealogical Records*. Salt Lake City: Ancestry, 1998.

Military Service Records in the National Archives of the United States. Washington, D.C.: National Archives and Records Administration, 1985.

Mills, Elizabeth Shown. *Evidence! Citation & Analysis for the Family Historian*. Baltimore: Genealogical Publishing Company, 1997.

National Union Catalog of Manuscript Collections. Washington, D.C.: Library of Congress, 1959–1993. Data entered online from 1986 forward; available at <http://lcweb.loc.gov/coll/nucmc/>. Choose one of the search types under "NUCMC Z39.50 Gateway to the RLIN AMC (Archival and Mixed Collections) file" to get to the search page.

Neagles, James C. *U.S. Military Records: A Guide to Federal and State Sources, Colonial America to the Present*. Salt Lake City: Ancestry, 1994.

Newman, John J. *American Naturalization Records, 1790–1990: What They Are and How to Use Them*. Bountiful, Utah: Heritage Quest, 1998.

Newspapers in Microform, United States. Washington, D.C.: Library of Congress, 1973–.

Ninkovich, Tom. *Family Reunion Handbook: A Complete Guide to Planning and Enjoying Family Reunions*. 2nd ed. Cincinnati: Betterway Books, 1999.

Parker, J. Carlyle. *Going to Salt Lake City to Do Family History Research*. Turlock, Calif.: Marietta Publishing Company, 1996.

Periodical Source Index [PERSI]. Fort Wayne, Ind.: Allen County Public Library Foundation, 1988–.

Renick, Barbara, and Richard S. Wilson. *The Internet for Genealogists: A Beginner's Guide*. 4th ed. La Habra, Calif.: Compuology, 1998.

Reunions Workbook & Catalog. Milwaukee, Wisc.: Reunions Magazine, latest edition.

Rose, Christine. *Nicknames: Past and Present*. San Jose, Calif.: Rose Family Association, latest edition.

Rose, Christine, and Kay Germain Ingalls. *The Complete Idiot's Guide to Genealogy*. New York: Alpha Books, 1997.

Rubincam, Milton. *Pitfalls in Genealogical Research*. Salt Lake City: Ancestry, 1987.

Saldaña, Richard H., ed. *A Practical Guide to the "Misteaks" Made in Census Indexes*. Bountiful, Utah: Heritage Quest, 1987.

Salmon, Marylynn. *Women and the Law of Property in Early America*. Chapel Hill: University of North Carolina Press, 1986.

Schaefer, Christina K. *Guide to Naturalization Records of the United States*. Baltimore: Genealogical Publishing Company, 1997.

——. *Instant Information on the Internet! A Genealogist's No-Frills Guide to the 50 States & the District of Columbia*. Baltimore: Genealogical Publishing Company, 1999.

Smith, Juliana Szucs. *The Ancestry Family Historian's Address Book: A Comprehensive List of Local, State, and Federal Agencies and Institutions and Ethnic and Genealogical Organizations*. Salt Lake City: Ancestry, 1997.

Smith, Kenneth. *Genealogical Dates: A User-Friendly Guide*. Camden, Maine: Picton Press, 1994. (Available with a computer disk for converting dates from Julian to Gregorian and back, translating liturgical dates, etc.)

Sperry, Kip. *Index to Genealogical Periodical Literature, 1960–1977*. Detroit: Gale Research Co., 1979.

——. *Reading Early American Handwriting*. Baltimore: Genealogical Publishing Company, 1998.

The Standard Periodical Directory. New York: Oxbridge Communications, 1964–1965.

Stevenson, Noel C. *Genealogical Evidence: A Guide to the Standard of Proof Relating to Pedigrees, Ancestry, Heirship, and Family History*. Rev. ed. Laguna Hills, Calif.: Aegean Park Press, 1989.

Strassburger, Ralph B. *Pennsylvania German Pioneers: A Publication of the Original Lists of Arrivals in the Port of Philadelphia From 1727 to 1808*. 3 vols. Edited by William John Hinke. Norristown, Pa.: Pennsylvania German Society, 1934, or reprints.

Stryker-Rodda, Harriet. *How to Climb Your Family Tree: Genealogy for Beginners*. Baltimore: Genealogical Publishing Company, 1983.

Szucs, Loretto Dennis. *Family History Made Easy*. Salt Lake City: Ancestry, 1998.

Szucs, Loretto Dennis. *They Became Americans: Finding Naturalization Records and Ethnic Origins*, Salt Lake City: Ancestry, 1998.

Szucs, Loretto Dennis, and Sandra Hargreaves Luebking, eds. *The Source: A Guidebook of American Genealogy*. Rev. ed. Salt Lake City: Ancestry, 1997.

Taylor, Maureen. *Uncovering Your Ancestry Through Family Photographs*. Cincinnati: Betterway Books, 2000.

Tepper, Michael. *American Passenger Arrival Records*. Baltimore: Genealogical Publishing Company, 1993.

Thorndale, William, and William Dollarhide. *Map Guide to the U.S. Federal Censuses, 1790–1920*. Baltimore: Genealogical Publishing Company, 1987.

Ulrich's International Periodicals Directory. New York: R.R. Bowker, latest edition. Section "Genealogy and Heraldry" includes family periodicals and periodicals of genealogical societies.

U.S. Bureau of the Census. *A Census of Pensioners for Revolutionary or Military Services*. Baltimore: Genealogical Publishing Company, 1967.

U.S. National Archives and Records Administration. *Guide to Genealogical*

Research in the National Archives. Washington, D.C.: National Archives and Records Administration, 1985.

U.S. Pension Bureau. *List of Pensioners on the Roll January 1, 1883; Giving the Name of Each Pensioner, the Cause for Which Pensioned, the Post-Office Address, the Rate of Pension per Month, and the Date of Original Allowance, as Called for by Senate Resolution of December 8, 1882*. Washington, D.C.: Government Printing Office, 1883. (Reprinted by Genealogical Publishing Company, 1970.)

Using Records in the National Archives for Genealogical Research. General Information Leaflet 5. Washington, D.C.: National Archives and Records Administration, 1990.

Using the Census Soundex. General Information Leaflet 55. Washington, D.C.: National Archives and Records Administration, 1997.

Warren, James W., and Paula Stuart Warren. *Getting the Most Mileage From Genealogical Research Trips*. 3rd ed. St. Paul, Minn.: Warren Research and Publishing, 1998.

Willard, Jim, and Terry Willard, with Jane Wilson. *Ancestors*. Boston: Houghton Mifflin Company, 1997.

Working Press of the Nation, vol. 1, Newspaper Directory. New Providence, New Jersey: R.R. Bowker, latest edition.

Index

Solve the Mystery of Your History with Betterway Books

A Genealogist's Guide to Discovering Your Immigrant & Ethnic Ancestors—Clear, authoritative instruction typifies both the content of this book and the reputation of its author, Sharon DeBartolo Carmack. Research techniques specific to your own ancestors' particular national and ethnic backgrounds enable you to learn where and how to find information that might otherwise elude you. *#70462/$18.99/192 pages/paperback*

A Genealogist's Guide to Discovering Your English Ancestors—Following basic, step-by-step instruction, you'll learn how to access the primary records you need to research your English ancestors. You'll also learn to document your findings properly and move beyond the names on your pedigree charts to understand the historical context in which they lived. *#70464/$18.99/192 pages/paperback*

A Genealogist's Guide to Discovering Your Female Ancestors—Discover special strategies for overcoming the unique challenges of tracing female genealogy. This comprehensive guide shows you methods for determining maiden names and parental lineage: how to access official documents; plus where to find information unique to women of ethnic origins. Also included is a glossary of terms specific to female genealogy, a detailed bibliography with more than 200 resources, plus an extensive source checklist. *#70386/$17.99/144 pages/paperback*

A Genealogist's Guide to Discovering Your Italian Ancestors—This easy-to-use reference guides you step-by-step through researching your Italian ancestors—as far back as the 1700s! You'll learn how to find—and read—Italian vital records; write letters requesting data from Italian officials; and use American records like census and naturalization records, and family letters and church records. You'll also find information on how to read foreign handwriting, and much more. *#70370/$16.99/128 pages/42 b&w illus./paperback*

A Genealogist's Guide to Discovering Your Germanic Ancestors—This hands-on guide addresses virtually every aspect of tracing you Germanic lineage. Here you'll learn how to plan your research, where to locate the vital records you need, and how to overcome the specific challenges associated with Germanic ancestral research. Includes a history of the Germanic countries' many changing boundaries and the key historical events that may have led your ancestors to emigrate. *#70446/$18.99/208 pages/paperback*

The Weekend Genealogist—Researching family history takes time—time that many people just don't have. This book shows you how to maximize your research efficiency by saving time and utilizing what little you have in the best way possible. Author Marcia Melnyk teaches how to make every minute count through step-by-step instruction and sidebars highlighting important tips and procedures. *#70496/$18.99/144 pages/paperback*

The Sleuth Book for Genealogists—From the author of the best-selling *Unpuzzling Your Past,* this guide focuses on research methods, showing you how to create a research "program" you can follow to achieve success. Emily Croom links her proven techniques to the advice of famous fictional detectives, such as Sherlock Holmes and Miss Marple, and organizes information into easy-to-read segments and sidebars. *#70453/$17.99/304 pages/paperback*

Bringing Your Family History to Life Through Social History—Most genealogy books show you how to fill in your pedigrees, but none teach you the hows and whys of your ancestry—until now. You'll find intriguing case histories, charts, sidebars and exercises along with step-by-step instruction on how to research college libraries and historical societies. And you'll learn to weave these historical facts with your own personal genealogies to form a unique family history narrative. *#70426/$19.99/176 pages/paperback*

Crafting Your Family Heritage Album—This inspirational, how-to guide for showcasing cherished family photos, documents and memorabilia combines two of today's hottest pastimes—genealogy and scrapbooking. It features visual, step-by-step instruction and page after page of elegant and imaginative ideas to help you capture and preserve the precious photos and keepsakes of your family history. *#70457/$23.99/128 pages/paperback*

Locating Lost Family Members & Friends—In this unique research guide, author Kathleen Hinckley combines her professional skills as a genealogist and private investigator to help you locate long-lost cousins, family members separated by divorce, missing heirs, biological parents and children, classmates, military buddies, first loves and more. She provides extensive tables, lists and charts to explain how *and* where to locate traditional 20th-Century documents, including U.S. and foreign vital records, social security information, phone directories, census records and more. *#70446/$18.99/176 pages/paperback*

Uncovering Your Ancestry through Family Photographs—Everyone keeps old family photographs, whether in frames, albums or shoeboxes. These photos house a treasury of genealogical information, revealing unique details about our ancestors' lives, personalities and everyday realities. Following this guide's step-by-step instruction, you'll learn how to identify different types of family photographs and determine their date, location, and in some instances, their photographer. Once these photos are collected and analyzed, you'll also learn how to preserve your family collection for generations to come. *#70452/$18.99/224 pages/paperback*

The Handybook for Genealogists, Ninth Edition—More than 750,000 copies sold! Since 1947, the Handybook has proven itself as the most popular and comprehensive research aid available for tracking down major state and county records essential to genealogists. Save countless hours of your research time by consulting its up-to-date listings of archives, genealogical libraries and societies. State profiles cover history and list sources for maps, census and church records. The county profiles tell you where to find custody records, property records and key addresses. Color maps are included of each state and their counties. *#70411/$34.99/380 pages/60 color maps/hardcover*

First Steps in Genealogy—If you're just stepping into the fascinating field of genealogy, this book will get you off to a successful start. Desmond Walls Allen, a recognized genealogical expert, will teach you step-by-step how to define your goals and uncover facts about the people behind the names and dates. Learn to organize your research with pedigree charts, group sheets and filing systems. Discover what sources are available for research, starting with your family scrapbook or attic. Also included are sample forms, a resource directory and glossary. *#70400/$14.99/128 pages/paperback*

Organizing Your Family History Search—Few hobbies generate more paperwork than genealogy. Sharon DeBartolo Carmack shows you how to successfully tackle the arduous process of organizing family research, from filing piles of paper to streamlining the process as a whole. With her flexible filing system and special research notebook, she reveals how you can free up time, conduct better research and become a more effective genealogist. #70425/$16.99/176 pages/paperback

The Genealogist's Companion & Sourcebook—115,000 copies sold! Uncover promising new sources of information about your family history. This hands-on guide shows you how to get past common obstacles—such as lost public records—and discover new information sources like church and funeral home records, government documents, newspapers and maps. #70235/$16.99/256 pages/paperback

Unpuzzling Your Past, Third Edition—Make uncovering your roots easy with this complete genealogical research guide. Step-by-step instructions, handy forms, sample letters, comprehensive resource lists, bibliographies and case studies help guide you every step of the way. #70301/$14.99/180 pages/paperback

The Unpuzzling Your Past Workbook—The perfect companion to *Unpuzzling Your Past*, this book provides you with 40+ forms and letters that make organizing, searching, record-keeping and presenting information easy and enjoyable. #70327/$15.99/320 pages/paperback

How to Tape Instant Oral Biographies, Second Edition—With fun interviewing techniques and exercises, family members of all ages will learn how to spark memories, recall treasured stories, and relate old family anecdotes, sayings, recipes and more. Comes complete with blank family history sheets and work pages. #70448/$12.99/144 pages/paperback

How to Write the Story of Your Life—This friendly guide makes memoir writing an enjoyable undertaking—even if you're a non-writer. Five hundred "memory sparkers" will help you recall forgotten events in each stage of your life and 100 topic ideas help add variety to your story. Includes excerpts from actual memoirs and plenty of encouragement to keep you moving your story towards completion. #10132/$14.99/230 pages/paperback

Writing Family Histories and Memoirs—Your family history and personal stories are too vital to lose. Turn them into a lively record for the next generation with this handy writing reference. You'll find helpful how-to advice on working from memories and interviewing family members, using public records, writing and publishing. #70295/$14.99/272 pages/paperback

Writing Life Stories—Author Bill Roorbach explains how to turn the engaging, untold stories of your life into vivid personal essays and riveting memoirs. You'll learn how to open up memory, access emotion and discover compelling material, shape scenes from experience, and populate stories with the fascinating, silly and maddening "characters" that surround you—your family members and friends. #48045/$14.99/224 pages/paperback

Reaching Back—Record life's most meaningful moments to share with future generations. This easy-to-use keepsake edition includes space for family stories, photos, heirlooms, family trees, and helps you research and record your family's unique history. #70360/$14.99/160 pages/paperback

Family History Logbook—Weave your personal history into the colorful web of national events. You'll find an extensive list of historical events spanning the years 1900 to 2000, along with a special section to record your own milestones. #70345/$16.99/224 pages/paperback

The Everyday Life Series—You've tracked down vital statistics for your great-great grandparents, but do you know what their everyday lives were like? These titles will give you a vivid and detailed picture of life in their own time. Learn what your relatives likely wore, what they ate, and how they talked. Social and religious customs, major occupations and family life are all covered. These "slice-of-life" facts will readily round out any family history.
The Writer's Guide to Everyday Life . . .
. . .during the Civil War
#10635/$16.99/288 pages/paperback
. . .from Prohibition to World War II
#10450/$18.99/272 pages/hardcover
. . .in Renaissance England
#10484/$18.99/272 pages/hardcover
. . .in Regency and Victorian England
#10545/$18.99/240 pages/hardcover
. . .in the 1800's
#10353/$18.99/320 pages/hardcover
. . .in the Wild West
#10600/$18.99/336 pages/hardcover
. . .in Colonial America
#10640/$14.99/288 pages/paperback
. . .in the Middle Ages
#10679/$14.99/256 pages/paperback

Creating Family Newsletters—This idea-packed book shows you how to write and design family newsletters that will bring "mail box cheer" to your friends and relatives the world over. More than 100 full-color examples—from hand-crafted to computer-generated—offer great ideas for creating your own unique newsletters for every occasion. #10558/$19.99/120 color illus./128 pages/paperback

Scrapbook Storytelling, Step by Step—Go beyond typical scrapbooking techniques! Here is how to recall your favorite family stories and combine them with cherished photos, collages and illustrations to create unique booklets, albums, gift items and more. #70450/$19.99/120 color illus./128 pages/paperback

Publishing Your Family History on the Internet—With this first-ever guide, even if you're a beginning computer user, you can design and publish your own genealogical Web sites. Learn how to display your family history data—including pictures, sounds and video—onto the Web. #70447/$19.99/320 pages/140 b&w illus./paperback

The Internet for Genealogists, Fourth Edition—This completely revised and updated guide to the latest genealogy Web sites will give you quick access to the resources you need. Includes more than 200 addresses to genealogy sites, libraries, catalogs, maps, gazetteers, bookstores, online databases and living persons directories. #70415/$16.99/192 pages/paperback